Sports Law in Lithuania

Sports Law in Lithuania

Martynas Kalvelis

This book was originally published as a monograph in the International Encyclopaedia of Laws/Sports Law.

Founding Editor: Roger Blanpain
General Editor: Frank Hendrickx
Volume Editor: Michele Colucci

Wolters Kluwer

Published by:
Kluwer Law International B.V.
PO Box 316
2400 AH Alphen aan den Rijn
The Netherlands
E-mail: lrs-sales@wolterskluwer.com
Website: www.wolterskluwer.com/en/solutions/kluwerlawinternational

Sold and distributed by:
Wolters Kluwer Legal & Regulatory U.S.
7201 McKinney Circle
Frederick, MD 21704
United States of America
E-mail: customer.service@wolterskluwer.com

ISBN 978-94-035-1596-0

e-Book: ISBN 978-94-035-1436-9
web-PDF: ISBN 978-94-035-1446-8

The Author

Martynas Kalvelis is first of all a sports fan and then a practising lawyer. Martynas is a football admirer with deep knowledge and passion for Italian football. His best childhood memories are strongly related to Roberto Baggio's goals in 1994 and 1998 FIFA World Cups. In 2000 he was struck by the magic of then-young Francesco Totti, and Martynas began following Totti's home club, AS Roma. It was love at first sight. Since then, Martynas has been known as a die-hard *romanista*. He rarely misses a match on TV and is able to comment on various aspects of *giallorossi* club, including organization, player selection and finance. However, being born in a country of basketball, Martynas, like any other Lithuanian, cannot be disturbed during an official match of Lithuanian men's national basketball team.

Martynas Kalvelis obtained his Master's in Law from Mykolas Romeris University, Vilnius, Lithuania, in 2009. In 2014 he gained a diploma of Master's in International Sports Law from *Instituto Superior de Derecho y Economía* (ISDE), Madrid, Spain.

Martynas' knowledge of the field is largely based on his practical experience. Martynas started his legal career in FK Ekranas, a then one of the top football clubs in Lithuania, back in 2007. After three years of intriguing experience, Martynas moved to Vilnius where he started practising business law with a strong emphasis on sports law and sports and commercial litigation. Martynas has been dealing with many different aspects of sports law. Martynas assisted sport clubs, leagues, federations and athletes in navigating through various legal matters. Sports litigation is his main field of professional interest. Martynas has successfully represented clients in FIFA DRC and FIFA PSC, Basketball Arbitral Tribunal (BAT), various national and international sports federation bodies and most importantly Court of Arbitration for Sport (CAS), where he successfully acted as counsel for clients. In 2020 Martynas founded LEXTRA, a sports law and commercial litigation firm, where he continues his professional career.

From 2011 until early 2015 Martynas Kalvelis was a member of the Legal Advisory Panel of the European Club Association. He has also taken part in rendering certain handball decisions while on duty as a member of the Commission for Law and Ethics of the Lithuanian Handball Federation.

The Author

Table of Contents

Table of Contents

List of Abbreviations

BAT	Basketball Arbitral Tribunal
BFDS	Betting Fraud Detection System
CAS	Court of Arbitration for Sport
CDE	Code of Discipline and Ethics of the LKF
CED	Commission for Ethics and Disciplinary of the LKF
Civil Code	Civil Code of the Republic of Lithuania, 2000 (as amended)
Constitution	Constitution of the Republic of Lithuania, 6 November 1992 (as amended)
Constitutional Court	Constitutional Court of the Republic of Lithuania
Court of Appeals	Lithuanian Court of Appeals
CPC	Civil Procedure Code of the Republic of Lithuania, 2002 (as amended)
Criminal Code	Criminal Code of the Republic of Lithuania, 2000 (as amended).
EU	European Union
FIBA	International Basketball Federation
FIFA	International Federation of Association Football
FIFA DRC	FIFA Dispute Resolution Chamber of the Football Tribunal
FIFA PSC	FIFA Players' Status Committee of the Football Tribunal
FIFA RSTP	FIFA Regulations on the Status and Transfer of Players, edition 2022
FIFA TMS	FIFA Transfer Match System
Government	The Government of the Republic of Lithuania
IOC	International Olympic Committee
ITC	International Transfer Certificate
Law on Sport	Law on Sport of the Republic of Lithuania, edition in force as of 1 July 2022 (as amended)
LFF	Lithuanian Football Federation

List of Abbreviations

LKF	Lithuanian Basketball Federation
LKL	Lithuanian Basketball League
LTOK	Lithuanian National Olympic Committee
MESS	Ministry of Education, Science and Sport of the Republic of Lithuania
NBA	National Basketball Association
NKL	National Basketball League
PAR	Players' Agent Regulations
RWI	Regulations on Working with Intermediaries
SAA	Sports Activity Agreement (Lithuanian *sporto veiklos sutartis*)*
Seimas	Parliament of the Republic of Lithuania
Supreme Court	Supreme Court of Lithuania
UEFA	Union of European Football Associations
UNESCO	United Nations Educational, Scientific and Cultural Organization
VAT	Value Added Tax
VCCA	Vilnius Court of Commercial Arbitration
WADA	World's Anti-Doping Agency
WADA Code	World Anti-Doping Code, edition 2021

* An agreement between a professional athlete or coach and a sports organization under which the professional athlete or coach undertakes to prepare for sports competitions or to train athletes, to participate in competitions by adhering to the set internal procedure of the sports organization, and the sports organization undertakes to pay remuneration for sports or coaching activities and guarantees the conditions of training for and participation in competitions, as well as undertakes to implement other terms and conditions provided for in the contract.

Acknowledgements

This assignment to elaborate on sports law in Lithuania to such an extent was an enormous honour for me. However, it was even more challenging. It was in particular very hard to complete this task due to several reasons: first of all, legal matters related to sport have never been systemized in Lithuania before; second, the scope of this monograph required analysis of so many different fields of law and legal matters, and last but not least, I am not a scholar and my academic experience is not notable, therefore it is an additional challenge to handle.

Therefore, I could not have finished this assignment without the help and support of various persons. I would first like to thank Michele Colucci for his trust and patience. Michele is also responsible for keeping my passion for sports law flying high due to his outstandingly vivid and explosive lecture given in ISDE course in Madrid back in June 2014.

I would also want to thank all my colleagues, in particular, Ingrida Maciūtė for her indispensable help in research stage and Marius Devyžis for support and tolerance. My special thanks go to my mentor Stanislovas Butkevičius for important lessons of life which I had to remember in order to finish this assignment. I am very grateful to all my friends who kept enquiring regarding 'that project I am working on', supported me and also distracted me by force from this project when I did need such distraction mostly.

Finally, I want to thank my family for their support and understanding (in particular, my grandma, nephews and football match and rock concert mate, brother-in-law Giedrius).

And last but not least, with my pleasure, I dedicate this book to (so far) the most important women of my life – my Mom and my sister Laura.

Acknowledgements

General Introduction

1. Sports law is relatively a new legal definition in Lithuania (the term 'sports law' was used by the Supreme Court in its 14 July 2017 ruling in Civil Case No. 3K-3-317-686/2017 to refer to regulations of sports federations; however, no detailed elaboration was provided by the court).[1] It is mostly used by practising lawyers to identify services to be provided to potential clients. Specific aspects which could be attributed to sports law, such as Sports Activity Agreements (SAAs), issues with doping and match-fixing become subjects of legal publications and master's or PhD thesis. However, sports law, as a general concept, had avoided particular attention of scholars so far. Therefore, nature of sports law in Lithuania, as well as the place of sports law in Lithuanian legal system, is not analysed thoroughly.

2. The essential question to be asked is, what is sports law? It is not easy to provide a straight answer. Simon Gardiner[2] states that 'dedicated legislation and case law have developed specific sports law-related doctrines and principles and will continue increasingly to do so'. According to Gardiner, 'a new legal area has been born [sports law] and is thriving in the "bloom of its youth"'. Some believe[3] that '"sports law" is nothing more and nothing other than an *amalgamation of elements* from different substantive areas of law that are relevant in the context of sport'. While there are authors who are in between the mentioned positions and state[4] that sports law 'has the capacity to develop into an independent area of law'. Further, such definitions as *lex sportiva* (usually referred to as jurisprudence of Court of Arbitration for Sport (CAS)), global sports law (described as 'transnational autonomous legal order created by the global private institutions that govern international sport'),[5] transnational sports law (described as 'law made by private parties, without the intervention of states and across their borders, and intended to regulate activities in the community concerned'),[6] *lex ludica* (rules of the game and their application and ethical standards),[7] public international sports law ('the struggle against apartheid and other forms of discrimination in sport, peacekeeping during

1. Current and further quotes from decisions of Lithuanian courts are translated by the author.
2. Simon Gardiner, *United Kingdom*, in International Encyclopaedia of Laws: Sports Law, Frank Hendrickx (ed.), p. 22 (Kluwer Law International, 2014).
3. Edward Grayson, *Sport and the Law*, 2nd edition, p. XXXVII (Butterworths, 1994).
4. Robert C.R. Siekmann, *Introduction to International and European Sports Law*, ASSER International Sports Law Series, p. 4 (Asser Press, 2012).
5. *Ibid.*, at p. 11.
6. *Ibid.*, at p. 12.
7. *Ibid.*

the Olympic Games and preventing and combating violence in connection with sporting events (matches), the prevention of and fight against doping in sport and the question of recognising a "right to sport" as a human right').[8]

3. Timothy Davis summed up a list of criteria[9] that should be taken into consideration when assessing whether sports law can be considered a separate field of law. Such criteria, *inter alia*, include, a unique application by courts of law from other disciplines to a specific context, factual peculiarities within a specific context that produce problems requiring specialized analysis, significant affection of nation's business, economy, culture, or society, publication of legal casebooks that focus on the proposed discipline, development of law journals and other publications specifically devoted to publishing writings that fall within the parameters of the proposed field. In accordance with criteria suggested by Davis as well as traditions of Lithuanian legal doctrine, at the moment it would be very courageous to conclude that separate field of law, sports law, exists in Lithuania. It could be suggested that the main reason for such lack of consideration is that Lithuania avoided issues related to sports which were very common in most European Union (EU) countries. For example, in countries like UK, Germany or Italy, important factors contributing significantly to development of sports law were general commercialization of sports, increased player salaries, sponsorships, fight against hooliganism, doping and match-fixing, distribution of income from media and broadcasting rights. Such issues did not appear in Lithuania to a more significant extent. Therefore, this resulted in lack of catalysts to develop sports law as a field of law. Moreover, due to relatively small national market, certain aspects which are hugely important in bigger countries (e.g., such as collective sale of broadcasting rights by football clubs or leagues) are not yet relevant in Lithuania.

4. However, it can be said that sports law in Lithuania is in the stage of development and initial recognition. As it will be further analysed in this monograph, lawmakers, public entities and national courts have to deal with matters related to sport more often. Therefore, certain applicable rules are being formed. It may be concluded that sport law will gain more significance in Lithuanian social and economic life and that steps will be made towards recognition of this field as a special area of law in the near future.

5. In order to explain development of sports law and governance, specific dualism of governance of sports matters will be analysed. First, an emphasis will be put on the state governance of certain matters related to sports. Second, rules and regulations of sports federations will be underlined too. Interaction of public and private governance will be explained as well. Most of the issues are analysed from a practical point of view; thus, the importance of case law of state courts, arbitration institutions has to be emphasized.

---

8. *Siekmann, supra* n. 4, at p. 13.
9. Robert C.R. Siekmann & Janwillem Soek (eds), *Lex Sportiva: What Is Sports Law?*, ASSER International Sports Law Series, p. 25 (Asser Press, 2012).

Chapter 1. General Background

6. Lithuania (the Republic of Lithuania) is a Northern European country. The Republic of Lithuania is an independent democratic republic. The area of the territory of Lithuania is 65,300 square kilometres. Lithuania has land borders with Latvia on the North, Belarus on the East, Poland on the South and Russian exclave of Kaliningrad Oblast on the South-West side. On the western side Lithuania has a 99-kilometre coast of the Baltic Sea. Lithuania's population is about 2.9 million. Over 86% of people are of Lithuanian ethnicity. The national language is Lithuanian, one of the oldest Indo-European languages.

7. Lithuania, first mentioned back in 1009, once was a European superpower, having territories from the Baltic Sea coast to the Black Sea coast at its peak in the fifteenth century. For more than 200 years (until 1795) Grand Duchy of Lithuania and the Kingdom of Poland formed a single state of Polish – Lithuanian Commonwealth before being divided. From then on, Lithuania had been striving to survive under the constant threat and occupation from the Russian Empire finally breaking free after declaring independence on 16 February 1918. Development of Lithuania as a modern and democratic state came to a stall during World War II. Lithuania was occupied by the Soviet Union in June 1940. In June 1941, Lithuania was occupied by Nazi Germany. Soviets returned in 1944 and Lithuania remained occupied by Soviet Russia for more than forty years. On 11 March 1990, the Act of Re-Establishment of the State of Lithuania was adopted by the Parliament of the Republic of Lithuania, the Seimas and Lithuania gained its independence once again. Since 2004 Lithuania has been a member of both the North Atlantic Treaty Organization and the EU.

8. Lithuania is an independent democratic state. The form of state of Lithuania is a parliamentary republic with attributes of semi-presidential republic.[10] The legislative power lies within the single house parliament, the Seimas, consisting of 141 elected parliament members. The Government of the Republic of Lithuania, the Government, holds executive powers. Meanwhile, the directly elected President of the Republic of Lithuania is the head of the state. Judiciary power lies within the courts. Besides being abided by the EU law, Lithuania is also a member of important international treaties and conventions, including but not limited to Universal Declaration of Human Rights, Charter of the United Nations, Vienna Convention on the Law of Treaties, New York Convention on the Recognition and Enforcement of Foreign Arbitral Awards, Convention for the Protection of Human Rights and Fundamental Freedoms.

9. Lithuania's legal system belongs to the tradition of the continental legal system where the legal act is a primary source of law. The following types of sources of law are distinguished in Lithuania[11] in accordance with their legal power:

---

10. Toma Birmontienė et al., *Lietuvos konstitucinė teisė,* p. 321 (Mykolo Romerio universitetas, 2012).
11. Linas Baublys et al., *Teisės teorijos įvadas*, pp. 162–163 (Mes, 2012).

(1) The Constitution.
(2) Legal principles.
(3) International statutory law, primary sources of EU law and international treaties. In accordance with 13 July 2004, Constitutional Act on membership of the Republic of Lithuania in the EU, provisions of the EU law are a part of the Lithuanian legal system. Moreover, in accordance with the Constitutional Court,[12] in case of conflict of laws, the EU law shall prevail over Lithuanian law as far as it does not contradict with the Constitution. The EU law has a direct effect on Lithuania. In accordance with the Law on International Treaties of the Republic of Lithuania, 1999, ratified international treaties area part of the Lithuanian legal system as well.
(4) National statutory law. Sources of national statutory law in accordance with their legal power are divided into the following:
   (a) Constitutional acts, i.e., law passed by Seimas by certain quorum. In accordance with the Constitution, two types of constitutional acts exist. First type of constitution acts are considered part[13] of the Constitution which supplement it and have legal power of the Constitution. Second type is not considered part of the Constitution. Procedures of adoption of both types differ as well.
   (b) Laws, i.e., laws passed by the Seimas in accordance with regular procedures.
   (c) Sub-statutory legal acts passed by the Government, ministries, state institutions, municipalities.
(5) Normative agreements, such as collective bargaining agreements.
(6) Legal customs.
(7) Jurisprudence of courts.
(8) Legal doctrine.

10. Lithuanian court system consists of ordinary courts, specialized courts (administrative courts) and the Constitutional Court. The function of the latter is to safeguard the superiority of the Constitution. Administrative court system consists of two regional courts and the Lithuanian Supreme Administrative Court. Ordinary court system provides three instances and consists of twelve county courts, five regional courts, the Court of Appeals and the Supreme Court. Although Lithuanian legal system does not recognize the rule of precedent in the same way as in common law countries, the role of the jurisprudence of the court is very important. The courts which render a decision in cases of certain category are bound by the decisions rendered by courts previously.[14] Interpretation of law by a court of higher

12. 9 November 2010 ruling of the Constitutional Court.
13. Vytautas Sinkevičius, *Konstitucinių įstatymų samprata: teoriniai aspektai*, 2008 2(104), Jurisprudencija: mokslo darbai, pp. 28, 31 (2008).
14. 24 October 2007 ruling No. 26/07 of the Constitutional Court.

instance is compulsory for lower courts (vertical effect) and to the same court of higher instance as well (horizontal effect).[15] The jurisprudence, once established, can be amended and changed only when it is necessary and can be justified by constitutional need.

15. 18 November 2008 decision of the Supreme Court in Civil Case No. 3K-7-465/2008.

Chapter 2. Sources of Sports Law

11. In Lithuanian legal doctrine, it is common to classify sources of certain areas of law into primary and secondary sources. Primary sources are in general judiciary sources classified in accordance with the legal power, i.e., hierarchy. Secondary sources are in general jurisprudence and doctrine.

12. Classification of sources of sports law is more complicated due to different areas of law involved in matters traditionally related to sports as well as due to the significant role of private regulations applicable to matters of sport and internal dispute resolution. However, sources of sports law in Lithuania can be divided into the following groups:

- legislative sources of sports law;
- private regulations: statutes, rules and regulations of national and international sports federations and bodies;
- jurisprudence of the courts;
- case law of national, international sports federations and arbitration institutions;
- legal doctrine.

§1. Legislative Sources of Sports Law in Lithuania

13. The Constitution is a primary source of sports law in Lithuania. Article 53 of the Constitution provides that the state promotes physical culture of society and *supports sport*. As a general rule constitutional provision, despite its formally brief nature, may consist of multiple provisions and principles.[16] Regardless of the broad nature of such provision, the content of it is considered to be wider:[17] this provision first of all provides a right for any citizen to freely choose a form of physical education and an area of sports such citizen admires. It also sets a priority for the state to promote healthy lifestyle in society. Finally, it also means that the state provides financial support and aid for promotion of sports and athletes.

14. Lithuania is a member of important international conventions in the field of sports: (1) the Anti-Doping Convention of the European Council, (2) Convention on the Manipulation of Sports Competitions, (3) the United Nations Educational, Scientific and Cultural Organization (UNESCO) International Convention against Doping in Sport. Signed international treaties are part of Lithuanian legal system; thus it is fair to conclude that globally accepted principles in the field of sports law are part of Lithuanian legal system as well.

15. As from 2004 Lithuania has been a Member State of the EU. Thus, EU law, namely the primary sources such as the Treaty on European Union and the Treaty

16. Egidijus Šileikis, *Alternatyvi konstitucinė teisė*, p. 53 (Teisinės informacijos centras, 2003).
17. Genovaitė Dambrauskienė, et al., *Lietuvos Respublikos Konstitucijos komentaras*, p. 494 (K. Jovaišos PĮ, 2000).

on the Functioning of the European Union as well as secondary sources which directly or indirectly regulate field of sports are applicable too.

16. The laws passed by the Seimas are very important part of sources applicable to sports. The key law governing the field of sports in Lithuania is the Law on Sport. It provides the main principles and determines the level of involvement of the state in the field of sports. Public financing of sports has been constantly a hot topic of debate, hence the Law on Sport which, *inter alia*, governs the said issue is subject to frequent amendments. Civil Code and Criminal Code, laws governing such issues like taxation, social security, sponsorship, advertising, fair competition are important and applicable to matters related to sports too. Law on Associations of the Republic of Lithuania, 2004 should also be mentioned as a legal act establishing grounds of activity of extremely important elements of organization of sports, sports federations.

§2. Regulations of National and International Sports Federations

17. Some of the most important matters in sports are governed exceptionally by the rules and regulations of international and national sports federations and bodies. One of the most crucial examples is the World's Anti-Doping Agency (WADA) and its regulations, namely the World Anti-Doping Code (WADA Code) establishing key principles and procedures applicable in the fight against doping. Regulations of international federations, such as International Federation of Association Football (FIFA), establish a set of rules and policies (e.g., related to the status of the football player) which are applied universally to the relationship between clubs and players with an international dimension with slightly small margin for the intervention of national law.

18. National sports federations which operate under the legal form of an association, enjoy a wide level of immunity from the intervention of state. Their rules and regulations are applicable to members, such as clubs, and athletes who accept the application of such regulations in order to participate in competitions organized or authorized by the association. Such regulations may have a very serious impact on the status and activities of clubs or players. For example, a player may be banned from participating in competition for a significant amount of time in accordance with the rules set forth in disciplinary regulations of a federation.

§3. Jurisprudence of Courts

19. In case of lack of legal certainty in certain legal regulations, the jurisprudence of national courts is very important. For example, as it will be seen further, a legal nature of SAA is not clearly defined by legislation; thus explanations of the jurisprudence of the courts and in particular the Supreme Court are essential. Interpretation of legal provisions by the court is also very important for proper application of such provisions. It should be noted that Lithuanian courts take into consideration case law and interpretation by the Court of Justice of the EU as well as the European Court of Human Rights.

§4. Case Law of National, International Sports Bodies and Arbitration Institutions

20. Case law of national and international sports federations and arbitration institutions, such as Basketball Arbitral Tribunal (BAT) and, most importantly, CAS is very particular. First of all, such case law is basically immune from the intervention of national courts and on many occasions it avoids involvement of national law as well. This is more common in the case of arbitration. Parties are free to choose to refer a particular dispute to the arbitration and decide, *inter alia*, on the applicable law which is not necessarily national law – parties are free to choose a set of rules other than national law, such as the FIFA Regulations on the Status and Transfer of Players (FIFA RSTP) or assign an arbitrator to decide the dispute *ex aequo et bono* (such applicable law option is included in the standard BAT arbitration clause). In many countries arbitral awards are respected and courts rarely interfere. Direct arbitration clauses in sports contracts are very popular: most basketball players and clubs include the BAT clause in their contracts. BAT awards, unlike most CAS Ordinary Division awards, are available to the public. It forms practice which brings uniform approach to similar issues.

21. International and national sports federations have their judicial bodies, mainly disciplinary bodies. However, some federations, such as FIFA, also have bodies which solve private disputes (contractual disputes between clubs, clubs and players or coaches, etc.). For example, FIFA Dispute Resolution Chamber (FIFA DRC) is a body which solves numerous international football disputes. In most cases, FIFA DRC avoids the application of any national law and applies statutes and regulations of FIFA, namely the FIFA RSTP. Through the years FIFA DRC established case law which in many fields is clear and consistent. Thus, a Lithuanian football club engaged with a foreign player is at 'risk' to be condemned by the FIFA DRC applying FIFA RSTP and its own case law in case the club fails to meet its contractual obligations. Most importantly, FIFA DRC decisions, as well as final decisions of the Lithuanian Football Federation (LFF) dispute resolution bodies are subject to appeal to CAS, i.e., the arbitration clause is established in the statutes thus preventing reference of the case to the courts. Therefore, case law of sports federation bodies as well as arbitration institutions, in particular CAS, is a very important source of sports law.

22. Jurisprudence of CAS must be emphasized in particular. CAS awards rendered by its Appeals Division which in most cases are open to public are essential sources of sports law. CAS Appeals Division deals with the most important global cases and sports issues, including doping, match-fixing, disciplinary cases as well as in private disputes, in particular contractual disputes in football. Lithuanian athletes are clubs also become parties of a dispute before CAS more often. Thus, importance of CAS jurisprudence in Lithuania will definitely rise.

§5. Legal Doctrine

23. Legal doctrine is important for the development of any area of law since it not only helps to understand elements of the field but also contributes to the development of it and provides guidelines to solve difficult issues. Despite the fact that, so far, there has been no systemic and thorough analysis of sports law as a potential area of law in Lithuania, general interest in this field has increased. Articles and academic projects on particular issues related to sports law, such as contractual relationship, doping or match-fixing, appear. Moreover, initiatives for seminars and conferences are also noted. Due to the general undeniable charm of sports, it is very likely that sports law will be an interesting matter of academic attention.

Chapter 3. Specificity of Sports and Lithuania

24. Before analysing the definition of the specificity of sports, it is worth paying attention to the term 'specificity'. Specificity of a certain subject simply means that such subject is specific, distinguishing from other subjects due to its exceptional attributes. Needless to say, sports fans think that sport is specific and charming in many ways. But it is important to understand how such specificity results in the application of law.

25. Specificity of sports is a definition which is first of all related to the EU and the EU law. Even though early treaties did not specifically address sports[18] European Court of Justice had to deal with issues directly or indirectly related to sport. In a very early decision in case *Walrave & Koch*[19] the European Court of Justice noticed that 'in regard to the objectives of the community, the practice of sport is subject to the community law only in so far as it constitutes an economic activity'. However, in the same *Walrave & Koch* the European Court of Justice noticed that 'prohibition on discrimination on nationality ... does not affect the composition of sport teams, in particular national teams, the formation of which is a question of *purely sporting interest* and such has nothing to do with economic activity'. Similarly, in *Donà v. Montero*[20] case the European Court of Justice stated that:

> Rules of national practice, even adopted by a sporting organization, which limit the right to take part in football matches as professional or semi-professional player solely to nationals of the state in question are incompatible with ... the Treaty unless such rules or practice exclude foreign players from participation in certain matches for reasons which are not of an economic nature, which relate to the particular nature and context of such matches and are thus of sporting interest only.

26. Couple of decades later in notorious *Bosman*[21] case, the European Court of Justice yet again had to analyse a rule potentially infringing EU law in the light of 'sporting interest'.

27. In *Meca-Medina*[22] case the European Court of Justice dealt not with the free movement of workers but with competition issues (even though the subject matter of the case was doping regulations) and stated that even if sporting rules do not constitute restrictions on freedom of movement due to their 'sporting interest' that fact

---

18. Term 'sport' was first mentioned in 1997 Amsterdam Treaty. Treaty of Lisbon assigned specific competence of the EU in the field of sport. Now Art. 165 of the Treaty on Functioning of EU governs involvement of the EU in the field of sport.
19. Case 36/74 *Walrave and Koch v. Union Cycliste Internationale and Others* [1974] ECR 1405.
20. Case 13/76 *Gaetano Donà v. Mario Mantero* [1976] ECR 1333.
21. Case C-415/93 *Union Royale Belge Sociétés de Football Association and others v. Bosman and Others* [1995] ECR I-4921.
22. Case C-519/04 *David Meca-Medina and Igor Majcen v. Commission* [2006] ECR I-6991.

does not mean that the sporting activity in question necessarily falls outside the scope of competition law provisions. However, *sporting nature* has to be taken into consideration.

28. The above-mentioned practice of the European Court of Justice demonstrates that the court may decide to exempt certain rules or practices from the application of the EU law or to provide specific treatment by recognizing its specific, i.e., sporting nature. Thus, sporting nature may provide recognition leading to exemption from application of competition law and internal market provisions, otherwise applicable to sport rules and practices as well. That specific sporting nature can be referred to 'specificity of sport'.

29. Siekmann[23] defines specificity of sport as 'legal concept (and method or instrument of appreciation or assessment) that is applied by the European Commission and the European Court of Justice to tackle this question on a case-by-case basis, in order to determine whether the sporting rules and regulations concerned are acceptable in EU law'.

30. The European Commission White Paper on Sports introduced the first definition of what is known as the 'specificity of sports' via two prisms approach:

(1) 'The specificity of sporting activities and of sporting rules, such as separate competitions for men and women, limitations on the number of participants in competitions, or the need to ensure uncertainty concerning outcomes and to preserve a competitive balance between clubs taking part in the same competitions.'
(2) 'The specificity of the sport structure, including notably the autonomy and diversity of sport organisations, a pyramid structure of competitions from grassroots to elite level and organised solidarity mechanisms between the different levels and operators, the organisation of sport on a national basis, and the principle of a single federation per sport.'

31. In general sporting rules and practices could fall into the scope of the EU law and would probably contradict it if not for the specific sporting nature, or 'specificity of sport'. Such specificity must be recognized and taken into consideration though it solely cannot grant exemption from the EU law.

32. National legal regulation in Lithuania does not stipulate any definition of specificity of sports. However, the Law on Sport provides the exception of the principle of equality and equal treatment which is applicable to the activity of sports and physical education: Article 3 of the Law on Sport specifically provides that 'separate sports competitions for men, women, disabled persons, sports competitions

23. Siekmann, *supra* n. 4, at p. 94.

according to age groups, limitation of the number of participants in sports competitions shall not be considered a violation of the principle of equal treatment'. This provision reflects a small element of what can be considered as specificity of sports.

33. The number of cases in the field of sports has not been significant yet in Lithuania; therefore, the concept of the specificity of sports is not developed by the jurisprudence of the courts of Lithuania as well. However, as it will be analysed further, specific attributes of sports is a circumstance which is taken into consideration by the courts while dealing with both civil and criminal cases.

Part I. Organization of Sport

Chapter 1. Sports Governance

§1. Historical Background of State Governance of Sports

34. Global roots of governance of sports as it is understood now lie in the second half of the nineteenth century and the beginning of the twentieth century. The beginning of modern governance of sports in Lithuania is related to the date of signing of the Act of Reinstating Independence of Lithuania on 16 February 1918. The modern state of Lithuania began to develop; thus various elements of social life and its governance were formed as well.

35. Understanding of sports organization and its governance as well as some popular sports, including basketball, is claimed to be brought to Lithuania by Lithuanian expatriates, mostly from the US.[24] The very first independent sports organization in Lithuania was established on 18 May 1919 and it was named as 'Lithuanian Sports Union'. Its statutes stipulated that the union was responsible for the coordination of activities of sports organizations. On 15 September 1920 Union of Physical Education of Lithuania that is responsible for the promotion of youth sports was founded.

36. The early predecessor of the Lithuanian National Olympic Committee (LTOK), the Lithuanian Sports League, was established in 1922. Lithuanian Sports League had a right to represent Lithuania in the Olympic movement and, accordingly, the Olympic Games. In 1924 athletes from Lithuania competed in the Olympic Games for the very first time. However, the activities of separate institutions and an increasing number of sports entities such as clubs were poorly coordinated.

37. In 1931, the very first law on sport in Lithuania was adopted, the Law on Physical Education of the Republic of Lithuania. Establishment of Physical Education Chamber ('Chamber') accountable to the Ministry of Education was an essential element of the new law. Chamber was responsible for setting up physical education programmes for schools. Moreover, their functions included construction

24. Information on history of sports governance in Lithuania is based on information provided in website of KKSD, translated by author (accessed on 17 May 2019). At the moment the website is no longer available.

and administration of sports infrastructure. It was also declared that all sports organizations actually belong to the Chamber. The law established that all international relationships of any sports organizations would be carried out through the Chamber.

38. The Chamber coordinated activities of the sports organizations. An increase in physical activity and capability was at the centre of attention of the Chamber. Key efforts were taken to increase the demand for physical activities among young generation. This task was of such importance that the 1938 Constitution of the Republic of Lithuania included a provision obliging the state to take steps to develop physical strength of young generation. In order to improve the level of physical education system and develop competence of experts in sport, high courses of physical education were introduced.

39. The year 1937 marks the first important achievements of Lithuanian athletes. Debut of Lithuanian national basketball in European Basketball Championship in Riga, Latvia, was marked by gold. Lithuanian team which included three US-based expatriates beat Italy in the finals and claimed first notorious victory. Two years later, in 1939, European Basketball Championship was organized in Kaunas, Lithuania. Specially built sports hall in Kaunas witnessed another triumph after Lithuania beat Latvia in the final 37:36.[25] Few would doubt that these victories laid deep foundations of basketball as the most admired sport and a phenomenon exceeding limits of sport as an activity of entertainment, in Lithuania for decades to come. Unfortunately, independent development of sports as well as other areas was brutally interrupted by events of World War II.

40. The date of 14 June 1940 marks the first occupation of Lithuania by Soviet Russia. Nazi Germany took over while advancing their Eastern front towards Russia and remained in Lithuania from 1941 to 1944, i.e., upon the return of Soviets. Terror began as many Lithuanian citizens, including athletes and sports officials, were killed, exiled by force. Sports bodies and structures were destroyed as well. Activities of national sports organizations were seized. Many athletes and sports professionals were exiled.

41. Yet under the Soviet seizure, Lithuanian athletes were able to demonstrate world-class results in such fields as swimming, boxing, rowing, cycling and most importantly, basketball. The 1980s marked battles between BC Žalgiris, a basketball team consisting of Lithuanian players only, and CSKA Moscow, a team which requested contribution to general glorification of the red army, consisting of basketball players from all around the USSR. Such basketball battles were more than a game of basketball. For most of the Lithuanians, the team in green, Žalgiris, fighting against the team from Moscow dressed in red, symbolized Lithuanian resistance and fight for freedom against the Soviet Union. It is widely believed that basketball victories against CSKA highly contributed in igniting pride and determination

25. By that time basketball final score used to be low compared to nowadays due to significant differences between the rules and dynamics of the game, however a very high scoring game was also registered in the very same event, when Lithuania beat Finland by a remarkable result of 112:9.

which did take a notable part in escaping the Soviet Union and re-establishment of independent Lithuania in 1990.

42. At the end of the 1980s and beginning of the 1990s, nationally based sports institutions were formed, the LTOK to name the first. After the re-establishment of the independence of Lithuania on 11 March 1990, the LTOK and Physical Education Committee[26] immediately addressed Lithuanian athletes encouraging them not to compete in Soviet competitions and not to represent USSR teams. Sports governance system began to transform. The Department of Physical Education and Sports under the Government of the Republic of Lithuania (KKSD) was formed. The LTOK gained Lithuanian Olympic movement and Lithuania became a member of the International Olympic Committee (IOC) in 1991 and immediately took part in 1992 Winter Olympic Games in Albertville and 1992 Olympic Games in Barcelona with decent success (gold in men's discuss event and bronze in men's basketball).[27] Following examples of other European states, club system was introduced and autonomy for federations was provided as well. Lithuanian sports organizations began to improve in various fields, including development of international relationship. The Paralympic Committee was established in 1991 as well. Seven medals were won in Barcelona Paralympic Games in 1992 by Lithuanian athletes.

43. In 1995 a Law on Sport was adopted by the Seimas which became the foundation of sports governance in Lithuania. At the time professional sports clubs began to develop, leagues were created. Lithuanian sports governance and organization began to shift towards European model. It should be noted the new edition of the Law on Sport introducing important amendments was adopted on 18 October 2018. Mainly due to ever-changing concept of public financing of sports, the Law on Sport is amended constantly. Evolution, structure and core principles of the Law on Sport shall be analysed in detail in §4 of the current part of the monograph.

§2. Public and Private Governance of Sports

44. There are two basic sources of sports governance in Lithuania: public and private regulation. Public governance is exercised by state and municipality authorities in accordance with competence assigned to such authorities by law. State and municipality authorities act in the field of sport by passing statutory legal acts: laws, regulations, orders, etc. Private governance is exercised by sporting organizations, such as federations, clubs and other bodies that enjoy an important level of autonomy and are protected by the law from interference of the public authorities.

45. Public governance of sports covers, *inter alia*, the following fields:

26. Institution which was later replaced by the KKSD.
27. Symbolically, the Lithuanian team had to face so-called Union of Independent States, i.e., a remainder of USSR, in a match for 3rd place.

- national sports strategy and policies and responsibility of state authorities in the field of sports;
- legal basis for the functioning of sports federations and clubs;
- legal status of athletes and players;
- financing of sports and athletes;
- prohibition of the use of doping and fight against match-fixing;
- safety of sports events;
- requirements for sports infrastructure;
- general commercial matters that are directly or indirectly related to sports (advertising, media and broadcasting, competition, taxes);
- other public regulations affecting sports.

46. Mostly, private governance of sports manifests in the following fields:

- rules of the game;
- competitions and their formats;
- statutes of athletes, coaches, referees and other participants;
- player transfers;
- systems to compensate training of players;
- formation of national teams;
- disciplinary issues;
- commercial matters.

§3. Sports and Physical Education (High Performance Sport and Physical Activity)

47. Two different types of physical activities may be noticed in legal regulation: sports and physical education. This issue starts with Article 53(3) of the Constitution which states that the state promotes *physical education* of society and supports *sport.*[28] Same approach is reflected in the main legal act governing sport in Lithuania, the Law on Sport.

48. Article 4 of the current edition of the Law on Sport clearly states that the system of sport in Lithuania contains two basic areas: physical activity (defined by Article 2(15) of the Law on Sport as 'personal physical activity aimed at strengthening health, improving physical and mental qualities and skills, without the aim of preparing for and/or participating in high-level sporting competitions, as well as activities aimed at educating the general public about sport, physical activity and the improvement of health achieved through it high performance') and high performance sport (defined by Article 2(2) of the Law on Sport as 'a person's form of physical activity, in the age groups of juniors, youth, young adults and adults other than veterans (in accordance with the age requirements set by the international (world) sports federation or the governing body of the Paralympic, visual, hearing,

---

28. Official translation available on website of the Seimas (accessed on 25 Jun. 2021) (http://www3.lrs.lt/home/Konstitucija/Constitution.htm).

mobility or intellectual disability sports or student sports movements (world or European)), competing against other persons (individually or in a team) in a high-level sporting competition (using animals and/or technical aids where appropriate) in accordance with specific rules, with the aim of beating competitors and improving one's physical and mental qualities and skills, as well as activities which improve a person's physical and mental qualities and skills with a view to preparing him/her adequately for high-level sporting competitions'. High performance sport is also considered to be a person's activity which, although it does not meet the criteria set out above, is generally recognized as high performance sport by tradition or other circumstances).

49. Thus, the main two pillars of sports which determined the scope of regulation of the Law on Sport are: (1) general physical activity, sports played 'for fun' or grassroots sport; (2) result-orientated high performance sport whereby certain element of professionalism is present.

50. Policy and governance of sports in Lithuania basically follow the above-mentioned two main directions: development of grassroots sports, including implementation of healthy lifestyle, creating conditions for sports activities, establishing general policies on education of sports and professional sport governance providing roles of state and private stakeholders in developing high performance athletes, financial conditions of such athletes. It is not possible to completely separate grassroots sports and professional sports governance as it supplements each other and interacts as well.

§4. The Law on Sport

51. The Law on Sport is the main legal act in the field of sport in Lithuania. The first edition of the Law on Sport was adopted back in 1995. The law was aimed to lay down the principles of sport; establish sports system and its governance; regulate the competence of state, municipal institutions and private sports organizations in the field of sport; regulate the organization of sport and examination of health of persons; set requirements for safety of sports events; govern financing of sport; implement policies of anti-doping.

52. Before adoption of the Law on Sport, different matters related to sport and its governance were governed by multiple laws and legal acts. However, due to the increasing importance of sport, it was decided to draft a single legal act covering all main issues. As from its adoption in 1995, the Law on Sport was amended on a number of occasions.

The most recent major overhaul of the Law on Sport took place in 2018. The new edition of the Law of Sport was passed by the Parliament on 18 October 2018 and came into legal force on 1 January 2019. The new edition of the Law on Sports not only changed foundations of public financing of sports but also introduced significant structural and institutional changes. The following major reasons for the introduction of the new edition of the law were indicated (as per the official explanatory notes of the draft of the new edition of the Law on Sport):

- Issues related to application of certain provisions of the Law on Sport in practice due to incompliance of the old regulation with contemporary realities.
- Lack of transparency and effectiveness of distribution of state funds to finance sports.
- Incompliance with the old regulation with the Law on Reduction of Administrative Burden of the Republic of Lithuania (complicated and ineffective distribution of powers among various institutions).
- Increased level of self-governance of sports federation which allows deregulation of certain areas.
- Aim to improve healthy lifestyle in society.
- High performance.

The main changes brought by the new edition of the Law on Sport (which came into legal force on 1 January 2019) are the following:

(1) *Structural reform*. One of the main reforms brought by the new edition of the Law on Sport was the decision to liquidate the Department of Physical Education and Sports ('KKSD') which was a special purpose state institution (accountable directly to the Government) responsible for implementation of the sports policy and administration of physical education and sport. The role and functions of KKSD were essentially transferred to the Ministry of Education, Science and Sport (MESS). The elimination of the KKSD and transfer of its functions to the MESS was aimed to reduce the administrative burden and bring effectiveness to sport governance. The KKSD was finally liquidated in December 2020. However, as per the current edition of the Law on Sports (which came into legal force on 1 July 2022), a new special purpose institution was set-up to administer specific functions in administration of sports in Lithuania, i.e., the National Sports Agency (accountable to the MESS).

(2) *Financial reform*. Lack of transparency and effectiveness in distribution of the state funds for sport[29] was one of the main factors for adoption of the new edition of the Law on Sport. The new edition of the Law on Sport brought the following important amendments:

   (a) The administration of state funds for sport was amended. In accordance with the previous edition of the Law on Sport, the state budget funds were distributed by both, the Sports Support Fund and the KKSD. The Sports Support Fund and the KKSD had a right to fund amateur sport (grassroots sport) and professional sport (high performance sport); however, there

29. For example, the President of Lithuanian Rugby Federation described state financing of sport system as 'not transparent' in interview. Interview available online (accessed on 26 Jun. 2021) (https://www.15min.lt/sportas/naujiena/regbis/regbio-federacijos-prezidentas-rytis-davidovicius-nusivyles-valstybes-finansavimu-671-512278).

were no clear criteria on the selection of fields and organizations to finance from state budget. The new edition of the Law on Sport introduced more clarity – the Sports Support Fund is now responsible to distribute funds for physical activity projects (grassroots sport) and infrastructure. The MESS is responsible for distribution of funds for high performance sport programmes only. What is more important, the methods of application for state funds were clarified: the physical activity and infrastructural matters are financed by distributing certain funds for organizations in accordance with submitted and confirmed planning documents, i.e., sports projects. The Law on Sport lays down the procedures for confirmation of sports project suitable to finance. The high performance sport is financed by the MESS by funding high performance sports programmes.

(b) The new edition of the Law on Sport sets forth strict requirements for sports organizations submitting high performance sports programmes for receiving state financing. Subject to failure of the organization concerned to meet such requirements, state funds cannot be granted. Moreover, a mechanism for return of state funds or suspension of funding was introduced for cases where organization fails to maintain certain requirements after the decision to fund programme of such organization is taken. These amendments set standards which will have to be followed by most organizations, in particular the national federations and, thus, the level of administration of sports organization will surely increase.

(c) The pool of organization which can be funded by the state was expanded. In accordance with the old legislation, only non-governmental institutions could be financed. However, in accordance with the new legislation, other legal persons (including private establishments) can apply for state funds by submitting sports projects or high performance sports programmes.

(d) The Law on the Fund for Support of Physical Education and Sports of the Republic of Lithuania lost its legal power. Due to the fact that the Sports Support Fund is not involved in financing of high performance sport its influence decreased. Now the principles of formation of the Sports Support Fund are included in the Law on Sport.

(e) Pursuant to the new edition of the Law on Sport, a certain part of state funds for sports financing will have to be designated for disabled sports only.

(f) Stricter criteria were added for state awarding and funding of individual athletes for the results achieved in high performance sports competitions. Moreover, the pool of persons which can claim state support or awards was limited.

(3) *Deregulation of aspects governed by international and national federations.* The old edition of the Law on Sport governed various fields which in accordance with contemporary practices are usually governed privately by international and national federations. In accordance with the old edition of the Law on Sport, such aspects as content of SAAs, formation of national teams, status of professional and amateur players, athletes' right to have agents, requirements for activities of player agents and representatives, right of athletes for collective representation were governed. The current edition of the Law on

Sport completely deregulates such areas thus recognizing right and competence of the national and international federations to govern such matters independently.

(4) *Simplification.* Due to multiple change of the old version of the Law on Sport, the structure of the law became complex. There were also certain confusions in terms of definitions and rules. For example, the law set forth multiple definitions of persons involved in sport (professional athlete, amateur athlete, sportsman) without providing any clear differences and legal meaning on such different definitions. The new edition of Law on Sport is more compact, provides less (but more clear) definitions and governs those fields which do require certain standards set by the state.

(5) *Safety of sport.* The new edition of Law on Sport stipulates clear responsibilities of persons in safety of sports competitions, compulsory examination of health of athletes. It also sets new requirements for persons conducting physical activity and sports trainings.

53. The current edition of the Law on Sport is structured as follows:

– List of definitions, principles and definition of system of sport in Lithuania.[30]
– Concept of permanent monitoring of the situation of sport in Lithuania.[31]
– Distribution of obligations in the field of governance of sport among states, municipality authorities and sports associations and federations.[32]
– Foundations of economic activities of athletes, coaches and referees.[33]
– Requirements for activity of physical activity or sport instructors and specialists.[34]
– Principles of organization of sport in educational system.[35]
– Requirements for safety of sports.[36]
– Public financing of sport.[37]

54. It is important to note that the Law on Sport is based on the following legal principles:[38] equality,[39] safety of sports events,[40]anti-doping,[41]

30. Articles 2–4 of the Law on Sport.
31. Article 5 of the Law on Sport.
32. Articles 6–8 of the Law on Sport.
33. Article 10 of the Law on Sport.
34. Article 11 of the Law on Sport.
35. Article 12 of the Law on Sport.
36. Articles 13–15 of the Law on Sport.
37. Articles 16–21 of the Law on Sport.
38. Article 3 of the Law on Sport.
39. This principle means that all persons, irrespective of their sex, race, nationality, language, origin, age, disability, religion or belief, sexual orientation, and social or economic status, shall have the same right to take part in sport.
40. This principle implies that all necessary measures must be taken to avoid adverse effects on the life, health and property of any person during the sporting event and to ensure that statutory requirements are not infringed, and that, if adverse effects do arise, or if statutory requirements are infringed, it is ensured that they are remedied (restored in accordance with the procedure laid down by the law) in the shortest time possible and with the minimum of possible damage.
41. This principle implies that, in order to protect the health of athletes and other persons who improve their health through physical activity and to ensure fair competition in sport, the State, municipal

prohibition of manipulation in sports competitions and ensuring integrity of sport,[42] continuity of sports activities,[43] free self-determination and choice of persons,[44] promotion of society to participate in physical activities.[45]

55. The provisions of the Law on Sport governing specific fields of sport will be analysed in broader detail further.

---

authorities and bodies, as well as non-governmental organizations active in the field of sport, shall take measures to combat anti-doping rule violations.

42. This principle implies that individuals are prohibited from manipulating sporting competitions and that the public's right to fair sporting competitions must be protected and the fairness of athletes competing in sporting competitions must be ensured.
43. This principle implies that state and municipal institutions and bodies, as well as non-governmental organizations active in the field of sport, are obliged, in the course of their activities, to create the conditions in which individuals are able to take part in sport in order to improve their health.
44. This principle means that individuals have the right to freely choose forms of physical activity and sports, to form associations of their members on the basis of sport, and to engage in sporting activities not prohibited by law.
45. This principle implies that public and municipal authorities and bodies encourage people to take part in sport as widely as possible.

Chapter 2. Governmental Institutions and Bodies

56. The Law on Sport distributes competence in sport governance to various governmental bodies and institutions in accordance with their status and hierarchy in the governmental institutional system. The following governmental institutions and bodies are provided with certain fields of competence by the Law on Sport:

- The Seimas.
- The Government.
- National Council of Sport.
- The MESS and National Sports Agency.
- Ministries of the Republic of Lithuanian and other state institutions.
- Municipalities.

§1. The Seimas

57. The Seimas is the legislative body of the Republic of Lithuania, which, first of all, adopts laws, including laws governing field of sports.

58. In accordance with Article 6(1) of the Law on Sport, the main competence of the Seimas in the field of sport is determination of the development directions of sports policy by approving the State Progress Strategy and adopting laws. The strategy contains priorities of the state in the field of sport, long-term goals, as well as directions of amendment of strategy.

59. By the resolution of 24 March 2011, the Parliament approved Strategy for State Development of Sports in 2011–2020. Following the termination of 2011–2020 strategy, no new strategy was approved by the Parliament. As it will be discussed further, sport is covered by strategic planning document prepared and implemented by the Government.

§2. The Government and National Council of Physical Education and Sport

60. The Government exercises executive power of the Republic of Lithuania. The Government is responsible for drafting and implementing another strategic document – National Progress Plan. In accordance with Article 6(2) of the Law on Sport, the Government is responsible to set goals and/or progress objectives of sports policy in the field of sport in the National Progress Plan. The Government is also under duty to foresee development programmes to implement objectives provided in the National Progress Plan.

61. The National Council of Sport is not a legal person, nor institution. It is a set of members from different institutions summoned by the Government. Candidates are proposed by the Minister of Education, Science and Sports from representatives of entities and institutions of state and municipalities as well as representatives of umbrella organizations acting in the field of sports policy. Members of the council shall have an impeccable reputation. Its primal goal as defined by Article 7(3) of the Law on Sport is to consult Seimas, the Government and the MESS on the formation and execution of state sports policy. The National Council of Sport considers state strategy on sport, goals of progress, priorities of sports policy, criteria for recognition of strategic areas of sport and other issues related to the development of sport.

62. The main task of the National Council of Sport is promotion of sport. The council must ensure that the development of sport is in compliance with the international regulations. In order to fulfil these tasks, the National Council of Sport informs the society on activities of governmental and non-governmental organizations while developing and promoting the sport and discusses drafts of legal acts submitted to the Government.

63. The National Council of Sport enjoys an important advisory role for the Government and although it does not constitute a body of a significant function in the field of government of sport, it possesses notable political power and influence.

§3. The MESS and the National Sports Agency

64. Before adopting the current edition of the Law on Sport on 18 October 2018, a central and most important institution in terms of sports governance was the KKSD. In accordance with the current edition of the Law on Sport, the KKSD does not exist, and its functions are transferred to the MESS. However, during the transitional period following the introduction of the new legislation, the KKSD remained operative and active throughout 2019. Finally, the KKSD was dissolved at the end of 2020 and its powers were assumed by the MESS.

65. The new edition of the Law on Sport does not provide an extensive list of competences of the MESS. In accordance with Article 6(3) of the Law on Sport, the MESS formulates the state sports policy, participates in the preparation of the National Progress Plan on the establishment of strategic goals and/or progress objectives of the sports policy, prepares the national development programmes implementing the sports policy progress objectives, organizes, coordinates and controls their implementation.

66. The main task of the MESS in the field of sport is to formulate the state policy in the field of sports, to organize, coordinate and control its implementation. In accordance with further provisions of the Law on Sport, the MESS possesses specific powers in the area of sport, in particular in financing of sport.

67. With the latest update of the Law on Sport (in legal force as of 1 July 2022), a notion of 'institution authorized by the Minister of Education, Science and Sports' was introduced. The institution authorized by the Minister of Education, Science and Sports is an entity which is assigned to perform the specific tasks laid down by the Law on Sport, including administration and distribution of finances to the high performance sport and national physical activity programmes, projects for sports competitions. As well as this, said institution is obliged by the Law on Sport to administer and finance primary, elementary and secondary education, in conjunction with sports education for pupils with exceptional sporting ability, provide consultancy services to sports federations, encourage athletes and their coaches to achieve excellence in sport and to carry out other duties as provided for in this and other laws or as delegated by the Minister for Education, Science and Sport. As from 1 July 2022, a newly incorporated state enterprise, the National Sports Agency, has been set-up to assume said functions. It is stated that the National Sports Agency shall implement the national sports policy in the fields of high performance sport and physical activity, assist sports federations and sports organizations in strengthening the principles of good governance, protect athletes' rights and sports infrastructure.

§4. Lithuanian Sports Centre

68. Before instruction of the 2018 edition of the Law on Sport, Lithuanian Olympic Sports Centre, now called Lithuanian Sports Centre (Olympic Centre), was mainly a state-funded entity accountable to the KKSD. Its main mission was to ensure proper preparation for the Olympic Games of individual athletes.

69. The Olympic Centre coordinated preparation activities of individual athletes for World or European championships and, most importantly, the Olympic Games. The Olympic Centre used to be responsible for the preparation of new generation of Olympic and national teams.

70. In accordance with criteria confirmed by the KKSD, the Olympic Centre was responsible for selecting candidates from lists presented by regional sports organizations to prepare for Olympic Games.

71. Currently, the functions of the Lithuanian Sports Centre are essentially reduced to ensuring the proper operation of the sports and residential infrastructure created by the State and entrusted to the centre for the purpose of training athletes, organizing high-level sports competitions and events, and for the purpose of other activities of benefit to society. In other words, the Lithuanian Sports Centre is mainly responsible for administration of State-owned sports infrastructure. As well as this, the centre administers Sports Medicine Department which is responsible for carrying out preventive medical examinations of athletes, functional tests of athletes, treating athletes who are injured or ill, providing outpatient rehabilitation services, and assisting athletes of sports teams during training camps or competitions. Moreover, the centre is responsible for managing national sports statistics.

§5. MUNICIPALITIES

72. Municipalities enjoy special status granted by the Constitution and the Law on Local Self-Government, 1994 and have independent functions (i.e., immunity from the interference of the state bodies subject to conditions set by law) in certain fields. There are sixty municipalities in Lithuania formed in accordance with a regional basis. The main governing body of the municipality is the municipal council, which possesses legislative power within municipality. Competence of municipalities in governance of sport manifests in powers provided by the Law on Sport to the municipal councils.

73. Pursuant to Article 8(1) of the Law on Sport, municipal council:

- taking into account the strategic goals and/or progress objectives of the sports policy set out in the National Progress Plan, the list of strategic sports approved by the Minister of Education, Science and Sport, and the needs of the local community, plans municipal sports development measures and projects, determines the areas of sport to be financed by the municipality's budget, and promotes public and public-private partnerships in sport;
- establishes the criteria and procedure for financing the activities of natural and legal persons operating in the field of sports from the municipal budget;
- on the basis of programmes or projects, finances and otherwise contributes to the activities of natural and legal persons operating in the field of sports operating in the territory of the municipality.

74. While implementing the sports policy in the municipal territory, the executive institutions of municipalities shall:

- analyse the state of sport in the municipality, ensure the implementation of the strategic goals and/or progress objectives of the sports policy set out in the National Progress Plan at the local level and the implementation of municipal sports development measures and projects to achieve them;
- carry out the development of sports facilities, ensure the accessibility of the services provided by them to the population;
- carry out educational activities, form a positive attitude of people living in the territory of the municipality towards the significance of sports for health;
- prepare and implement other measures for the development of physical activity and high mastery sports in the municipality.

75. Role of municipalities is very important in developing children and youth sports activities policy, development of sports facilities and infrastructure as well as financing activities of clubs and other sports organizations (sport organization is a wider term than sport club, it covers other entities, such as sports schools and academies, institutions providing education in relation to sports, organization of sports sponsors) and athletes.

Chapter 3. National Olympic Committee and Federations

§1. Lithuanian National Olympic Committee

76. Legal form of the LTOK is association. It is an independent non-profit organization which belongs to the global Olympic movement.

77. The main function of the LTOK is to ensure conformity with the Olympic Charter in Lithuania. The other functions include[46] promotion of Olympic principles, protection of cultural aspects of Olympic movement, promotion and development of sports, promotion of educational activities, fight against discrimination in sports and use of doping, cooperation with government and non-governmental institutions, selection of athletes for Olympic Games (while cooperating with the sports federations), representation and defence of interests of athletes and coaches. The main obligation of the LTOK is to ensure Lithuanian competition in the Olympic Games and to form national Olympic delegations.

78. The LTOK is free from any financial support of the state. Activity of the LTOK is financed by the IOC and two private sources: UAB 'Olifėja' (a company which is licensed to organize nationwide lottery games and is partially owned by the LTOK) and Lithuanian Olympic Fund (an organization owned by the LTOK whose function is fundraising via commercial activities).

79. The LTOK managing bodies are:

- General Assembly.
- Executive Committee.
- President.
- Commission for Revision.
- Council for Olympic Matters.

80. The main body is the General Assembly which consists of a maximum number of sixty-seven members (national sports federations, athletes who participated in Olympic Games, etc.). Each member possesses one vote in the meeting of the General Assembly. The General Assembly has a competence to decide on the most important issues of the LTOK, including but not limited to the amendment of statutes, setting the strategic goals, confirming annual financial reports, confirming annual budget, election of the Executive Committee and the President, etc.

81. The Executive Committee is a collegial body consisting of thirteen members. The Executive Committee governs the LTOK during the absence of General

---

46. Information and documents on activities of the LTOK are also available on the website of the LTOK (accessed on 21 Jun. 2021) (https://www.ltok.lt/apie-mus/).

Assembly sessions.[47] The Executive Committee is elected for a four-year term of office. The main functions of the Executive Committee are to monitor the implementation of Olympic Charter, establish internal structure of the LTOK, decide on establishment of legal persons, branches and subsidiaries, decide upon admission and dismissal of the General Secretary of the LTOK.

82. President of the LTOK is a sole managing body. The main function of the President is to manage activities of the LTOK, represent the LTOK in national and international organizations, to represent the LTOK in courts and arbitration institutions, to take care of daily issues of the LTOK.

83. The LTOK is an important institution for financing Olympic athletes. However, there are no clear rules which define precise responsibilities of the LTOK in financing sport.

§2. Federations

84. In accordance with the Law on Sport, two definitions of sports federations are distinguished. Sports federation is considered as a non-governmental organization acting upon the principle of membership, which is responsible for development of a certain area of sport within a certain territory (territorial based, or nationwide) and which develops said area of sports, represents interests of representatives of such sport area, sets forth specific requirements of such area of sport and ensures compliance with said requirements, prepares and implements measures for promotion of said area of sport. The Law on Sport also defines 'International Sports Federation' as non-governmental organization acting upon the principle of membership which sets principal rules of certain sports area on a global (or European) level uniting federations of said sport established and acting in several countries. The Law on Sport provides no specific requirements or duties to federations. However, federations willing to receive state funds have to comply with strict criteria set out by the Law on Sport.

85. Federations in Lithuania operate under a legal form of association. Therefore, the Law on Associations of the Republic of Lithuania ('Law on Associations') is applicable first of all. Associations are provided with the autonomy and they are protected by the law against interference from the state authorities. This protection is stipulated by Article 14 of the Law on Associations. The Law on Associations sets forth the order of establishment of an association, management of association, order of dissolution and guarantees of activity.

86. It is important to notice that the Law on Associations requires an association to have at least two governing bodies: (1) meeting of members (it may be called in

47. Usually a session of the General Assembly takes place once a year. Extraordinary session may be called upon request of one-third of the members. An electoral session, where the President and the Executive Committee members are elected takes place every four years.

any other name, such as assembly, congress, conference), (2) managing body (sole or collegial). Any additional bodies and their composition is a subject of discretion of an association. Most of the sports federations have more bodies. Every association is requested to adopt their statutes. Statutes are essential for the activity of association. It is very important to indicate purposes and goals of activity of an association. Associations are restricted to take part in some activities, including provision of loans, donating its assets, receiving loans from the member of association against the payment of interest, buy an asset for an obviously unreasonable price, etc.

I. Lithuanian Basketball Federation

87. Basketball is the number one sport in Lithuania. It is no surprise when prominence of sport is measured by the results of men's national team. Lithuanian national men's basketball team managed to appear on the elite basketball stage before World War II and as mentioned earlier won European championships in 1937 and 1939. Lithuania repeated this success in 2003. Lithuania won European silver on three occasions (1995, 2013 and 2015), and in 2007 the team won bronze. Lithuanian national basketball team won three Olympic bronze medals in 1992, 1996 and 2000, respectively. Lithuania finished 3rd in 2010 International Basketball Federation (FIBA) World Championship. Since re-establishment of independence in 1990, Lithuanian national men's basketball team had managed to advance to every single Olympic Games tournament. It alone says that every four years Lithuania manages to assemble a very strong team. Lithuanian national basketball women's teams were less successful despite the 1997 gold medal in European Championship. This consistency of success and remarkable popularity of basketball makes Lithuanian Basketball Federation (LKF) one of the most important and powerful sports federations in Lithuania.

88. The LKF was established in 1991 and in the same year the LKF became a member of the FIBA.[48]

A. Legal Form, Membership, Governance

89. Legal form of the LKF is association. Only legal persons can be members of the LKF. More precisely, registered entities, organizations, formal and non-formal education entities, basketball federations of cities and counties and other entities which promote and develop the sport of basketball and which abide by the LKF Statutes and which share similar goals and values as the LKF. Legal person willing

48. The roots of basketball in Lithuania can be traced to year 1921. Lithuania was admitted to FIBA in 1936. At that time LKF did not exist and the Basketball Committee of the Lithuanian Ball Games Union was admitted by the FIBA. Information provided by the website of LKF (accessed on 19 Aug. 2017) (http://www.musukrepsinis.lt/lkf/istorija/).

to become a member of the LKF must submit a request to the LKF's Executive Committee. A decision to approve the candidate is taken by the Executive Committee.

90. The main governing bodies of the LKF are:

– Conference of the LKF (assembly of members) is a main governing body of the LKF.
– As from December 2021, a new collegial body, the Strategic Management Board, was established.
– Executive Committee is a collegial executive body of the LKF.
– President of the LKF is a sole governing body of the LKF.
– General Secretariat of the LKF managed by the General Secretary.

LKF Council of Honour (advisory body) and LKF Commission for Ethics, Disciplinary and Appeals (legal disciplinary body) also form bodies of the LKF which are assigned to specific tasks by the LKF Statutes.

B. *Conference*

91. Conference is the main governing body of LKF. It has an exclusive power to decide on most important matters of the LKF, including amendment of the statutes, election of the Executive Committee and the President, approval of annual financial reports, approval of annual basketball event schedule. Conference is usually convened on an annual basis. Every four years 'elective' Conference takes place for election of the Executive Committee, the President and other elected officers. Extraordinary Conference may also be summoned by request of one-third of members, the President or the Executive Committee. Decisions in Conference are taken by majority of votes of participating members. Specific matters (e.g., amendment of the statutes) require a quorum of two-thirds of members participating in the meeting. On 7 October 2020, there were 135 members of the LKF.[49] Most of them are basketball clubs, basketball schools and academies.

C. *Strategic Management Board and Executive Committee*

92. As from the establishment of the LKF, the Executive Committee was a principal collegial governing body of the LKF assuming typical roles and functions of a collegial governing body of a sports association. However, in December 2021, new Statutes of the LKF were adopted establishing a new collegian governing body of the LKF, the Strategic Management Board. The Strategic Management Board

49. The list of LKF members is published in the website of LKF (accessed on 21 Jun. 2021) (https://ltu.basketball/wp-content/uploads/2021/04/LKF-nariu-sarasas_20201007.pdf).

was assigned to run functions previously assumed by the Executive which are considered to be more strategic than casual tasks of the Executive Committee. In particular, the Strategic Management Board is now responsible for adopting and monitoring strategies and plans of development of sport of basketball in Lithuania. As well as this, the Strategic Management Board has a power to decide on issues like membership of the LKF in various organizations, incorporation of institutions accountable to the LKF.

93. The Strategic Management Board consists of nine natural persons, i.e., the President and eight vice-presidents (four vice-presidents are appointed by the President, two vice-presidents are selected by the President from representatives of the LKF members and two of them are selected from the members of the Executive Committee).

94. The Executive Committee consists of twelve natural persons: the President, and eleven members delegated from various basketball organizations (e.g., leagues, coaches' association, referees' association). Executive Committee is elected by the Conference for an office term of four years. Executive Committee is competent to decide on matters which are not expressively attributed to the exclusive competence of the Conference. The Executive Committee, *inter alia*, decides upon confirmation of basketball competition regulations, approves candidacy of the General Secretary, approves candidacies of head coaches and coaches of national basketball team,[50] approves calendar of preparation of national team, decides upon approval of new member or suspension or exclusion of the existing member, supervise the implementation of annual budget.

D. President

95. President is the sole governing body. President is elected by the Conference for an office term of four years. President leads the Executive Committee and the Strategic Management Board. President is not allowed to hold any other office related to basketball. Specific conditions on the reputation of candidate for President are also applied. A person may not be elected as the President for more than two consecutive terms of office. Main duties of the President are to run daily operations of the LKF, represent LKF before courts, state and municipality authorities, in relationship with third persons, issue annual reports and annual financial reports. President has the discretion to convene Conference. President of the LKF is considered to be a very important person in the field of sport.

50. This privilege is considered to be very important in Lithuania. Chair of men's basketball national team is always a hot topic. Attention of the society to the coach election procedure is significant.

E. Other Bodies and Finances

96. LKF Secretariat is responsible for administrating daily activities of the LKF. The LKF Secretariat is managed by LKF Secretary who is appointed by the Executive Committee upon proposal of the President.

97. LKF Commission for Ethics, Discipline and Appeals. The commission is competent to hear disciplinary matters, hear certain disputes between federation, leagues, players, coaches and other official persons and as well as this also serves as an appeals body to hear appeals against decisions of leagues and their bodies.

98. In 2019–2020 annual budget of the LKF varies from EUR 3 million to EUR 4 million. About two-thirds of the budget is generated from marketing and commercial activities (such as sponsorship) and about one-third of the budget is collected from the state funds.

II. Lithuanian Football Federation

99. Despite basketball being the most popular sport football is very popular as well. The roots of football in Lithuania can be traced back to 1912 when the first intercity match was played between cities of Vilnius and Kaunas. Football branch of Lithuanian Sports League organized a first football championship in 1922. On 21 May 1923, Lithuania was admitted to FIFA, and one month later a first international football match was played against Estonia.

100. During the years of Soviet occupation, football was an important sport as well. In 1982 football club FK Žalgiris (Vilnius) consisting of home-grown players only was promoted to the top Soviet division. The same team finished third five years later conquering first Union of European Football Associations (UEFA) competition spot. Similar to the basketball club BC Žalgiris (Kaunas), it is widely believed that results of FK Žalgiris had similar social effects boosting the moods of Lithuanian resistance against Soviet oppression.

101. After the re-establishment of independence, the LFF was established and the Lithuanian national team was summoned. Lithuania was readmitted to FIFA. Unlike basketball teams, Lithuanian football teams have never experienced any significant international success. Lithuanian national team has never advanced to the FIFA World Cup or the UEFA European Championships. However, LFF, together with LKF, remains one of the most important sports organizations in the country. Affairs of the LFF are always at the centre of attention of football stakeholders and society as a whole.

102. The statutes of the LFF are the backbone of activity of the LFF. The statutes of the LFF have been the target of critics of stakeholders for several years. It is claimed that the statutes of the LFF significantly limit possibilities of new members to gain membership (potential members have to be approved by the Conference and the Executive Committee), it does not ensure proper representation of all football stakeholders (players, clubs are not directly represented), it established an exhaustive list of members, majority of Executive Board members are automatically approved.

103. In September 2016 a task force was summoned to analyse the existing situation and to propose potential amendments of the statutes.

104. Task force issued a report which identified[51] key problems of the LFF governance:

- lack of involvement of all stakeholders into activities of the LFF;
- disproportional representation of various stakeholder groups in current membership of LFF;
- lack of uniform order and transparency in appointing delegates to the Conference by members;
- disproportional structure of the Executive Committee;
- lack of transparency and clarity of activities of functional federations, members of the LFF;
- lack of publicity and transparency in activities of the LFF.

105. Following amendments were, *inter alia*, proposed:

- to annul an exhaustive list of members provided in the statutes and to ensure that clubs, association of clubs, association of players, association of coaches and association of referees are accepted as members of the LFF;
- decision on accepting candidacy of a new member or expulsion of members has to be taken by the Executive Committee only;
- only one delegate of a member having one vote should participate in the Conference;
- to expand the composition of the Executive Committee including three independent members;
- introduce requirements of impeccable reputation for elected offices.

106. In May 2017 the LFF Statutes were amended; however, amendments were very symbolic comparing to the proposals of the task force.[52]

---

51. Report of the task force is available in website of LFF (accessed on 26 Jun. 2021) (http://lff.lt/files/documents/189/Darbo%20grupes%20raporto%20projektas.pdf).
52. Executive Committee was expanded to twenty members, including seats for presidents of clubs' association, players' union and an independent female member. Maximum limit of terms of office (three) was introduced. Moreover, powers of the President were minimized significantly. Limitation of at least five-year activity in the field of football as criteria for membership was cancelled as well. It should be noted that new edition of the LFF Statutes have not yet been made public thus the author

107. In accordance with the current edition of the LFF Statutes (amended once again in 2020), the main bodies of the LFF are the following:

- The Conference.
- The Executive Committee.
- The President.
- General Secretary.
- Vice Presidents.
- Legal Bodies (Disciplinary Committee, Appeals Committee, Club Licensing Committee, Licensing Appeals Committee, Committee for Ethics).
- Permanent Committees (Referee Committee).
- Other bodies.

108. Role of each of the bodies is analysed further.

A. *Conference*

109. Conference is an assembly of LFF members. Only a legal person can be a member of the LFF. Candidate member of the LFF has to meet not only procedural requirements laid down by the LFF but to be approved by both the Executive Committee and the Conference. The members may be expelled from the Conference by the Conference with the opinion of the Executive Committee. The Conference may suspend the member's rights as well. The Executive Committee has a right to suspend the membership of certain members under specific circumstances (breach of the statutes, failure to comply with decision of the LFF, etc.) as well.

110. Each member has a right to delegate five persons having one vote to the Conference, i.e., each member possesses five votes in the meetings of the Conference. The Conference decides on essential issues of the LFF, including, but not limited to an amendment of the statutes, election of part of the Executive Committee and the President and vice presidents, approval of annual financial reports.

111. The LFF member list is provided directly in the statutes. At the moment, the LFF has nineteen members. Nine members of the Conference are representing certain fields of football which are referred to as 'functional federations' (Lithuanian Association of Football Referees, Lithuanian Futsal and Beach Football Association, Association for Grassroots Football of Lithuania, Association for Children and Youth Football Development of Lithuania, Lithuanian Women's Football Association, Lithuanian Association of Football Clubs 'A Lyga', Lithuanian Union of Football Players, Association for Training of Coaches, Lithuanian Student Football Association) and ten members are representing certain regions of Lithuania. Regional federations have an equal number of votes regardless of their size in area

---

had to rely on information provided by the website of the LFF. Information on amendment of the KFF Statutes is available online (accessed on 17 May 2019) (http://lff.lt/news/3892/priimti-atnaujinti-lff-istatai/).

or population or professional clubs belonging to regional federation. Before 30 September 2017, there was no direct representation of football players and football clubs in the Conference. Currently, the clubs are represented by Lithuanian Association of Football Clubs 'A Lyga'. However, it can be easily argued that the Lithuanian Union of Football Players is barely functional as majority of professional football players are represented by newly established (2020) Union of Professional Players. However, the latter organization, despite support of majority of professional players, still lacks recognition from the LFF.

112. Decisions of the Conference are passed by the majority of votes. Each member can appoint five delegates possessing one vote per delegate in the Conference. Specific issues require a quorum of two-thirds of votes (e.g., amendment of the statutes). The Conference takes place every calendar year. However, extraordinary Conference may be convened upon request of the Executive Committee.

B. Executive Committee

113. The Executive Committee is a collegial governing body of the LFF. It decides on the important issues of the activity of the LFF, including appointment of General Secretary, chairmen and members of LFF Legal Bodies and Permanent Committees, appointment of head coaches and coaches of national teams, deciding on financial matters of the LFF, submission of financial reports, decisions on LFF budget and approval of activity programme. It is important to notice that the Executive Committee possesses wide discretion related to competitions. The Executive Committee approves the regulations of competitions. Usually, the regulations provide the right for the Executive Committee to render final decisions in case of any contingencies.[53]

114. Prior to the amendment of the statutes in May 2017, the Executive Committee consisted of thirteen members: President, six presidents of all six functional federations (Lithuanian Association of Football Referees, Lithuanian Futsal Association, Association for Grassroots Football of Lithuania, Lithuanian Association for Football Technical Development, Association for Children and Youth Football of Lithuania, Lithuanian Women's Football Association) and six representatives elected from ten regional associations. Thus, seven members used to be permanent members of the Executive Committee and six members were elected by the Conference for a term of office of four years. After the amendment of the statutes in May 2017, the Executive Committee was expanded to a potential number of twenty members. Presidents of all regional associations together with presidents of functional federations are now considered as members of the Executive Committee. Moreover, in accordance with the statutes, an additional member proposed by members of the LFF can also act as the twentieth member of the Executive Committee. It is required by the statutes that such twentieth member shall be female member.

---

53. For example, Art. 269 of current edition of the LFF's competition regulations (2021 edition).

115. The meetings of the Executive Committees are held at least once in a quarter of a year. Decisions are taken by majority of votes. President and three members of the Executive Committee form what is known as the Committee for Exceptional Matters which decides in case of unforeseen circumstances.

116. As from April 2022, a person can hold an office of a member of the Executive Committee for a maximum of two consecutive terms.

C. President

117. For many years the President of the LFF used to be one of the most important offices in terms of sports governance in Lithuania. President used to be the sole governing body of the LFF, elected directly by the Conference for a term of four years via complex election system. President was authorized to conclude transactions on behalf of the LFF, sign documents, operate assets of the LFF. The President was responsible for due preparation of annual activity plan and financial report of the LFF. The President was also responsible for maintenance of the relationship between the LFF and its members, FIFA, UEFA, political and other organizations and institutions.

118. However, President's powers were minimized significantly after amendments of the statutes of May 2017. Most of the previous functions of the President were transferred to the General Secretary and the Executive Committee.

119. As from April 2022, a person can hold office of the President for a maximum of two consecutive terms.

D. Other Bodies

120. With the minimization of President's powers, General Secretary gained more authority. General Secretary runs the administration of the LFF and is appointed for an unlimited term. General Secretary is authorized to conclude transactions on behalf of the LFF, sign documents, operate assets of the LFF. General Secretary is now responsible for the due preparation of the annual activity plan and the financial report of the LFF. General Secretary is appointed by the Executive Committee. General Secretary can be withdrawn from office by the Executive Committee under a quorum of two-thirds. As from April 2022, a person can hold office of the General Secretary for a maximum of two consecutive terms.

121. Legal bodies of the LFF consist of the Disciplinary Committee, Appeals Committee, Club Licensing Committee, Licensing Appeals Committee, Committee for Ethics.

122. The Licensing Committee is responsible for functioning and implementation of the club licensing system. In accordance with the UEFA Club Licensing and

Financial Fair Play Regulations 2015, Lithuanian top and second-tier clubs have to undergo licensing procedures and have to obtain a licence permitting to participate not only in local competitions but in UEFA competitions as well. The clubs have to meet certain criteria, including sporting, legal, financial, administrative and infrastructural requirements. Licensing system was first launched by the LFF back in 2004, and it contributed to improvement of clubs, their legal structure, infrastructure and competence of staff. Decisions of the LFF Licensing Committee, including decisions on refusal to issue licence, are subject to an appeal to the Licensing Appeals Committee.

123. Disciplinary bodies of the LFF are the LFF Disciplinary Committee and the LFF Appeals Committee. The LFF Disciplinary Committee is competent to decide on disciplinary matters, including imposition of sanctions. Decisions of the LFF Disciplinary Committee are a subject of appeal to the LFF Appeals Committee. The latter is also competent to hear private disputes between members of the LFF, clubs (e.g., regarding payment of a training compensation), players (e.g., a contractual dispute between the player and the club regarding payment of salaries) as sole instance.

124. Article 61 of the statutes of the LFF includes the CAS arbitration clause. It states that any final decision of the body of the LFF is subject to an appeal of CAS. CAS is not competent to hear disputes related to the rules of the game and decisions of the LFF bodies to impose sanction on a natural person not exceeding disqualification of four matches.

Chapter 4. Other Sports Institutions

§1. LEAGUES

125. In general, a sports league is considered to be an entity formed by clubs for competition among each other. Unlike the US,[54] European sports leagues are based on a 'pyramid structure of competitions from grassroots to elite level'.[55] It means that teams in the leagues slightly change every season since some teams are relegated to the lower division and some teams are promoted to the higher division. Most important leagues in Lithuania, top-tier basketball and football leagues are of European sport model tradition.

126. A term 'league' is not defined by the Laws of the Republic of Lithuania. Usually, leagues in Lithuania are organized under a legal form of association (however, there are exceptions, e.g., Lithuanian Women's Basketball League is organized under form of public entity) or organized directly by responsible federation without establishment of a separate legal person. Teams participating in competition organized by the league do form the league. The status of the league depends on its relationship with certain federation.

127. Lithuanian top football championship is actually named as 'league', i.e., '*A Lyga*'. Depending on the financial and factual situation it is organized by the Lithuanian Football Club Association 'A Lyga' in accordance with the agreement with the LFF or by the LFF itself. In accordance with the statutes of the Lithuanian Football Club Association, only clubs which obtained LFF club licence to participate in top division can be admitted to members of the association. Members automatically lose their membership rights when they lose licence permitting to play in the league. It should be noted that the Lithuanian Football Club Association has been a relatively new organizer of the competition. It was established only in 2015, and it has been responsible to organize top football competitions for 2016, 2017 and 2018 footballing seasons[56] only. Before that, the LFF was responsible for the organization of top-tier football competitions. It should be also noted that nevertheless the status of Lithuanian Football Club Association as league organizer under agreement, '*A Lyga*' is organized and conducted in accordance with the LFF Competition Regulations. Disciplinary matters are a responsibility of the LFF as well. The second division or '*I Lyga*' is organized directly by the LFF. A club at the very bottom of '*A Lyga*' is relegated to '*I Lyga*' and champion of '*I Lyga*' is promoted to the top division. Penultimate team of '*A Lyga*' and vice champion of '*I Lyga*' have to play a round of home-away games.

---

54. In the US most know professional sports leagues, such as NBA, the Major League Soccer, the Major League Baseball, the National Football League and the National Hockey League are closed leagues; i.e., the teams are not relegated, nor promoted. The equality between franchises is ensured by such measures as draft system allowing the worse team to sign the best rookie and thus improve significantly, coordinated marketing and commercial activity ensuring equal share of income.
55. *See* the White Paper on Sport.
56. Football season in Lithuania starts in March and finishes in November due to weather conditions, thus a season corresponds to a calendar year.

128. Slightly different practices apply in basketball. The top division of basketball is called Lithuanian Basketball League (LKL). LKL is association and clubs are members of association. The second division of Lithuanian men's basketball is called National Basketball League (NKL). NKL is also association whose members are basketball clubs possessing right to participate in the championship. Membership in NKL is directly linked to the right of a club to participate in the said division. However, unlike Lithuanian football leagues, LKL and NKL operate under their own competition regulations (approved by LKF). LKL and NKL have their own disciplinary bodies and disciplinary systems. There is promotion/relegation relationship between the LKL and the NKL as well. LKL and NKL have sufficient opportunities to exploit their media rights and marketing.

§2. Clubs

129. In accordance with the Law on Sport, sports club is defined as an enterprise or a subdivision thereof, the purpose of which is to unite individuals for physical activity, healthy lifestyle and/or sports, to achieve qualitative and quantitative results in physical activity and/or high performance sport.[57] Sports clubs are assigned by the Law on Sport to organizations developing physical activity and high performance sport. The Law on Sport does not distinguish any specific rights or obligations for sports club.

130. Laws do not specify any legal form for sports club. It is upon the decision of the founders of sports club to choose a legal form subject to general legal provisions. However, Regulations of sports federations may introduce certain requirements. For example, in accordance with the LFF Club Licensing Regulations, a club cannot operate under legal form of budget office (an entity established by the state or municipal authority which is financed directly from the state or the municipality).

131. The most popular legal forms of sports clubs are an association or public institution.[58] All top division basketball and football clubs are either public institutions or associations. One of the main reasons behind such choice is that associations and public institutions are recognized as beneficiaries in terms of the Law on Charity and Sponsorship of the Republic of Lithuania 1993 and thus can receive financial support from providers of such support. Such income is subject to tax

---

57. Article 2(24) of the Law on Sport.
58. A term 'public institution' does not necessarily mean that legal person is controlled by state or municipality, i.e., public sector. Public institution is a non-profit legal person with an objective to entertain public interests in the field of education, science, culture, medicine, protection of environment, physical education and *sports*. Term 'public' refers to public interest. The main difference between public institution and association is that the establishment of public institution does not require specific number of association members. Stakeholder of public institution can have different proportions of stakes, whereby in association one member usually holds one vote. Stakes in public institution may be transferred to the other person whereas membership right is not subject of such transaction.

privileges. Companies which provide financial support, i.e., the sponsors, benefit from it as contributed financial support may be considered as allowable deductions in terms of corporate tax.

132. Sports clubs depending on their membership are further governed by the private regulations of national federations. LFF Club Licensing Regulations sets forth a very comprehensive list of criteria which have to be met by the clubs. Basketball clubs have to meet certain requirements set by the leagues before they are accepted to participate in competitions.

§3. Sports Schools and Academies: Promotion of Sports in Educational System

133. A sport school or sports academy is not defined by laws. However, said terms are heard and used very often in practice. Sports schools and academies are entities which carry out educational activities in the field of sports and train children and young athletes. Such entities usually form children and youth teams which participate in certain level of organized competitions.

134. A sport school and academy may function under various legal forms. Most of them are, as clubs, associations or public institutions. However, many of them operate as budget offices. Thus, private and public schools and academies exist. Moreover, schools and academies may be controlled by both public and private persons.

135. Most of the public sports schools and academies are controlled by municipal authorities and are directly accountable to them. Spread of such structures may be explained by the regulation of the Law on Local Self-government of the Republic of Lithuania which assigns organization of physical education and sports to the independent functions of the municipality. Thus, the municipalities have a duty to ensure the organization of sports within their territory and grant access to sports for citizens. Besides, in general, all sport infrastructure objects with rare exceptions are a property of the state and are controlled by municipalities. Due to the historic popularity of certain sports within certain regions, tradition of sports schools controlled by municipality remained.

136. The issue related to the control of sports infrastructure contributes to the fact that privately funded sports schools and academies find it hard to compete against municipality-owned entities, *inter alia*, due to the inability to use sports infrastructure. However, ideas of joining forces of the private sector, a sports club (which possess know-how and may provide additional value due to its name and fame) and public sector (budget funds and infrastructure) are developing.

137. Professional football clubs are encouraged to develop their own youth and children training structures. Football clubs must develop a youth system inside their club structure in order to obtain licence in accordance with the LFF Club Licensing

System. This can be done by developing structures inside the club or establishing separate legal entities controlled by the club. As well as this, football clubs are encouraged to develop their own children and youth education systems due to participation of the club in local and FIFA-governed training compensation and solidarity contribution systems: the more the club is involved in the education of future professionals, the more money the club can expect due to successful career of the player and his or her future transfers. Finally, UEFA Solidarity Programme payments are distributed by the LFF for clubs after taking into consideration the level of youth team education system developed by a club. These factors push football clubs to develop their own youth academies and schools which may result in competition between private and public sports schools and academies.

Unlike football clubs, basketball clubs, as well as clubs of other areas of sports, are not encouraged by solidarity and training compensation systems applicable to them. Thus, with rare exceptions, children and youth development is usually carried out by public basketball schools or academies. Major part of municipalities does control a single entity which conducts education activities in multiple areas of sports.

It should also be noted that schools and academies which gained a right to conduct programmes of non-formal education in accordance with the Law on Education of the Republic of Lithuania, 1991, are subject to additional requirements provided by the mentioned law.

138. The Law on Sport sets basic principles on organizing physical activities in educational system. In accordance with Article 12(1) and 12(2) of the Law on Sport, a minimum amount of time per academic week for physical activities is provided for schools. Article 12(4) of the Law on Sport obliges universities to provide an option in their academic programmes for students to select a subject related to physical activities.

Chapter 5. Public Financing of Sport

139. Financing of sport in Lithuania is one of the most important issues related to governance of Lithuanian sports and certainly one of the hottest topics of public discussion. Most of the professional sports in Lithuania are directly or indirectly funded by the budget funds. It also applies to professional football and basketball clubs. Even top Lithuanian basketball and football clubs do not generate all of their income from private sources (sponsors, sale of tickets, sale of TV rights, transfers of players). They are actively supported by the funds of budget as well, and for some clubs budget funds are key income.

§1. Principles and Sources of Financing of Sports

140. Article 53(3) of the Constitution stipulates that the state promotes physical education of society and supports sport. This provision should be understood in the sense that the state supports sports, *inter alia*, in financial terms. Further the financing of sports from the budget of the state or municipalities is mainly governed by the Law on Sport.

141. One of the main reasons for the introduction of the new edition of the Law on Sport in 2018 was a will to amend governance of public financing of sport and to make it more transparent. In accordance with Article 16(1) of the Law on Sport, the financing of sport is composed by: (1) funds of state budget; (2) funds of budgets of municipalities; (3) other funds.

142. As mentioned in paragraph 140, a duty of the state to finance and support sport derives directly from the Constitution. Pursuant to Article 8(1)(3) of the Law on Sport, municipalities have the duty to fund (or to support by different means) natural or legal persons conducting activities of sport within the territory of municipality concerned.

143. The Law on Sport distinguishes and governs three basic methods of financing sport from funds of the state and municipalities: (1) financing of physical activity and improvement of sports facilities from funds of state and municipalities' budget; (2) financing of high performance sports programmes from the state and municipalities' budgets; (3) awarding and supporting active and former athletes from funds of the state and municipalities' budgets.

144. Further, the main methods of financing of sport are explained in detail.

I. Financing of Physical Activity and Improvement of Sports Facilities

145. As from 2022, physical activity and the improvement of sports facilities are financed by the state budget through the allocation of funds, in accordance with the procedure laid down by the Minister for Education, Science and Sport, for national physical activity programmes (a four-calendar-year physical activity planning document of a national umbrella non-governmental organization, which sets out the goals, objectives and measures for their implementation, the timeframe, the criteria for evaluating the implementation of the measures, and the values of the measures that comply with the requirements set out by the Minister for Education, Science and Sport), for national and regional physical activity projects (a document describing the temporary activity of a legal entity, the unique and specific quantitative and/or qualitative results related to physical activity, the objectives, targets and measures of these activities, the timeframe for their implementation, the expected results and the resources and sources of funds needed to achieve them) and for projects for the improvement of sports facilities (a document describing the temporary activities of a legal entity to achieve unique and specific quantitative and/or qualitative results related to the improvement of sports facilities, the objectives, targets and measures of these activities, the timeframe for their implementation, the expected results and the funds and sources of funds needed to achieve them).

The list of national physical activity programmes and their requirements are established by the Minister for Education, Science and Sport. National physical activity programmes are financed by the state budget in accordance with the procedure laid down by the Minister for Education, Science and Sport. Umbrella organizations providing national physical activity programmes, which apply for state budget funds for the implementation of these programmes, must meet the criteria laid down in the Law on Sport (Article 17(3) of the Law on Sport). National and regional physical activity projects and projects for the improvement of sports facilities are selected using the following general evaluation criteria: relevance and importance of the project, effectiveness, impact and continuity of the project, financial and economic justification of the project, and project management.

The institution authorized by the Minister for Education, Science and Sport (the National Sports Agency) administers programmes and projects for the improvement of physical activity and sports facilities, including the organization of project selection, the organization of public procurement, the adoption of decisions on the allocation of funds, and the supervision of the implementation of contracts for the implementation of the projects or programmes.

The municipal executive authority or its authorized bodies, in accordance with the procedure for the financing of physical activity projects and sports facilities improvement projects financed by municipal budgets established by the municipal councils, are assigned to carry out the selection of physical activity projects and sports facilities improvement projects submitted to the municipality and take decisions on their co-financing.

146. The year 2022 is the first year of funding physical activity and improvement of sports facilities through four-year-long programmes and projects. The results of the new financing physical activity could be assessed in the period of several years only.

II. Financing of the High Performance Sports Programmes

147. High performance sport is funded by state and municipal budgets. High performance sport is financed by the state budget in accordance with the procedure established by the Minister of Education, Science and Sport.

148. High performance sport is financed by allocating funds for high performance sport programmes (a four-calendar-year planning document for high performance sport, which specifies the objectives, tasks and measures for the implementation of the activities of the legal entity, as laid down in its statutes, regulations, statutes or any other founding document, as well as the deadlines for implementation, the criteria for evaluation of the implementation of the measures, the criteria and the values of the measures, the need for funds for the period of the implementation of this document in the course of the each calendar year, as well as the planned sources of these funds), the National Anti-Doping Programme (a four-calendar-year planning document setting out the National Anti-Doping Organisation's activities related to the implementation of the World Anti-Doping Code, the measures for their implementation, the timeframes for the measures, the financial requirements for the implementation of this document in each of the current calendar years, and the planned sources of these funds), and the institutions enabling conditions for preparation of athletes.

149. High performance sport is financed by allocating funds for Olympic, Paralympic, visual, hearing, mobility or intellectual disability sport, student sport movements in Lithuania, the functions performed by the leading non-governmental organizations and sports federations in Lithuania in relation to the training of athletes and their participation in international high performance sport competitions, and sports training, the organization of high performance sports training camps and sports events, the selection and training of children with exceptional sporting abilities, the development and strengthening of club activities, the implementation of the World Anti-Doping Code, the prevention of brutal behaviour of spectators, and the combating of manipulation of high performance sports competitions. These organizations are required to develop programmes for high performance sport, including corresponding measures to achieve their goals.

150. The criteria for a legal entity to be entitled to receive state budget funds for the implementation of a high performance sport programme are set out in detail in Article 19 of the Law on Sport. Such requirements include, *inter alia*, administrative requirements, sporting requirements (e.g., the requirement for athletes representing the federation to participate in a certain level of competition), organizational requirements (requirements for the governance structure of the federation or organization, rotation of governing bodies).

151. It should be stressed that the funding of high performance sport takes into account, among other things, the priorities set by the state for the sport concerned. The Minister of Education, Science and Sport determines the criteria for strategic sports to be funded by the state budget for a period of four years and approves the list of strategic sports. Federations or other organizations of sports on this list have a better chance of receiving state funding.

152. The Law on Sport also provides for the financing of the organization of international competitions of high excellence in Lithuania included in the calendar of an international sports federation. Such funding is carried out in accordance with the procedure laid down by the Minister of Education, Science and Sport, by allocating state budget funds to projects submitted for international sports competitions. The selection of projects for international sports competitions shall be based on the following general evaluation criteria: relevance and importance of the international high performance sport competition, the place of the international high performance sport competition in the system of international high performance sport competitions in the sport branch, the financial and economic justification of the international high performance sport competition, the state of the sports facilities where the international high performance sport competition will be held, the activity of the international federation of the sport branch, the international high performance sport competition, the participants in the international high performance sport competition, the promotion of the international high performance sport competition, and the partnership.

153. High performance sport is also financed by municipal budgets in accordance with the procedure laid down by municipal councils.

154. Article 20 of the Law on Sport provides mechanisms preventing abuse of the use of state budgets. Article 20(1) sets forth the list of circumstances which constitute the ground to deny application of an organization for funds to finance their high performance sports programmes. Such list includes circumstances related to suspension of activity of an organization, pending obligations to tax authorities, pending seizure of assets of an organization, failure to provide authentic data to the authorities providing funds, records of failure of an organization to comply with agreement for use of state, incompliance of the project of high performance sports programmes with the anti-doping regulations, criminal record of an organization or a person involved in management of an organization.

155. Article 20(2) of the Law on Sport provides an instrument to state institutions to suspend or to recover funds provided to the organization which does not comply with the requirements set forth in Article 20(1) of the Law on Sport. Such instruments, *inter alia*, are a right to withhold the payment or request of return of funds if circumstances related to incompliance become known after confirmation of a high performance sports programme.

156. As the system of funding sports projects, the funding of high performance sports programmes is relatively new, and it is too early to provide reasonable conclusions on its effectiveness and legal clarity.

§2. FUNDING OF SPORTS BY MUNICIPALITIES

157. Pursuant to Article 8(1)(3) of the Law on Sport, municipalities have the duty to fund (or to support by different means) natural or legal persons conducting activities of sport within the territory of municipality concerned. Besides, the Law on Sport provides that the municipalities can finance both physical activity and high performance sports programmes and projects implemented in the territory of certain municipality. However, the laws do not prevent municipalities from financially supporting sports in other forms as well. The key basis for funding sports by municipality is Law on Local Self-Governance of the Republic of Lithuania which states that development of physical education and sports is independent function of municipality. There are two main directions of financing of sports from municipality budgets:

(1) Funding of non-budget institutions: In order to receive funds from municipalities, sports organizations, for example, regional federation or sports clubs, have to apply to the municipality concerned. Each municipality distributes money in accordance with their own regulations, therefore procedures and other aspects do differ from municipality to municipality. However, they all share the principle of financing in accordance with the programme system. Sports organizations willing to receive funds from municipalities have to submit a project of annual programme such sports organizations are willing to carry out. Such projects are assessed by municipality bodies. If approved, a financing is granted and usually agreement for use of municipality funds is signed between municipality or its institution and sports organization.
(2) Funding of budget institutions: budget offices of municipalities, such as football or basketball schools, or budget offices are responsible for the administration of municipality-owned sports infrastructure are generally funded straight from the budget without any submission of programme, i.e., such funded institutions are considered as managers of municipality appropriations. Certain amount to be provided for budget office is directly included in a decision of municipality council to approve annual budget.

158. A lot of professional sports clubs, including top basketball and football clubs,[59] are financially supported by municipalities. For many clubs such support is the main part of their budget. Decision of municipality to fund or not to fund certain club is subject to various hardly foreseeable factors, such as economic situation and political tense. Therefore, a club financed by municipality for many years may suddenly lose an important source of income. Thus, dependence of sports clubs from public sector money and fragility of their self-sustainability is one of the biggest challenges of professional sports in Lithuania. Besides, practices of funding clubs from public money could infringe state-aid issues in accordance with the EU law governing state aid. For the past years, Lithuanian clubs escaped troubles

59. For example, in 2016 Vilnius City Council granted BC Lietuvos Rytas and FK Žalgiris a little less than a million Euros each. Information available in news portal online (accessed on 26 Jun. 2021) (https://www.basketnews.lt/news-94633-vilniaus-savivaldybe-mazina-parama-lietuvos-rytui.html).

related to potential state aid; however, the latest actions of the Competition Council of the Republic of Lithuania demonstrate that practices of municipalities funding sports clubs will be viewed under much more intense scrutiny.[60]

§3. State Support of Athletes

159. Lithuanian legal regulation provides framework for financial support and promotion of individual athletes including support for athletes who terminated their sporting careers. Article 22 of the Law on Sport provides that the state ensures implementation of equality principle and rewards athletes for their sporting achievements while taking into consideration different systems for selection of athletes and quotas for countries, level of competition, number of athletes or countries participating in specific sports events. The main instruments of state support for athletes are: (1) state prizes for achieved results in high performance sports competitions; (2) state grants for athletes; (3) state support for former athletes (the system of rents).

I. State Prizes

160. In accordance with Article 23 of the Law on Sport, athletes and their coaches are rewarded by state for sporting achievements in high performance sports competitions. Amounts of rewards are set by the Government and are paid from the state budget.

161. A person has a right to receive a state reward if he or she achieved specific milestones provided by Article 23(2) of the Law on Sport while representing Lithuania in international competitions organized by international sports federations or other international sports organizations. Athletes who won 1st to 8th places in Olympic Games, 1st to 3rd places in World or European championships, 1st to 4th places in Paralympic Games are awarded.

162. The 16 August 2000 Decision No. 927 of Government on Promotion of High Performance Athletes and Other Members of National Teams ('Government Decision') stipulates amounts of grants and payments including exception for payments of higher amount subject to extraordinary circumstance. It should be noted that bonuses may also be provided for team sports athletes and staff as well.

163. Analysis of the content of the Government Decision confirms particular attention of the state to achievements in the Olympic Games. For example, a gold

60. On 4 Sep. 2017 the Competition Council of the Republic of Lithuania issued a statement declaring that the decision of Vilnius municipality to grant financial support of EUR 500,000 for FK Žalgiris and Basketball Club Lietuvos Rytas might be illegal due to failure to consult the European Commission on potential state-aid issues. Municipality was requested to inform on the course of the issue (accessed on 26 Jun. 2021) (https://kt.gov.lt/lt/naujienos/parama-profesionaliems-sporto-klubams-gali-buti-neteiseta).

medal in Olympic Games is rewarded by payment of approximately EUR 140,000 to an athlete. Meanwhile, a gold medal in world championship of an Olympic sport is valued by approximately EUR 27,000 only.

164. It is important to notice that achievements of disabled athletes in Paralympic Games, World and European championships are awarded too. Municipalities are also entitled to pay grants and bonuses for athletes in accordance with their regulations.

165. Article 23(4)–23(5) of the Law on Sport provide cases when the state awards cannot be paid or, if paid, have to be returned by the athlete. Such cases are related to criminal conviction or annulment of sports results constituting right for state award due to violation of anti-doping rules or participation in manipulation of sports competition.

II. State Grants

166. In accordance with Article 24 of the Law on Sport, athletes who achieved exceptional sporting results while representing Lithuania (and possessing Lithuanian citizen shop) have right to receive a state payment (state grant) payable on a monthly basis. Results obtained in Olympic Games, World and European championships, Paralympic Games and other competitions may constitute the ground for athlete to be supported by the state in the form of state grant.

167. An amount of grant is set on the basis of basic social payment and a coefficient determined by the world ranking of an athlete or his or her position in world championship. A motion to provide a grant has to be submitted by an athlete to an institution authorized by the Government.

168. The law also provides the grounds for dismissal of application for payment of state grant or suspension of payment of state grant. Such grounds are, *inter alia*, related to circumstances as criminal conviction, violation of anti-doping rules or participation in match-fixing, annulment of sports results giving ground for payment of state due to violation of anti-doping rules or participation in match-fixing, representation or preparation to represent another country. Naturally, the state grant is seized to be paid upon the termination of sporting career of an athlete.

III. Financial Support of Athletes after Termination of Career

169. Citizen of the Republic of Lithuania has a right to receive monthly payment ('rent') after termination of sporting career if he or she achieved specific sporting results while possessing citizenship of the Republic of Lithuania and while representing Lithuania.

170. A rent is payable only for athletes who achieved at least one of the following sporting milestones:

– he or she had become Olympic champion or had won Olympic medal; or
– he or she had become World or European champion in Olympic sports; or
– he or she had become Paralympic champion or won 2nd place.

171. The amount of state rent is fixed to twenty-seven basic social payment per month.

172. Rent is not payable if, *inter alia*, a person concerned loses Lithuanian citizenship is disqualified due to violation of anti-doping rules or involvement in match-fixing. The rent will not be paid if an athlete decides to reopen his or her sporting career.

173. Payment and amounts of rents are important topics in Lithuania. Legal disputes emerge among athletes and the former institution responsible for allocation of state rent, KKSD, as well. On 21 November 2013, Lithuanian Supreme Administrative Court rendered a ruling in Administrative Case No. A502-2131/2013 related to the grounds of payment of a rent. An athlete, very successful Lithuanian kayak rider Alvydas Duonėla, challenged the decision of the KKSD director not to approve rent payment to the athlete. Mr Duonėla claimed rent in accordance with the following ground which was stipulated in the old version of the Law on Sport: 'He or she had become world champion *and* world record holder in non-Olympic event of Olympic sport.' Mr Duonėla was in fact world champion of non-Olympic event of Olympic sport, i.e., 200 metres in double Kayak. Mr Duonėla also claimed to have set a world record in the said event. KKSD argued the latter element, i.e., the world record. KKSD claimed that Mr Duonėla did not set a world record, but rather a 'best time' which is not considered as a world record. KKSD claimed that sport events strongly related to external influence, such as weather conditions and acts of nature, are not subject to 'records'. The court stated that the athlete failed to prove that he did set a world record. The court concluded that 'best time' does not correspond to 'record' in accordance with procedures of logging world records. The court concluded that the lawmakers defined criteria for the provision of rent with precision and interpretation of related provision of Law on Sport by an athlete could not disprove the essence of legal regulation. The court further stated that expanded interpretation of the essence of record could constitute unjust privileges, which would result in the undermining of sporting achievements and contribution to Lithuania sports by other athletes from society's point of view. Even though the legal provision giving rise to said dispute is no longer valid, the considerations on the court are important for further assessment of a right of a former athlete to receive state grant.

Chapter 6. Fundamental Rights

§1. Basic Human Rights

174. Basic fundamental rights and freedoms of a person in Lithuania are guaranteed by the sources of national and international law. Main rights and freedoms of a person are established directly by the Constitution, a legal act of the highest legal power and direct effect. Therefore, these legal values can be defended by a person referring directly to the Constitution.

175. Depending on the content,[61] fundamental rights and freedoms directly protected by the Constitution are classified as:

- Civil (personal).
- Political and economic.
- Social and cultural.

176. Basic civil (personal) rights and freedoms are: (1) right to life which is protected by Article 19 of the Constitution, (2) right to personal liberty (Article 20 of the Constitution), (3) immunity and personal dignity of a person (Article 21 of the Constitution), (4) inviolability of private life of a person (Article 22 of the Constitution), (5) inviolability of property and house of a person (Articles 23 and 24 of the Constitution), (6) right to possess own convictions and freely express them and freedom of thought (Articles 25 and 26 of the Constitution), (7) freedom of movement (Article 32 of the Constitution).

177. Main political and economic rights include, *inter alia*, (1) right to participate in the governance of their state both directly and through democratically elected representatives (Articles 33 and 34 of the Constitution), (2) freely form societies, political parties and associations, and (3) right of assembly (Articles 36 and 37 of the Constitution).

178. Social and cultural rights, *inter alia*, include (1) a right to freely choose a job or business, and have proper, safe and healthy conditions at work, as well as to receive fair pay for work and social security in the event of unemployment (Article 48 of the Constitution), (2) right of strike of employees (Article 51 of the Constitution).

179. Said principles are safeguarded and also further implemented by laws and other regulations of the Republic of Lithuania. As mentioned earlier, each of the said right and freedom may be protected by the court with direct reference to a legal act of a highest and direct power, the Constitution.

---

61. For classification of basic rights *see* Birmontienė et al., *supra* n. 10, at p. 363.

180. Lithuania is also a member of the Council of Europe and accordingly is a consignee of the Convention for the Protection of Human Rights and Fundamental Freedoms ('the European Convention on Human Rights') and its additional protocols. In accordance with Article 138 of the Constitution, ratified international agreements are a constituent part of the legal system of the Republic of Lithuania. Therefore, the European Convention on Human Rights and its protocols are an integral part of the Lithuanian legal system. The Constitutional Court underlined the importance of the European Convention on Human Rights by stating[62] that the European Convention on Human Rights and decisions of the European Court of Human Rights have constitutional dimension and thus the European Convention on Human Rights may determine the principles for the interpretation and the content of human rights. The European Convention on Human Rights is applied directly in Lithuania. The Constitutional Court also determined[63] that jurisprudence of the European Court of Human Rights is an important source of interpretation of law which contributes to interpretation and application of the Lithuanian law.

181. As of 2004 Lithuania is a member of the EU. The Constitution Act on Participation of the Republic of Lithuania in the EU passed by the Parliament on 13 July 2004 sets forth the constitutional background of validity and application of the EU law in Lithuania. Article 2 of the said act establishes that the norms of EU law shall be a constituent part of the legal system of the Republic of Lithuania. Where it concerns the founding treaties of the EU, provisions of EU law are applied directly, while in the event of the conflict of laws EU provisions have supremacy over the laws and other legal acts of the Republic of Lithuania. Upon entry into force of Lisbon Treaty in 2009, Charter of Fundamental Rights of the European Union came into legal force for Member States of the EU, including Lithuania. Despite the fact that the Charter of Fundamental Rights of the European Union is applied when implementing EU law, it is believed[64] that the importance of the Charter of Fundamental Rights of the European Union for Lithuanian legal system will grow.

182. As will be discussed in further chapters, fundamental rights and principles are reflected in public regulation related to sports, as well as in private regulation of sports organizations and federations.

§2. Autonomy of Association

183. Lithuanian Laws and Lithuanian courts recognize the freedom and autonomy of association, which is the basis of existence of national and international sports federations operating under a legal form of an association.

62. 5 Sep. 2012 Ruling of the Constitutional Court.
63. 29 Dec. 2004 Ruling of the Constitutional Court, 29 Sep. 2005 Ruling of the Constitutional Court, 21 Dec. 2006 Ruling of the Constitutional Court, 15 May 2007 Ruling of the Constitutional Court.
64. Birmontienė et al., *supra* n. 10 at p. 394.

184. In accordance with Article 35 of the Constitution, citizens shall be guaranteed the right to freely form societies, political parties and associations provided that the aims and activities thereof are not contrary to the Constitution and laws. No one may be compelled to belong to any society, political party, or association. Said constitutional provision established a principle of freedom of association which is further stipulated by the Law of Associations of the Republic of Lithuania.

185. Article 14 of the Law on Associations of the Republic of Lithuania establishes[65] that state and municipal institutions and officials in the cases and procedure which are not laid down by law, political parties and political organizations, other organizations and persons shall *be prohibited from interfering in activities of an association and in its internal affairs.* The Constitutional Court noticed[66] that the most essential element of association is its autonomy from public governance (government or state and municipality entities). Autonomy of association before public authorities stipulates, *inter alia*, its constitutional right to independently regulate its own internal matters by means of internal legal acts (statutes, regulations, rules, etc.) in compliance with the Laws of the Republic of Lithuania.

186. The Supreme Administrative Court of Lithuania in its practice[67] stated that Article 14 of the Law of Associations of the Republic of Lithuania establishes two concepts of freedom of association: first, the right of association to self-regulate is preserved by the state; second, this provision guarantees the protection of association from interference in their casual business from public authorities. Such interference may be justified by the necessity of intervention due to safety and protection of society, aim to prohibit violations of public order or criminal act, to protect health and morale and rights and liberties of natural persons.

187. Thus, in general, the decisions of sports associations (federations) are a matter of their autonomy and usually the state does not intervene. However, if such interference is justified by the general exception of the autonomy of association, i.e., the necessity of intervention due to safety and protection of society, aim to prohibit violations of public order or criminal activity, to protect health and morale and rights and liberties of natural persons, such interference might take place.

188. One of the methods of the state's intervention to association matters is the court's review of the decisions taken by the association (subject to a claim of person possessing *locus standi*). Article 17(1)(11) of the Law on Resolution of the Administrative Cases of the Republic of Lithuania, 1999 establishes that administrative courts are competent to hear disputes related to, *inter alia*, validity of acts of general nature passed by associations. In such case, a court would assess whether decisions taken by the association meets the requirement of proportionality.

65. Official translation provided in website of the Seimas (accessed on 26 Jun. 2021) (https://e-seimas.lrs.lt/portal/legalAct/lt/TAD/066670f3168011e5bfc0854048a4e288?jfwid=-9dzqnu8gj).
66. 1 Jul. 2004 Ruling of the Constitutional Court and 8 Jul. 2005 Ruling of the Constitutional Court.
67. 14 Feb. 2013 ruling of the Lithuanian Supreme Administrative Court in Administrative Case No. I-261-2-13.

189. For example, the Supreme Administrative Court of Lithuania[68] annulled the decision of the Executive Committee of Lithuanian Judo Federation to the extent where it was decided that athletes obtaining certain qualification would not be included into Lithuanian national Judo team and that they would be disqualified for a period of one year (lifetime ban for subsequent violation) should they participate in competition of alternative wrestling (*sambo, alysh and kurash*). Such practice provides possibility to tackle general acts of association, including statutes, regulations applicable for all members, etc.

190. It should be noted that such federations, like LKF and, in particular, LFF, enjoy an additional level of protection from state interference. In accordance with the FIBA General Statutes, national associations shall 'manage their affairs independently and with no influence from third parties' (Article 9.7). Failure to meet such requirement may lead to suspension of national association from FIBA. Article 19(1) of the FIFA Statutes also states that each member association shall manage its affairs independently and without undue influence from third parties. The same rule is provided by Article 7*bis*(2) of the statutes of UEFA. Article 9(1*bis*) of the statutes of UEFA establishes more details:

> Member Association may in particular be suspended if state authorities interfere in its affairs in such a significant way that: a) it may no longer be considered as fully responsible for the organisation of football-related matters in its territory; b) it is no longer in a position to perform its statutory tasks in an appropriate manner; c) the smooth running of a competition organised under its auspices is no longer guaranteed; or d) the free election of its executive body or the totally independent election or appointment of its other bodies is no longer ensured.

191. Thus, whenever the state authorities attempt to interfere in the affairs of the LKF (member of FIBA) or the LFF (member of both, UEFA and FIFA), a risk of national basketball or football association being suspended or expelled from membership of international federation occurs. In such event, national federation would most likely lose membership privileges, including the ability to field national team in international tournaments or to delegate national clubs to international club competitions. A price of potentially very negative reaction from supporters and society may prevent such intervention.

68. *Ibid.*

Chapter 7. Tort Law/Conditions

§1. Criminal Liability and Sports

I. General Introduction on Criminal Liability

192. Criminal liability is the most serious form of liability. This position is based not only on the severity of sanction applicable in case of criminal liability (which can lead to life imprisonment) but to the essence of criminal liability, i.e., the condemnation of a person in the name of the state and the use of force of the state against such person. Criminal liability arises as a result of commitment of activities forbidden by the Criminal Code. Activities stipulated in the Criminal Code are distinguished from other violations by the nature and degree of their dangerous nature, contrariety to the law and by legal consequences.[69]

193. In order to convict a person in Lithuania, like in other jurisdictions, it is necessary to prove by a certain standard that a person had committed a crime or a criminal offence. To conclude that certain dangerous activity is a crime or a criminal offence in accordance with the Criminal Code, it is necessary to prove that all elements of certain criminal activity are present. Although it is not specified or explained in the Criminal Code, a concept of 'body of crime' is applied in Lithuanian criminal law. In other words, every single crime stipulated in the Criminal Code should be viewed as a body, composition of specific attributes which vary depending on a crime. Body of crime is the totality of objective and subjective attributes stipulated by the Criminal Code which describe dangerous acts as certain crime or criminal offence.

194. Objective attributes concern 'visible'[70] part of a crime. Principal objective attributes are values protected by criminal law, dangerous act (which can be an active act or omission), consequences (only applicable in the case of material body of crime, if a crime consists of formal body of crime, consequences are not required), causational link between an act and consequences, age of charged person. Optional objective attributes are time, date, manner of committing a crime, tools and measures and other aspects.

195. Subjective attributes relate to 'invisible, internal, mental side of crime'.[71] Principle subjective attributes are legal capacity of charged person and guilt. Optional subjective attributes are the purpose and motive of a crime.

196. A court hearing a criminal case must be convinced that all attributes of a body of certain crime are proved. It is very important to analyse the content of every attribute with scrutiny. Failure to prove a single attribute could result in an acquittal. Convicted persons are punished by measures stipulated in the Criminal Code,

---

69. Armanas Abramavičius et al., *Baudžiamoji teisė: bendroji dalis: vadovėlis*, p. 129 (Eugrimas, 2003).
70. Vytautas Piesliakas, *Lietuvos baudžiamoji teisė: pirmoji knyga*, p. 180 (Justitia, 2006).
71. *Ibid.*

such as deprivation of public rights, deprivation of the right to be employed in a certain position or to engage in a certain type of activities, community service, a fine, restriction of liberty, arrest, fixed-term imprisonment, life imprisonment.[72]

II. Crimes in the Field of Sports: Direct Provisions of Criminal Code

197. The Criminal Code includes two crimes directly related to sports, i.e., manipulation in sports competition (match-fixing) and possession of specific doping materials.

198. As from 1 January 2017 an amendment to the Criminal Code including new provision, Article $182^1(1)$, came into legal power. Article $182^1(1)$ of the Criminal Code provides punishment for a crime of manipulation of sports results. It states that whoever illegally effected fair course or outcome of *professional* sports competitions shall be punished by community service or by a fine or by restriction of liberty or by arrest or by imprisonment for a term of up to four years. Article $182^1(2)$ of the Criminal Code provides that a person who committed said crime shall be exonerated if he or she did inform law enforcement institutions on an illegal activity before gaining the status of suspect and did cooperate actively in the investigation of such crime.

199. This provision is brand new and courts have not yet elaborated on the composition of Article $182^1(2)$ of the Criminal Code. Therefore, it is too early for a thorough analysis of the content of attributes of the body of crime. However, it is very likely that courts are going to have issues to interpret the said provision. For example, a provision in question relates to 'professional sports' only. The Law on Sport or any legal act does not explain what is considered to be 'professional sport'.

200. As from 2016, Article 276^1–276^2 was introduced to the Criminal Code. Said provisions define a crime of 'illegal disposition [with the intent to distribute], distribution or prompt the usage of materials indicated in the Law on Control of Certain Doping Materials of the Republic of Lithuania'. Law on Control of Certain Doping Materials of the Republic of Lithuania, 2015 restricts the circulation of certain materials, *inter alia*, with the intention to prevent doping and to protect the health of society.

201. No other provisions of the Criminal Code describe crimes directly related to sport. Further potential involvements in other crimes and criminal offences with relation to activities of sports are analysed.

72. Execution of death penalty in Lithuania was suspended in 1996 and death penalty was ultimately abolished in 1998.

III. Hooliganism

202. From 2000 Lithuania is a member of the European Convention on Spectator Violence and Misbehaviour at Sports Events and in particular at Football Matches. Article 3(1)(c) provides that parties undertake to apply or, if need be, to adopt legislation which provides for those found guilty of offences related to violence or misbehaviour by spectators to receive appropriate penalties or, as the case may be, appropriate administrative measures.

203. Spectator violence and hooliganism is an important issue in sports due to its dangerous nature and total incompatibility with the principles sports relates to. Although spectator violence and hooliganism is not a very notable issue in Lithuania,[73] the Criminal Code foresees sanctions for involvement in activities which may be attributed to spectator violence. Article 283 of the Criminal Code defines crime of 'riot' and establishes attributes of such crime:[74]

> A person who organises or provokes a group of people to engage in public violence, destruction of property or other grave violations of public order, also a person who, during the riots, uses violence, destroys property or otherwise gravely violates public order shall be punished by arrest or by imprisonment for a term of up to five years.

204. If an armed weapon or explosive device is used while committing the crime, period of imprisonment may lead to six years. It is important to notice that body of such crime (riots) contains other crimes, such as cause of physical pain or minor bodily injury (Article 140 of the Criminal Code), or minor health impairment (Article 138(1) of the Criminal Code) and destruction or damaging of assets (Article 187 of the Criminal Code). More significant crimes which are committed during a riot, such as grievous bodily harm or murder are counted as separate crimes.

205. Article 284 of the Criminal Code provides a definition of public order disturbance. This crime is not necessarily related to the behaviour of a crowd or in the crowd and is more related to the fact of disturbance of public order and (or) public peace. Conviction of such crime can lead to imprisonment for a period of two years.

206. Spectators in arenas and stadiums may witness other troubling crimes which are not necessarily related to physical harm. Acts related to various forms of racial, ethnic and other discrimination and abuse unfortunately do occur in arenas

---

73. A tension between the fans of domestic basketball and football does exist, however their brawls are not very common. Besides there is no culture for using cold weapons in Lithuania, thus serious injuries are usually avoided. Most notable incidents are related with the visit of foreign fans, namely football supporters from Croatia, Poland, Russia, including death of Lithuanian football fan after UEFA Intertoto Cup match between local FK Atlantas and Spartak Moscow in 2004.
74. Translation used from online source (accessed on 22 Aug. 2021) (https://e-seimas.lrs.lt/portal/legalActPrint/lt?jfwid=-9dzqnu9t0&documentId=a84fa232877611e5bca4ce385a9b7048&category=TAD).

and stadiums. A person committing these acts may be charged with public order disturbance (Article 284 of the Criminal Code) or crime of incitement against any national, racial, ethnic, religious or other group of persons (Article 170 of the Criminal Code).

IV. Use of Violence in Sports Competition

207. One of the most interesting and important issues in the crossroad between criminal law and sports is criminal liability for injury or death in sports competitions. Unfortunately, sports events which are intended to entertain people and promote healthy lifestyle sometimes end in tragic manner: participants or spectators get injured or, most tragically, lose their lives.

208. In contact sports an event of loss of life may in fact form the objective body of a crime of serious bodily injury (Article 135 of the Criminal Code) or even a crime of murder (Article 129 of the Criminal Code). A basic example would be a serious injury or death of an athlete during a boxing fight. However, heavy injuries and events giving rise to the risk of a life do happen in other popular sports as well. For example, during a football match a player can be seriously injured by tackle of an opponent. Serious injury may be caused even without a foul play by an opponent as well. On the contrary, a player can intentionally harm the opponent by reckless tackle or a predetermined kick to the body of an opponent, i.e., commit an act which has nothing in common with practices of a certain sports event. In any case it is not easy to conclude to what extent the rules of the Criminal Code would apply. Therefore, it is important to understand how the case of an injury or death of an athlete or spectator would be treated in accordance with the legal framework of Lithuania.

209. Case law related to this specific issue is not developed therefore considerations on a theoretical level should be done. In accordance with Lithuanian authors,[75] bodily injuries or death may have immunity from criminal jurisdiction due to the fact that the state consents certain scope of risk while tolerating sports. However, a legal basis is needed in order to implement such immunity. Other authors[76] suggest that section V of the Criminal Code 'Circumstances Eliminating Criminal Liability' and more precisely Article 34 which governs justifiable professional or economic risk as a ground for elimination of criminal liability could serve as a legal basis. This institute establishes conditions eliminating criminal liability even if activities which formally would fall into the scope of certain body of crime or criminal offence are committed. It is suggested that a ground for elimination of the criminal liability in such cases should be a lack of one of the necessary objective attributes of a crime, i.e., dangerous nature of activity.[77]

75. Salomėja Zaksaitė, *Nusikalstamas elgesys sporto srityje*, ISSN 1392–1274, 2010 74, pp. 136, 145, Teisė (2012).
76. Aurelijus Gutauskas & Linas Žalnieriūnas, *Fizinio smurto sporte baudžiamasis teisinis įvertinimas*, ISSN 1392–6195, 2014 21 (3), Jurisprudencija, pp. 885, 888 (2014).
77. Vytautas Piesliakas, *Lietuvos baudžiamoji teisė: antroji knyga*, p. 16 (Justitia, 2008).

210. Article 34(1) of the Criminal Code stipulates that a person shall not be held liable under the Criminal Code for the actions which, although they incur the consequences provided for by a criminal law, have been carried out with a *justifiable professional or economic risk and for a publicly beneficial purpose*. Article 34(2) of the Criminal Code provides that the 'risk shall be deemed justifiable where the committed act is in line with the contemporary science and technology, and it was not possible to attain the specified objective by carrying out the actions not involving risk, and where the person taking the risk has taken the necessary precautions to prevent damage to the interests protected by the law'.

211. In order to determine what kind of events of bodily injury or death can 'escape' criminal liability it is necessary to analyse different types of violence manifestation in sports competitions and their legality in accordance with the rules of certain sports games defined by the governing sports body. Lithuanian authors, basing on Canadian sociology scientist Mike Smith, distinguish[78] the following types of sports violence that could fall into immunity from criminal jurisdiction: (1) Strong physical contact – it occurs where the rules of the game allow physical damage of the opponent in order to eliminate him or her (boxing, mixed martial arts, etc.), (2) Marginal violence – it occurs where the force is not directly addressed to the body but its use is justified by the purpose not related to the opponent (a drive of a player to the basket with the intention to score a bucket, tackle in rugby in order to stop an opponent from scoring a try, sliding tackle in football, etc.), (3) Quasi-violence – it occurs where under certain customs of the game, although not allowed by the rules, certain level of violence is tolerated (the best example is boxing on ice between ice hockey players). These types of violence should fall out of the scope of the Criminal Code with potential reference to Article 34(1) of the Criminal Code.

212. However, a fourth type of sports violence exists, i.e., 'criminal violence'.[79] Criminal violence should be understood as rough use of bodily force against body of opponent *in serious breach of the rules* of the game and *with an intention to harm the opponent*. Such type of violence should not escape the application of the Criminal Code and anyone acting in said manner should be charged with certain criminal offence. Same approach should be applied not only to situations of clear and distinguishing violence in serious breach of the game rules (kick in the head of lying opponent during football match), but also to the events when an offence externally is similar to the playing situation, but is in breach of rules of the game and is aimed to injure the opponent[80] (e.g., a reckless sliding tackle of a football player aiming not the ball, but the knee or an ankle of the opponent). The aspect of the consent of an athlete of certain risk is also important. If certain rules of the game do allow the use of force, it can be assumed that an athlete understands the risks and by accessing the competition assumes such risks. However, one should not foresee and assume to be intentionally punched in the face with an elbow during a basketball

78. Gutauskas & Žalnieriūnas, *supra* n. 77, at p. 891.
79. *Ibid.*
80. *Ibid.*, at p. 894.

game. Such aspect is important in accordance with the authors[81] because the court while dealing with an issue of application of the Criminal Code in such cases would have to contemplate on the scope of consent of an athlete.

213. There is very little jurisprudence of the Lithuanian courts in this field. Vilnius District Court had to deal with an issue of application of Article 140 (cause of physical pain or minor bodily injury). Dangerous activity allegedly took place during a brawl in an amateur football match. Defendant allegedly had punched the victim to his head area during a brawl. The court did annul the verdict of the Court of First Instance and did acquit the defendant stating that he had not committed any criminal offence. The court also noticed that[82] every athlete who, in accordance with his talent and needs, chooses certain area of sports which is governed by rules of game allowing certain physical contact (marginal violence) assumes risks that he or she might suffer pain, minor bodily injury or trauma during the match. The court further stated that brawling during the match is *a common situation* which is not subject of criminal law, thus the criminal liability for such act cannot be applied. Most importantly, the court stated that 'cause of physical pain or minor bodily injury in sports arena or stadia has immunity from criminal liability since the state accepts such risk. Otherwise, sports competitions would lose its attraction and it would create a precedent that due to breach of rules of the game (and quasi-rules) causing cause of physical pain or minor bodily injury, the perpetrator would be charged with criminal offence'. However, the court concluded that it does not mean that the conflict which started on the field could be further developed outside the field after the end of the game. The court also noticed that the Court of First Instance, while assessing 'ordinary typical situation of football game' expanded limits of criminal liability without reasonable justification. Thus, the court did consider that a brawl in a football match is a common situation which falls into quasi-rules of the game. The case was brought to the Supreme Court. Unfortunately, the Supreme Court[83] did not elaborate on the limits of violence in sports competitions and confirmed acquittal merely on the ground of lack of evidence. Therefore, the issues of use of violence in sports are subject to further development.

V. Criminal Liability for Death or Injuries of Participants and Spectators: Safety of Sports Events

214. Injuries or death in sports events do not necessarily happen when a participant in sports competitions harms the other participant. Spectators or participants get hurt or lose their lives due to other external risks related to the environment of an event as well. For example, every type of automobile race, be it rally, formula races, circuit racing, drift, are indeed very dangerous activities. Drivers push their vehicles with enhanced power to the very limits while trying to control a source of potential hazard. A single mistake in the nick of a second can be fatal for the driver

81. *Ibid.*, at p. 896.
82. 5 Nov. 2015 verdict of Vilnius District Court in Criminal Case No. 1A-693-149/2015.
83. 16 Jun. 2016 ruling of the Supreme Court in Criminal Case No. 2K-164-895/2016.

or a spectator as well. Therefore, serious measures of safety have to be taken for racing events and other events as well. In accordance with Article 15(1) of the Law on Sport, organizers of sports practices, sports competitions, physical activity practices and other sports events are responsible for the safety of participants and spectators during the competition and event.

215. Under certain circumstances participants and organizers may be charged with crimes and criminal offences, namely negligent murder (Article 132 of the Criminal Code), severe health impairment caused through negligence (Article 137 of the Criminal Code), or non-severe health impairment through negligence (Article 139 of the Criminal Code).

216. Element of negligence, in accordance with jurisprudence of the Supreme Court,[84] can be manifested through criminally false assumption (if a person who committed the act had anticipated that his act or omission may cause the consequences provided for by the Criminal Code, but recklessly expected to avoid them) or criminal negligence (if a person who committed it had not anticipated that his act or omission might cause the consequences provided for by the Criminal Code, although the person could and ought to have anticipated such a result based on the circumstances of the act and his personal traits). Practical application of such provision is carried out in jurisprudence of the courts.

A. *Drift Accident Case*

217. On 23 May 2009, a drift race driver, after finishing his stage, decided to show off a couple of more stunts in the deceleration lane. However, he failed to maintain control of his vehicle and skidded off the track hitting seven spectators who experienced various injuries.[85] Both, the organizer and the driver of the car were charged with a criminal offence of non-severe health impairment through negligence (Article 139 of the Criminal Code).

218. The Court of First Instance found both of the defendants guilty. Both the defendants did appeal to Kaunas District Court which however confirmed the verdict of the Court of First Instance.[86] In accordance with Kaunas District Court, the organizer did not obtain permission to organize the drifting event. Despite the fact that the race was considered illegal, the court maintained that nevertheless, certain safety measures had to be imposed by the organizer in the venue. The court further noticed that:

> Competing with vehicles requires exceptional safety measures since many emergency situations do occur due to various reasons. Because of the fact that

84. 18 Mar. 2014 ruling of the Supreme Court in Criminal Case No. 2K-90/2014.
85. Video of the incident can be found here (accessed on 26 Jun. 2021) (https://www.youtube.com/watch?v=6ql7f4DHVgU).
86. 14 Mar. 2014 verdict of Kaunas District Court in Criminal Case No. 1A-51-579-2014.

> in such competitions the result is obtained by competing in a source of a high-risk (automobile), organizers, cars, drivers, tracks must comply with exceptional safety requirements.

219. The court concluded that safety requirements were not followed. Especially, the court emphasized the absence of barriers in the deceleration lane which meant that there was nothing in between the crowd of spectators and the vehicles.

220. However, a conviction of a driver is a more interesting aspect of the case. Normally, one would not think that a racer could be held liable for skidding off the track since it is ordinary and a typical part of the race. However, the court, first of all, established that the race, as a sporting event, was illegal. The court invoked Article 28(2) of the previous version of the Law on Sport defining a term 'sports competition', i.e., competition of two or more athletes, teams, sports clubs *in accordance with rules advertised in advance pursuant to the rules set forth by the federation of a sport in question.* The court established that regulations of the Lithuanian Automobile Sports Federation set forth two types of automobile competitions: classified and non-classified. The latter is not included in the calendar of the Lithuanian Automobile Sports Federation nevertheless it should be organized and conducted in accordance with the Code of Automobile Sports of the Lithuanian Automobile Sports Federation. Thus, the drift race and its regulations and safety measures had to be confirmed by the Lithuanian Automobile Sports Federation. However, it was not done in this case and thus the race was considered as illegal by the court. It is important to notice that further, the court emphasized that:

> in case the competition was confirmed by the Lithuanian Automobile Sports Federation, its participant could only be liable for the breach of regulations set forth by the Lithuanian Automobile Sports Federation and liability for the safety of competitors and spectators would be held by organizers. Competitors of illegal sports competitions must assume responsibility for potential consequences regardless of the fact whether it has complied with the regulations or not.

221. The court further analysed that the driver was fully aware of the illegality of the race and that car racing, i.e., use of the source of high hazard, requires higher standard of care. The court also emphasized that the driver could have controlled the vehicle in the deceleration lane should he had acted with care.

222. The driver further submitted the claim of cassation to the Supreme Court. The court of highest instance maintained the position of previous courts and further stated that:[87]

> it is evident that the driver did not foresee that consequences stipulated by the Criminal Code could arise due to his acts, however considering circumstances

87. 2 Dec. 2014 ruling of the Supreme Court in Criminal Case No. 2K-507/2014.

of the activity and his personal features he could have and should have foreseen it. By verdicts of the courts it is established that the driver being aware of that he was competing in illegal (forbidden) race and being aware of the fact that that the racetrack had not been safe did act recklessly: he chose unsafe speed and improper operation of the vehicle, lost control of it and hit the spectators.

223. The case is an example of application of criminal liability not only for organizers but also for participants of illegal sport events.

224. The case is an example of application of criminal liability not only for organizers, but for participants of illegal sport events.

B. Kayaking Tragedy Case

225. On 9 December 2014 the Supreme Court rendered another decision in criminal case related to allegedly improper organization of sports event.[88] Two organizers of an extreme sports competition (certain version of triathlon where participants had to run long distance and to ride double kayak) were charged with criminal offence stipulated in Article 132 of the Criminal Code (negligent murder). Participants had to ride double kayak through the river. A kayak equipped by two athletes departed from a planned route and found itself in a fish ladder of a river dam. One of the athletes could not escape the whirlpool and drowned. The organizers were accused of failing to ensure race safety, namely marking of the racetrack and shore exit spots.

226. The Supreme Court acquitted both of the defendants. The court stated that the race was legal and it was intended to be extreme. The court established that participants, including the victim, were experienced athletes. Further, it was established that before the race, all participants, including the victim, had signed an agreement for legal responsibility and thus assumed the risk. Moreover, such agreement, in accordance with the court, contributed to the awareness of competitors on risk brought by competing in the race. Further, the court established that athletes were duly informed on the dangers in the track by the organizers, including the dam. The athletes were instructed to exit to the shore before the dam and to carry their kayaks to the further sport. The athletes were given maps marking dangerous spots.

227. Most importantly the court underlined that the victim and his partner could have easily spotted the dam and escaped it until the very last moment: the dam was easily notable, the sound of falling water was very clear and warning, and, despite that, the water before the dam was still and calm, the current was very weak; thus the athletes could have easily spotted and avoided the danger.[89]

88. 9 Dec. 2014 ruling of the Supreme Court in Criminal Case No. 2K-512/2014.

89. In fact, the Court of First Instance did determine that the athletes took a dangerous decision to swim on kayaks through the dam intentionally.

228. The Supreme Court of Lithuania finally summarized:

> Any sports event, especially race taking place in open water, is related to certain volume of risk which is comprehended by competitors themselves. Organizers are undoubtedly responsible for ensuring safe conditions of the event as far as required by specificity of the event (degree of risk, age and experience of the competitors, potential number of spectators and etc.), however such requirement cannot be only considered in the way that in case of an accident in the event, the organizers would have to inevitably assume criminal liability for the loss of life or injury.

229. The court concluded that the tragic event was simply nothing but an accident. Analysed jurisprudence shows that the courts would not automatically hold organizers liable and would analyse all aspects of the case, including awareness and experience of the victim.

§2. Civil Liability

I. General Introduction

230. Civil liability is defined by Article 6.245(1) of the Civil Code as 'a pecuniary obligation one party of which shall have the right to claim for compensation of damages (damage) or demand payment of the penalty (fine, interest), and the other party shall be bound to make compensation for damages (damage) arising therefrom, or pay the penalty (fine, interest)'.[90]

231. The Civil Code separates two types of civil liability: contractual civil liability and non-contractual civil liability. In accordance with Article 6.245(3), contractual liability is 'a pecuniary obligation resulting from a failure to perform a contract or from its defective performance where one party of the obligation has the right to claim for compensation of damages or demand payment of penalty (fine, interest), and the other party is bound to make compensation for damages, or to pay penalty (fine, interest) caused by the failure to perform the contract, or by a defective performance thereof'. Pursuant to Article 6.245(4), non-contractual liability is a 'pecuniary obligation which is not related with contractual relations, except in cases where it is established by laws that non-contractual liability shall also result from damage related with contractual relations'.

232. In order to establish civil liability of a person, all elements of the defendant's civil liability have to be present. Such elements are:

– Unlawful acts of a defendant (debtor). Unlawful acts derive from non-performance of a duty established by laws or a contract (unlawful refrainment

---

90. Official translation provided in website of the Seimas (accessed on 26 Jun. 2021) (https://e-seimas.lrs.lt/portal/legalAct/lt/TAD/TAIS.245495).

from acting), or from performance of actions that are prohibited by laws or a contract (unlawful acting), or from violation of the general duty of care (Article 6.246(1) of the Civil Code).

- Damage of the claimant (creditor). Damages are an amount of the loss or damage of property sustained by a person and the expenses incurred (direct damages) as well as the incomes of which he has been deprived, i.e., the incomes he would have received if unlawful actions had not been committed (Article 6.249(1) of the Civil Code).
- Causal link between unlawful act and damages. Causal link establishes factual or legal, direct or indirect link (Article 6.247 of the Civil Code) between actions (including omission) of the defendant and damages of the claimant.
- Fault of the defendant which is understood as subjective (factual) dishonesty, i.e., failure of a person to act with care, caution and attention.[91] The Civil Code also establishes the concept of civil liability 'without fault', or so-called strict liability. Generally, the fault of the debtor is presumed thus the creditor bears no burden to prove the condition of fault.

233. Civil liability is important to the field of sports. First, contractual civil liability is applicable to the cases where a contractual dispute arises. Contractual disputes between sports organizations or a sports organization and an athlete are very common disputes in the world of sports. Contractual civil liability arises in the party in breach of the contract, which results in certain performance, usually payment of debts and a forfeit. Second, issues related to non-contractual liability may arise in a sports-related situation between parties not related by a contract, for example, in case of responsibility of an owner of sports infrastructure and spectator due to injury. Further, both of civil liability types are analysed in more detail.

II. Contractual Liability

234. In accordance with Article 6.245(3), contractual liability is a pecuniary obligation resulting from a failure to perform a contract or from its defective performance where one party of the obligation has the right to claim for compensation of damages or demand payment of penalty (fine, interest), and the other party is bound to make compensation for damages, or to pay penalty (fine, interest) caused by a failure to perform the contract, or by a defective performance thereof. Basically, the Civil Code provides two types of general consequences of a civil liability: compensation of damages *or* payment of penalty.

235. Damages are governed by Article 6.249 of the Civil Code and are applicable both for contractual liability and for non-contractual liability. Where the amount of damages cannot be proved by the party with precision, it shall be assessed by a court. Article 6.250(1) of the Civil Code provides for non-pecuniary

91. Algis Norkūnas, *Kaltė kaip civilinės atsakomybės sąlyga*, 28(20); Jurisprudencija, pp. 112–118 (2002).

damage which is understood as a person's suffering, emotional experiences, inconveniences, mental shock, emotional depression, humiliation, deterioration of reputation, diminution of possibilities to associate with others, etc., evaluated by a court in terms of money. Article 6.250(2) of the Civil Code further establishes that non-pecuniary damage must be compensated only in cases provided for by laws. Non-pecuniary damage must be compensated in all cases where it is incurred due to crime, health impairment or deprivation of life, as well as in other cases provided for by laws. The court in assessing the amount of non-pecuniary damage must take into consideration the consequences of such damage sustained, the gravity of the fault of the person by whom the damage is caused, his financial status, the amount of pecuniary damage sustained by the aggrieved person, also any other circumstances of importance for the case, likewise to the criteria of good faith, justice and reasonableness.

236. Article 6.258(1) sets that it may be provided for by laws or a contract that the party guilty for non-performance of an obligation or defective performance thereof shall be bound to pay a penalty (fine, interest). The parties may agree upon certain amount of penalty which would be paid to the injured party by the creditor as a result of a breach of contract. Parties may agree upon the size of interest applicable in case of failure to respect contractual obligations (e.g., for late payment of money, etc.). Article 6.258(2) establishes that the sum stipulated as a penalty (fine, interest) may be reduced by the court when it is unreasonably excessive, or if the creditor has benefited from the partial performance of the obligation. However, this sum may not be reduced below the amount due to damages payable for the non-performance of the obligation or defective performance thereof. The latter provision demonstrates that there is a link between damages and penalty: the penalty may not be reduced below the amount of damages.

237. This link is very important since the actual damages may be higher than the penalty or the penalty may be excessive and may significantly exceed actual damages. As it is mentioned above, in case the penalty may not be reduced below actual damages. Article 6.251(1) established the principle of 'full compensation of damages' (*restitutio in integrum*). The provision states that the damages incurred must be compensated in full, except in cases when limited liability is established by laws or by a contract. Thus, if the damages are higher than the penalty, the court would award damages exceeding the amount of penalty in case such damages are duly proved. The penalty would be credited to the damages.

238. The purposes of penalty are to prevent the counterparty from breaching contractual obligations and to ease the proving of damages of the creditor. The penalty is considered as minimal damages of the creditor. In the jurisprudence of the Supreme Court, it is established[92] that the Civil Code does not establish punitive penalties. It allows the situation where the penalty is 'reasonably higher' than actual damages; however it should not be excessive. For example, the Court of Appeals[93]

92. 12 Oct. 2007 ruling of the Supreme Court in Civil Case No. 3K-7-304/2007.
93. 21 Dec. 2009 ruling of the Court of Appeals in Civil Case No. 2A-726/2009.

acknowledged that penalty of EUR 25 per day for late payment of salary to a basketball player was not excessive since 'the claimant is professional basketball player whose sporting career is risky and closely determined by his state of health, injuries and lasts considerably short period of time. Thus, the salary and its timely payment is vital factor for the player to choose a team and to sign a contract with professional basketball clubs'.

239. The institute of 'damages calculated by the parties in advance' or, as it is known in common law system jurisdictions, the 'liquidated damage' is not considered as part of Lithuanian legal system.[94] In accordance with the Supreme Court, 'liquidated damages' are close to the institute of 'penalty' set forth in the Civil Code; however the purposes and manifestation of such remedies are different.

240. It is very common for parties, including athletes and clubs, or club and sponsor include clauses providing penalties. In particular, clubs tend to include a clause stipulating amount of penalty to be paid by player in case of premature termination of contract by player or by club due to the fault of a player. Sometimes, very large penalties are inserted. Clubs consider a player as an asset who can be later sold to other clubs for significant amount money and draft penalty clauses accordingly. However, excessive penalty clause could be disregarded by Lithuanian courts. Penalties can also be applied to an athlete for failure to comply with disciplinary regulations of the club (e.g., reduction of a salary due to failure to appear for an official match). However, the right of club to apply such sanctions and procedure of application must be discussed in contract.

III. Non-contractual Liability

241. Non-contractual liability is a pecuniary obligation which is not related to contractual relationship, except in cases where it is established by laws that non-contractual liability shall also result from damage related to contractual relations. In general, non-contractual civil liability is related to breach of obligation provided not by the contract, but by law or by breach of the duty of care. General duty of care is related to obligation to obey such set of rules that would prevent causing harm to any other person (Article 6.263 of the Civil Code).

242. Certain laws set forth responsibility in the field of sports. For example, in accordance with Article 15(1) of the Law on Sport, organizers of sports practices, sports competitions, physical activity practices and other sports events are responsible for the safety of participants and spectators during the competition and event. Thus, failure of an organizer to provide for a secure environment of sports competition leading to an injury of an athlete may be ground for civil non-contractual liability of the organizer and award of damages.

94. 25 Apr. 2016 ruling of the Supreme Court in Civil Case No. 3K-3-234-248/2016.

243. Civil Code establishes cases whereby the non-contractual civil liability does not require the element of fault, i.e., the strict civil liability. Cases which may be related to sport concern the liability of an owner of a building (e.g., stadium, arena, racetrack) (Article 6.266 of the Civil Code) or liability for damage caused by a source of high risk (Article 6.270 of the Civil Code), for example a racing car.

IV. Disciplinary (Sporting) Liability

244. Disciplinary or sporting liability should be understood as negative consequences caused to athlete or other person (staff member, coach, official, a club, etc.) for breach of statutes or regulations and rules of certain sports organization (federation). Sports liability is not defined by laws in Lithuania and derives from regulations of sports federations. Athletes who participate in sports competitions, be it team sports or individual sports, by certain form accepts to obey the regulations of a sports organization (federation, organizer, etc.). Such regulations might provide rules of game, format of certain competition. Very often such regulations set forth disciplinary rules which provide a list of certain disciplinary violations, disciplinary procedures and sanctions for breach of regulations.

245. One of the examples can be doping regulations – sports federations have their anti-doping regulations which define anti-doping infringements and sanctions for it. The presence of banned substances in the system of an athlete will surely result in cancellation of sporting result and will probably lead to a period of disqualification. Football or basketball players can be disqualified for a certain period for unsporting behaviour (e.g., pushing a referee). The most serious sanction almost in every sport is the lifetime ban for an athlete or a coach or an official. If such sanction is determined a person is no longer able to participate in certain organized sport. Usually, lifetime bans are given for very serious offences, such as repeated anti-doping violations or participation in match-fixing activities.

246. Bodies of a federation or other sports organization[95] are responsible to carry out the investigation and to take a decision. Such decision might be subject to appeal to an appeals body within the same federation. Final decision of federation is usually subject to further appeal to the court or arbitration, namely CAS.[96]

95. Many domestic football championships are organized by leagues (a certain legal person formed by clubs performing the championship) and not federations. Thus, the leagues may be competent to impose sanctions related to certain competition.
96. Most of the world's international sports federations recognize the CAS as appeal institution regarding final decisions of such federations. Moreover, international associations require that their members; i.e., continental and national federations would recognize CAS as an appeal institution for related disputes. Thus, most of the disciplinary procedures within sports federations can end up in CAS.

247. The legal basis of disciplinary sanctions for athletes and other natural or legal persons[97] is their direct or indirect membership in such federation. By entering the competition athletes and clubs acknowledge certain regulations and accept that consequences provided in such regulations may be imposed on them should they fail to respect said regulations. The Supreme Court in its 18 May 2017 ruling in Civil Case No. e3K-3-238-686/2017 established that relationship between a football club and the LFF in relation to participation in competition organized by the LFF are contractual. Even though courts did not elaborate on the nature of relationship between athletes and association in terms of disciplinary matters in competition, considering the element of an athlete's acceptance that the statutes of sports organizations are applicable, it is possible to conclude that such relationship is contractual as well. Therefore, it can be concluded that sporting or disciplinary liability of athletes and clubs are a specific form of civil contractual liability.

97. A club, as a legal person, has the right to be sanctioned as well, for example, expelled from competition for fielding ineligible player.

Chapter 8. Tax Issues

248. There is no special treatment of sports in terms of tax regulation of Lithuania. It is necessary to distinguish taxation matters related to legal persons (federations, companies, clubs) and individual persons (athletes).

249. Main taxes in Lithuania are:

- individual income tax (simply referred to as income tax);
- corporate income tax;
- value added tax (VAT);
- lottery and gaming tax;
- inheritance tax;
- land tax;
- real estate tax;
- excises.

250. Certain taxes have to be paid subject to the activities of a person concerned. For example, provider of tobacco or alcohol will have to pay excise meanwhile a company owning land and real estate will have to pay land tax and real estate tax. A betting company is obliged to pay lottery and gaming tax.

251. Legal persons, including limited liability companies, associations or public institutions are subject to corporate tax. It should be noted that a tax relief is applied to corporate tax in relation to financial support or 'sponsorship'. Received financial support by a club does not always fall in the scope of tax base to a certain extent. Moreover, companies who provide support can include part of such amounts in allowable deductions.

252. Taxable persons engaged in the provision of goods or services in Lithuania must register as VAT payers and calculate and pay VAT to the budget of the state. However, it is not mandatory if the amount received by a payer from the goods and/or services supplied as part of routine business activities does not exceed EUR 45,000 during the last twelve months.

253. It should be noted that most of the clubs and federations operate under a legal form of association or public institution which are considered to be non-profit organizations. Such status may add certain specificities in taxation. The State Tax Authority issued Guidelines on Taxation of Non-Profit Organizations, 2017 which explains certain aspects of non-profit organizations related to corporate income tax, VAT, etc. For example, non-profit organizations which collect less than EUR 300,000 per year have not to pay any tax from part of EUR 7,500.

254. Employers have to pay certain taxes and related payments due to employment of their employees. Such taxes and payments include personal income tax paid for an employee, social security payment, compulsory health insurance payment and payments to the Guarantee Fund. An employer would have to pay taxes for an employee, which would amount to approximately 60% from the net salary of an employee.

255. Taxes imposed on athletes and related duties of athletes as taxpayers differ depending on the status of the athlete from taxation point of view. An athlete can be considered as an employee or self-employed. An athlete who is under SAA is considered as an employee from taxation point of view[98] and athletes who take care of their activities independently are not dependent on single sports organization are considered as self-employed. An athlete who is considered as an employee is not responsible for paying taxes and additional payments as their employers, i.e., clubs are responsible to do so if not agreed otherwise. Meanwhile, self-employed athletes are responsible for the timely declaration of income and payment of relevant taxes.

256. An income tax is payable from income earned by both, an employed athlete and a self-employed athlete. Tax base might differ depending on the status of an athlete. An employed athlete must take into consideration that amounts in SAAs are considered to be gross unless stipulated otherwise. Thus, he or she must make sure that the correct amount is inserted.

257. Employed and self-employed athletes have to pay compulsory health insurance payments as well as income tax. They are calculated from annual income; however certain parts have to be paid on a monthly basis. Usually clubs pay such payments for employed athletes. Meanwhile, self-employed athletes have to pay it themselves.

258. Finally, social security payment has to be paid by both employed and self-employed athletes. It is paid on a monthly basis. Clubs have to pay social security payments for players under SAAs; meanwhile self-employed athletes have to pay it themselves.

---

98. It must be stressed that an athlete under SAA is in general not considered as an employee or worker from labour law point of view.

Chapter 9. Dispute Resolution and Sport Justice

§1. General Introduction

259. This chapter shall relate to resolution of disputes between private parties, i.e., disputes of a civil nature. Criminal and administrative jurisdiction will not be subject of this chapter. Civil disputes cover all standard disputes arising in the field of relationship between, in general, private parties, such as contractual disputes (performance of contract, award of compensation, illegal termination of contract, etc.), disputes between members and/or managing bodies of a legal person (e.g., dispute among stakeholders of a football club, dispute raised by member of a basketball federation against decision of congress, etc.), disputes related to disciplinary matter between players and clubs or official persons on one side and federations and its disciplinary bodies on the other side.

260. Such disputes will be further grouped into disputes solved by (1) ordinary civil courts; (2) arbitration; (3) alternative dispute mechanisms. It must be stressed that labour disputes shall not be elaborated since athletes and coaches under SAAs, are not considered as employees in accordance with the Laws of the Republic of Lithuania, and disputes between them and their employers, sports organizations, are solved in accordance with general order,[99] thus the specificities applicable to labour disputes are not analysed.

261. Sport justice is not defined by the Laws of the Republic of Lithuania and jurisprudence. There is no specific public body or institution competent to deal with what could be known as 'sports justice' in Lithuania. Associations are free to establish their internal rules and regulations. Sport associations or federations establish rules of game, formats of competitions. As well as this, sports federations establish rules governing internal sanctions for its members, participants of competitions, for breach of regulations. Therefore, sports justice in Lithuanian regulation could be understood as a form of private enforcement of rules of the game and principles of integrity and fair play by the internal means of association. Sports justice is procedure for ensuring compliance of athletes, officials, referees, clubs and other persons with the regulations and rules of the sports federations.

---

99. However, it should be noted, that in accordance with the Law on Sport, coaches and sports organizations (clubs or schools) may conclude either SAA or simple labour agreement. It is common that private organizations, including sports clubs or private sports schools and academies and coaches tend to conclude SAAs. However, public owned or controlled organizations, usually sports centres and schools and their coaches often sign labour agreements.

§2. Civil Disputes

I. Procedure in Civil Courts

262. Civil disputes (contractual disputes, civil liability disputes, disputes among stakeholders, copyright disputes, etc.) are generally solved in civil courts, arbitration and by alternative dispute resolution mechanisms.

263. In accordance with the Constitution and the Civil Procedure Code (CPC) access to court is granted for every person whose rights or interests were violated. Usually, civil courts hear disputes deriving from civil, family, labour, intellectual property, competition, bankruptcy, restructure, public tender and other private legal relationship. Civil courts do not hear disputes between private party and state or municipal authority deriving of a public context (however, disputes between private entities and state or municipal authorities of a civil nature are heard by civil courts).

264. General court procedure includes three instances and possibility of reopening procedures of a closed case under specific circumstances. Courts operate by three instances system, Court of First Instance, Court of Appeal and court of cassation, the Supreme Court. Depending on the amount of monetary dispute, a county or a district court may act as a Court of First Instance. If a case in first instance is heard by county courts, district courts then act as appeal instance. When a district court renders a decision in a case in first instance, such decision is subject to appeal to the Court of Appeals.

265. Less complicated pecuniary disputes can be solved by so-called court order or by documental procedure which, depending on actions of the respondent, may lead to significantly quicker decision.

266. In accordance with the Justice Scoreboard Report[100] prepared by the European Commission, Lithuania is one of the leading countries in time of civil case hearing. If a dispute goes through all instances, a decision may be expected from 1.5 to 2 years.

267. Interim measures are usually applied if the claimant proves prima facie validity of the claim (the case should be plausible) and danger that the decision could not be implemented partially or fully in case of a decision favourable for the claimant.

268. Binding decisions are enforceable documents. Decisions are enforced in accordance with the enforcement procedure set by the CPC. Decisions of courts of EU Member States are recognized relatively fast (a single judge of the Court of Appeals examines if a decision meets formal requirements) in accordance with Council Regulation (EC) No. 44/2001 of 22 December 2000 on jurisdiction and the

100. Available online (accessed on 26 Jun. 2021) (http://ec.europa.eu/justice/effective-justice/files/justice_scoreboard_2016_en.pdf).

recognition and enforcement of judgments in civil and commercial matters. Decisions of courts other than EU Member States require more thorough recognition procedure. In accordance with EU Regulations No. 805/2004, European Enforcement Order may be enforced in Lithuania.

269. Hearing disputes in civil courts is the most popular way to solve a contractual dispute between Lithuanian athlete and Lithuanian sports club subject to nonexistence of arbitration clause. Usually, such disputes arise due to failure of a club to perform its financial obligations to the player. Applying the court with clear and evident financial obligations usually results in the instant application of interim measures and considerably fast procedure in court.

II. Commercial and Sports Arbitration

A. General Information

270. In accordance with Article 23 of the CPC, the parties are allowed to submit any dispute to arbitration except disputes which cannot be submitted to arbitration in accordance with the Laws of the Republic of Lithuania. If the arbitration clause is concluded by the parties, the court would not admit a civil claim at all. In case it appears that arbitration clause is concluded at the later stages of a court case, a ground to dismiss a case would exist.

271. The Law on Commercial Arbitration of the Republic of Lithuania (Law on Arbitration) was only adopted in 1996; thus arbitration is relatively a new way of dispute resolution. However, admiration for arbitration has been constantly growing in Lithuania. Lithuanian legal system is very friendly to arbitration as a very high percentage of awards of non-Lithuanian arbitration courts is recognized in Lithuania. The Supreme Court formed a jurisprudence which prevents the courts from re-examining arbitral awards on the merits of the case without sufficient justification and allows the challenge of arbitral awards in exceptional cases mostly.

272. Law on Arbitration is drafted in accordance with the UNCITRAL Model Law ('Model Law'). Article 5(4) of the Law on Arbitration actually provides that the interpretation of this law and the terms used in it should be subject in a subsidiary manner to the Model Law.[101]

---

101. Provisions of the Law on Arbitration are quoted in accordance with unofficial translation which can be found online (accessed on 26 Jun. 2021) (http://www.infolex.lt/portal/papildomiok/20121212_the_republic_of_lithuania_law_on_commercial_arbitration.pdf).

B. Arbitration Clause

273. The Law on Arbitration (Article 10(1)) sets requirements for arbitration clause: an arbitration agreement may be in the form of an arbitration clause in a contract or in the form of a separate contract concluded by the parties. Article 10(2) sets forth that the arbitration agreement has to be concluded in writing and will be considered to be valid if:

- it is executed as a joint document signed by the parties; or
- it is concluded by exchange by the parties of letters (electronic communications including) or other documents providing the fact of conclusion of an agreement; or
- concluded through electronic communications, provided that the integrity and authenticity of transmitted information is ensured; or
- the parties exchange a claim and an answer to the claim where one of the parties claims that parties have concluded the arbitration agreement and the other party does not object it; or
- there is other written evidence demonstrating that the parties have concluded or recognize the arbitration agreement.

274. In terms of sports, most common arbitration procedures derive from arbitration agreement stipulated in agreement of parties: for example, basketball players and clubs very often include BAT arbitration clause and, thus, in case of a dispute, a matter is forwarded to BAT. Direct CAS arbitration clauses, bypassing FIFA DRC or FIFA Players' Status Committee (FIFA PSC) and saving a significant amount of time, were very common in contracts between clubs and players before the change of the FIFA Statutes and the FIFA Disciplinary Code back in 2011 which resulted in the removal of enforcement of CAS Ordinary Division cases from FIFA Disciplinary Committee's function. However, major amount of arbitration disputes in CAS arrive in the form of appeal, i.e., by appealing the decision of national or international federation. The source of arbitration clause in latter situations lies within the statutes of federation. For example, Articles 61–63 of the LFF Statutes state that LFF members, LFF bodies, leagues, clubs, players, officials settle any dispute related to the national affairs, arising from or related to the LFF Statutes or members' statutes, the rules, regulations and other documents adopted by the LFF or members, the decisions of the LFF bodies, in the last instance only at CAS, without recourse to the ordinary courts, unless the LFF Statutes, rules, regulations or other documents of FIFA, UEFA and the LFF provide otherwise or/and Lithuanian law prohibits it directly.

275. In a fairly recent case, the Supreme Court had to decide on the existence of arbitration clause established in the LFF Statutes referring to CAS a dispute between a club and body of the LFF.[102] The court stated that arbitration agreement may be concluded by reference to the document containing arbitration clause. The

102. 14 Jul. 2017 ruling of the Supreme Court in Civil Case No. e3K-3-317-686/2017.

court concluded that arbitration clause in the LFF Statutes is valid and it meets requirements of the Law on Arbitration.[103]

276. Another initiative to increase admiration for sports arbitration in Lithuania was taken by one of the most established Lithuanian permanent institutions of arbitration, Vilnius Court of Commercial Arbitration (VCCA). VCCA had adopted a special set of rules for arbitration deriving for sports legal relationship.[104] Said rules establish certain exceptions from general arbitration rules of the VCCA and additional provisions. Regulations are designed to meet the demand of what is actually searched in terms of sports disputes – the speed of procedures. Regulations provide for one arbitrator instead of a standard three, a rule obliging arbitrator to strive for solving dispute in a single hearing, set a shorter deadline for decisions: three months as from submission of case file to arbitration court instead of standard six months provided in general regulations. However, sports arbitration in VCCA is not popular at all.[105]

C. Arbitrable and Non-arbitrable Disputes

277. The Law on Arbitration provides two groups of non-arbitrable disputes: objective (disputes deriving from certain legal relationships are not arbitrable) and subjective (certain persons are restricted to settle disputes in arbitration).

278. Article 12 of the Law on Arbitration regulates disputes which cannot be referred to arbitration (objective non-arbitrability). Article 12(2) of the Law on Arbitration specifies that arbitration may not resolve disputes which should be heard under administrative proceedings or hear cases, the examination of which falls within the competence of the Constitutional Court. Disputes arising from family legal relationships and disputes regarding the registration of patents, trademarks and design may not be referred to arbitration as well. Disputes arising from employment and consumption contracts, except for cases where the arbitration agreement was concluded after the dispute arose may not be referred to arbitration too.

279. Article 12(3) of the Law on Arbitration states that disputes may not be referred to arbitration when a state or municipal enterprise or institution or organization, except for the Bank of Lithuania, is a party to, *unless* the consent of the founder of such enterprise, institution or organization regarding the arbitration agreement had been obtained (subjective non-arbitrability).

103. This approach is consistent with the earlier ruling of the Supreme Court, i.e., 18 May 2017 ruling in Civil Case No. e3K-3-238-686/2017.
104. Available online (accessed on 26 Jun. 2021) (http://www.arbitrazas.lt/arbitrazo-reglamentas.htm).
105. As from the introduction of regulations for sports disputes no arbitration cases had been heard.

D. Arbitral Award and Its Recognition

280. Award of court of arbitration rendered by arbitral tribunal with the seat in Lithuania is final and binding and is enforceable. Article 50(3) of the Law on Arbitration sets forth the excessive list of grounds giving rise to challenge the arbitral award to the Court of Appeals:

- one of the parties to the arbitration agreement was in lack of legal capacity under the applicable laws or the arbitration agreement is not effective under the laws applicable by the agreement of the parties, or if the parties have not agreed on arbitration regarding the laws applicable to the arbitration agreement, according to the laws of the state in which the arbitral award was rendered; or
- the party against which the arbitral award is intended to be invoked was not properly notified of the appointment of the arbitrator or the arbitral examination or otherwise was not provided with a possibility to present its own explanations; or
- the arbitral award was rendered in respect of the dispute or the part of the dispute that was not referred to arbitration; or
- the composition of the arbitral tribunal or the arbitration proceedings did not meet the agreement of the parties and/or compulsory provisions of the Law on Arbitration; or
- the dispute may not be referred to arbitration according to the Laws of the Republic of Lithuania; or
- the arbitral award is against the public policy of the Republic of Lithuania.

281. Decision of the Court of Appeals regarding the annulment of the arbitral award is subject to further appeal to the Supreme Court.

282. The Convention on the Recognition and Enforcement of Foreign Arbitral Awards ('New York Convention') was signed and ratified by Lithuania in 1995. Therefore, the recognition of foreign arbitral awards procedure is conducted in accordance with the requirements of the New York Convention. In fact the Law on Arbitration does not specify grounds for refusal to recognize foreign arbitral award and refers directly to the text of the New York Convention. In order to recognize foreign arbitral award, an application must be filed to the Court of Appeals. Decision of the Court of Appeals on recognition matters is subject to appeal to the Supreme Court.

E. Kęstutis Marčiulionis v. BC Žalgiris: *Status of Player and Recognition of Foreign Arbitral Awards*

283. Very important issue for arbitrability and also recognition of a foreign arbitral award is the nature of contractual relationship between athletes and clubs.[106] As it is mentioned before, the Law on Arbitration does not allow reference of labour

106. This issue will be analysed in more detail in Part II of this monograph.

dispute to arbitration in case the arbitration clause was not concluded after the rise of a dispute. Many jurisdictions consider contractual relationship of an athlete and a club as labour relationship. In such case disputes between clubs and players deriving from their contracts could not go to arbitration in accordance with the Lithuanian regulation. Moreover, foreign arbitral awards, including CAS and BAT awards in cases between clubs and players deriving from their contracts, would not be possibly recognized in Lithuania.

284. In 2011 the Supreme Court had to deal with a case of recognition of arbitral award rendered by the Court Commercial Arbitration of Lugano, Switzerland. An arbitral award was rendered in a case between former Lithuanian national basketball team player, a winner of Olympic bronze medal in Sydney 2000, Kęstutis Marčiulionis and BC Žalgiris. The court of arbitration awarded an amount of USD 233,412 for the player. The player submitted a request to the Court of Appeals for recognition of Swiss arbitral award. The Court of Appeals[107] adopted a ruling refusing to recognize the arbitral award due to reasons related to objective arbitrability – the court considered that contractual relationship between athletes and clubs are 'more labour than civil' and concluded that arbitral award could not be recognized due to provision of the Law on Arbitration restricting arbitration in labour matters. The player appealed to the Supreme Court.

285. On 21 February 2011 the Supreme Court[108] overruled the ruling of the Lithuanian Court of Appeals and recognized the arbitral award. The key argument of the Supreme Court was that the disputed relationship between the player and the club deriving from SAA could not be considered as of labour nature and thus restriction to arbitrate such dispute was not applicable. The Supreme Court ruling made way that most of the potential arbitral decisions in the field of sports would be respected by courts.

F. Interperformances Inc. v. Javtokas: *Restriction to Review Arbitral Awards in Essence*

286. Another important dispute was heard by the Supreme Court in the field of sports relating relationship between a basketball agent and basketball player. The importance of dispute is not only based on the fact that it related to a very specific aspect of sports industry but the decision of the Supreme Court revealed the court's assumption of validity of arbitral award and refusal to review the dispute on the merits if no extraordinary circumstances are present.

287. The dispute arose between the then Lithuanian national basketball team player Robertas Javtokas and his former agent Luciano Capicchioni. Basketball agency related to Mr Capicchioni, i.e., Interperformances Inc. submitted a request to the Court of Appeals regarding recognition of arbitral award from arbitration

107. 28 Sep. 2010 ruling of the Court of Appeals in Civil Case No. 2T-164/2010.
108. 21 Feb. 2011 ruling of the Supreme Court in Civil Case No. 3K-3-65/2011.

institution of the Chamber of Commerce and Industry of Ticino, Switzerland. An amount exceeding EUR 325,000 was awarded from Mr Javtokas to his former agency due to allegedly illegal termination of representation contract.

288. On 29 December 2014 the Court of Appeals[109] issued a ruling refusing to recognize the arbitral award due to alleged contradiction of the said award with the public order of Lithuania. More precisely, the court decided that the award was in contradiction with the public order and Lithuanian regulation since (1) fifteen-day term for notice on termination of representation agreement was not aimed to protect the agent from surprise termination of an agreement but rather to encumber possibilities of a player to terminate the said agreement; (2) penalty stipulated in the contract was not of nature of compensation but rather *punitive penalty* which is not allowed in by the Laws of Lithuania. The agency appealed to the Supreme Court of Lithuania.

289. The Supreme Court rendered final decision on 25 September 2015.[110] The court annulled the ruling of the Court of Appeals and recognized the arbitral award. The Supreme Court emphasized the importance of prohibition for a court to review the content of an arbitral award and merits of the case. The court concluded that the Court of Appeals exceeded the limits of review of foreign arbitral award. The court further stated that the evaluation whether penalty was excessive would require the assessment of facts of the case which means nothing less than a review of the merits of arbitral award. Such review, according to the Supreme Court of Lithuania, could not be conducted.

290. This decision of the Supreme Court summarizes a general approach of Lithuanian courts to arbitral awards, including the ones rendered in foreign arbitrations: the courts treat arbitral awards with respect and possibilities to challenge the arbitral award are very limited.

III. Alternative Dispute Resolution

291. In accordance with the CPC, access to court is granted for every person whose rights or interests were violated. However, the CPC includes provisions preventing persons from the access to court should certain conditions are not met. One of such conditions is the requirement for a party to exercise so-called pre-court dispute resolution procedure before applying to the court. In case the party applies to the court without exercising mentioned pre-court dispute resolution procedure court may hold the claim inadmissible, dismiss the claim or leave the claim unheard. Therefore, compliance or non-compliance with the pre-court dispute resolution procedures shall create aforementioned procedural circumstances resulting in various limits of the right to court.

---

109. 29 Dec. 2014 ruling of the Court of Appeals in Civil Case No. 2T-96/2014.
110. 25 Sep. 2015 ruling of the Supreme Court in Civil Case No. e3K-3-483-421/2015.

292. In accordance with Article 22(1) of CPC the cases of compulsory alternative dispute resolution provided by the Laws of the Republic of Lithuania are considered as the 'pre-court dispute resolution procedures'. The Laws of the Republic of Lithuania provide clear cases of multi-tier dispute resolution obliging the parties to refer the dispute to alternative dispute resolution institution at first before applying to the court. Such regulation leaves the parties no choice but to exercise alternative dispute resolution system in order to gain the right to go to court.

293. It must also be mentioned that agreement of the parties to submit the dispute to mediation is also considered as 'pre-court dispute resolution procedure' in accordance with systemic interpretation of the CPC and the Law on Conciliatory Mediation in Civil Disputes of the Republic of Lithuania, 2008 (Law on Mediation).[111] In accordance with Article 3(1) of the Law on Mediation conciliatory mediation shall be used on the basis of a written agreement between the parties to a dispute. The parties to the dispute may agree on conciliatory mediation either after the dispute has arisen or prior to it. In accordance with Article 3(2) of the Law on Mediation where parties to a dispute agree to settle the dispute through conciliatory mediation, they must attempt to settle the dispute by this procedure before referring to court or arbitration. If a conciliatory mediation agreement sets time limits for the termination of conciliatory mediation, the party to the dispute may refer to court or arbitration only after the expiry of these time limits. Where no time limits for the termination of conciliatory mediation have been set in the conciliatory mediation agreement, the party to the dispute may refer to court or arbitration one month after suggesting to the other party in the dispute in writing to settle the dispute through conciliatory mediation. Thus, in accordance with aforementioned provisions of the Law on Mediation whereby the parties include a mediation clause in the contract, they will not be able to apply to court without attempting to solve the dispute via mediation.

294. Meanwhile, the agreement of parties to solve the dispute amicably (whereby no reference is made to mediation or arbitration) arising out of the contract which is not subject to compulsory alternative dispute resolution (e.g., a labour contract would be a subject of compulsory alternative dispute resolution) is not recognized by the Laws of the Republic of Lithuania as the 'pre-court dispute resolution procedure'.

295. It must be stressed that certain federations have dispute resolution mechanisms between members. The best example is the LFF. The LFF Disciplinary Committee and the LFF Appeals Committee, *inter alia*, hear disputes between clubs related to transfers, training compensation and solidarity mechanism and contractual disputes between clubs and players. It is not a rare event when parties include a clause in contract providing that a dispute between parties would be referred to the 'bodies of the LFF'. Lithuanian courts had dealt with the issue when a party in the dispute, usually the respondent, challenges jurisdiction of the court by claiming

111. Official translation of Seimas can be found online (accessed on 26 Jun. 2021) (https://e-seimas.lrs.lt/portal/legalActPrint/lt?jfwid=-l5uh8wlo8&documentId=TAIS.330591&category=TAD).

that the contract foresees 'pre-court dispute resolution procedure'. However, the courts did not recognize that such agreement had constituted a ground to conclude parties had agreed to submit the dispute 'pre-court dispute resolution procedure'.[112] The courts specify that the regulation of the LFF allows parties to choose where to apply to – the LFF or the civil court.

§3. Sports Justice

I. Disciplinary Regulations

296. Unpredictability of a sports event is one of the key elements which make sports so great. In order to provide teams or athletes with the same amount of opportunity to fight for a victory compliance with certain regulations must be assured. First of all, everyone must comply with the rules of the game. Rules of the game are usually confirmed by the international federation of certain sports, but not necessarily. For example, laws of the game of football are confirmed not by FIFA, but by the International Football Association Board, whose member is FIFA and four national football associations from the UK. FIBA approves the basketball rules of the game; however, the rules in the NBA or the National Collegiate Athletic Association are different. Despite their differences rules of the game are designated to ensure that all participants play the game fairly.

297. Despite the fact that rules of the game provide certain instant disciplinary measures (e.g., a red card in a football match, disqualifying a sprinter for repeated false start in track and field, sending off a basketball player due to two technical fouls, etc.), certain situations require more thorough investigation and might result in more serious negative consequences for the violator. Moreover, certain conditions have to be met by competition organizers ensuring the safety of the competitors and spectators, making sure that sports competition would not become a place for discrimination and abuse of any kind. Therefore, sports federations or organizers of competitions adopt their regulations protecting the integrity of the game and ensuring safety, dignity and well-being of the athletes and the spectators. Usually, those regulations are called disciplinary regulations or disciplinary codes. They provide remedies against violations which are outside of instant control of the match official. Such violations will not necessarily be related to the events on the pitch. It might also be the events outside the stadia (e.g., crowd trouble or attempted match-fixing).

298. Disciplinary regulations are a matter of sports federations and associations. All sports federations have internal regulations and, more precisely, disciplinary regulations which are the basis to impose sanctions to the athletes, coaches, clubs, referees, officials. Moreover, federations form internal legal bodies which are responsible for the procedure of imposition of sanction.

112. 21 Oct. 2014 decision of Panevėžys District Court in Civil Case No. 2A-692-425/2014 and 14 Aug. 2014 decision of Panevėžys District Court in Civil Case No. 2A-484-280/2014.

299. The state normally would not interfere in this field unless the disciplinary violation is so serious that it would fall into the scope of other areas of law. For example, a player who committed match-fixing violation may face disciplinary actions from the federation and, moreover, he could be charged with the crime of manipulation in sports competition as well. Finally, such player could also face civil liability and compensate damages to the club or other injured persons.

300. Further, the disciplinary regulations of the LFF and the LKF are analysed. Material regulations governing the type of violations and sanctions and principles of the application of sanction and the procedural regulations governing procedures of application of sanction are distinguished.

A. *LFF Disciplinary System*

1. Material Regulation

301. The LFF Disciplinary Code is a core document of the LFF disciplinary system. The LFF Disciplinary Code is applicable to all competitions organized by the LFF or persons authorized by the LFF.

302. The material part of the LFF Disciplinary Code provides a list of sanctions and violations. Different sanctions can be imposed for natural persons (players, coaches, official persons) and legal persons (clubs). The most obvious sanction for a player is a caution (yellow card) and sending off (red card). A player may also be fined financially or may be banned from playing for a certain amount of time (there are automatic disqualifications as in the event of a number of yellow or red cards collected throughout the season, or a player might be banned for a number of games and even for life for certain violations). Official persons, club staff, including coaches, may also receive fines and certain restrictions (such as ban from football activity). Clubs may be sanctioned by fines, restriction to register players, a game behind closed doors, annulment of match result, deduction of points, exclusion from competition, forced relegation, etc.

303. Said sanctions are applied for various violations which are also stipulated by the LFF Disciplinary Code. The first type of violations can be assigned to the in-game violations such as fouls or unsporting conduct. It must be stressed that at first sight, one would think that only a player or an official person may get involved in such violation. One of the most important rules of the LFF Disciplinary Regulations is the 'strict liability rule' of a club.[113] In accordance with this rule,[114] a club

113. It is very well established in UEFA and FIFA disciplinary regulations as well. Moreover, 'strict liability' is confirmed by numerous of CAS awards, including 5 Dec. 2013 award rendered in Case No. CAS 2013/A/3139 *Fenerbahçe SK v. UEFA the CAS*, 3 Jun. 2003 award rendered in Case No. CAS 2002/A/423 *PSV Eindhoven v. UEFA;* 20 Apr. 2007 arbitral award rendered in Case No. CAS 2007/A/1217 *Feyernoord Rotterdam v. UEFA CAS.*

114. Article 27(5) of the LFF Disciplinary Code, edition 2021.

will be held liable for the acts of its players, staff and even supporters. Thus, in case of racial conduct of home supporters against away team players, the home club will be held liable regardless of the fact that it could simply have no control whatsoever on the violation.[115] The club would also be held liable in cases where its players, without awareness of the club, get involved in a manipulation in competition (match-fixing). Other groups of violations consist of technical infringements – for example, fielding of an ineligible player,[116] or failing to show up at the match venue, or failure to guarantee proper conditions for the match. The last group of violations consists of violations against the integrity of sports: forgery, match-fixing and doping.

2. Procedural Regulations

304. In accordance with the LFF Disciplinary Code, referees and disciplinary bodies have the competence to provide certain sanction. Obviously, the decisions of referees take place instantly during match time. Decisions of a referee are final and not appealable. However, in extraordinary cases, disciplinary bodies may overview the sanction imposed by the referee (e.g., a red card for simulation which appeared to be not a simulation after review of the match video).

305. In accordance with the statutes of the LFF, the LFF contains two disciplinary bodies: the LFF Disciplinary Committee and the LFF Appeals Committee. Members of such bodies are appointed by the Executive Committee for a four-year term. Grounds for sanctions, as well as, competence of the Disciplinary Committee and disciplinary procedures are provided in detail by the LFF Disciplinary Code. The main responsibilities of the Disciplinary Committee are to decide on the imposition of sanctions in events stipulated by the Disciplinary Committee and to examine protests.

306. The LFF Disciplinary Committee initiates disciplinary procedures after becoming aware of potential violation. Such potential violations usually are noticed in match reports signed by referees and match delegates. Certain information, for example, a potential match-fixing violation might come from a different source after a game, such as SPORTRADAR, UEFA or police.

307. A protest is a document issued by one of the clubs involved in the match and it concerns certain dispute related to the match. Usually, clubs submit protests

115. In case of application of the UEFA or FIFA Regulations, actions of the club or federation responsible for the fans are important and might be a key factor for potential mitigation of fine – *see* CAS 27 Jun. 2013 arbitral award in Case No. CAS/2013/A/3090 *Bulgarian Football Union v. FIFA*.

116. Fielding ineligible players on the field by mistake caused Polish football club Legia Warsaw drop-out of the UEFA Champions' League despite beating Celtic F.C. 6-1 on aggregate. *See* further online (accessed on 26 Jun. 2021) (http://www.dailymail.co.uk/sport/football/article-2722612/Legia-Warsaw-outline-plan-fight-against-Champions-League-elimination-fielding-ineligible-player-against-Celtic.html).

to the LFF Disciplinary Committee against the decisions of the referee which, as mentioned, cannot be appealed. However, a club may notice that an ineligible player is fielded by an opponent and issue a protest which may later determine that the protesting club could be awarded a victory by default.

308. LFF Disciplinary Committee usually issues decisions in the meetings. However, the chairman has the discretion to issue certain decisions solely. Excisions of the LFF Disciplinary Committee may be appealed to the LFF Appeals Committee which evaluates the legality of the Disciplinary Committee's decision and refuses to accept new evidence.

309. In accordance with the LFF Disciplinary Regulations and the statutes of the LFF, decisions of the LFF Appeals Committee may be appealed by filing an appeal to the CAS Appeals Division within thirty days after receipt of the LFF's final decision. The statutes of the LFF provide a CAS appeal clause which prevent clubs or players appeal against LFF decisions in a civil court. There were several events whereby clubs tried to circumvent the CAS arbitration clause and submit the claim to the court; however their claims were not admitted.[117]

B. Disciplinary in Basketball Competitions

310. The main document in terms of disciplinary regulations of the LKF is the Ethics and Disciplinary Code of the LKF (ECD). The ECD is applicable to all competitions organized within the jurisdiction of the LKF and for the members of the LKF and their staff, staff of the LKF, clubs and their staff, players, agents, official persons, other legal and natural persons.[118] The ECD first of all provides ethical standards which should be followed by players, clubs and official persons. The ECD distinguishes two groups of violations: violations during matches and unsporting and inappropriate conduct. As well as the LFF, the LKF also established the strict liability rule for clubs for the conduct of supporters which allows the disciplinary body to apply sanctions to the club for the misconduct of their supporters.

311. Natural persons may be sanctioned by reprimand, fine, disqualification, stripping of the titles and prohibition to participate in basketball-related activities. The same sanctions are applicable to the legal persons as well.

312. Different from the LFF, the LKF provides that disciplinary matters may be heard and the sanctions set by the Code of Discipline and Ethics of the LKF (CDE) may be applied by *the bodies of the leagues*. In fact, the LKF has only a single disciplinary body, the Commission for Ethics and Disciplinary (CED). It is established that in general, bodies of leagues and competitions have the authority to decide upon disciplinary matters, and in such case, the CED would act as an appeal institution.

117. 28 Oct. 2016 ruling of Vilnius District Court in Civil Case No. e2S-1430-881/2016 and 5 Nov. 2012 ruling of Vilnius District Court in Civil Case No. 2S-1381-302/2012.
118. However, it is very doubtful that effective sanction could be applied against the spectator.

However, the CDE also provides that in case the regulations of leagues and competitions contradict the principles of the CDE, the CED then would interfere and act as a disciplinary body. The CDE provides that the decision of the CED is final and is subject to no appeal whatsoever. The CDE does not provide for the arbitration clause; thus final decisions of the CED could be appealed to the court.

C. *Resolution of Private Disputes by Federations*

1. Competence of LFF

313. It is common practice that certain private disputes are solved by the bodies of a sports organization as well. The best example is the FIFA DRC which hears disputes between clubs and players and coaches or between the clubs in matters related to training compensation and solidarity mechanisms. The FIFA PSC hears disputes between clubs which are usually related to the performance of transfer and loan agreements.

314. There can be several reasons to submit certain disputes to a sports organization, rather than the court: (1) solving a dispute within the sports federation can be time saving, (2) bodies of the sports federation would normally understand the specificity of certain matters better than an external judge, (3) the procedure of enforcement of a decision of a sports body may be faster and more reasonable,[119] (4) some regulations may provide very favourable material rules for one of the parties,[120] (5) dispute resolution in sports organization can help avoid jurisdiction issues when dispute is related to international element or is heard between the parties from different countries, (6) certain organizations apply a set of rules which is quite clear for all parties regardless of their own jurisdiction and which have a certain level of immunity from the application of national law.[121] An alternative to solve certain disputes in the bodies of the federation is also provided by the regulations of the LFF.

315. The LFF Player Transfer Regulations (Article 26.1) provide that all disputes related to contracts and sports employment may be submitted to the LFF Appeals' Committee of the LFF *or* the court by the choice of the parties. Moreover,

---

119. Usually, the means of sports federations to enforce the decision are very effective. For example, in accordance with the FIBA Regulations, basketball club would be banned from registering new players in case it failed to cover debts for an ex player under an arbitral award of the BAT.
120. For example, LFF Regulations used to establish that the LFF can terminate the contract between the player and the club subject to failure of the club to pay salary in amount of two monthly salaries.
121. For example, the FIFA DRC very rarely applies national law of the parties concerned and usually applies the FIFA RSTP and established jurisprudence. This allows the parties to the dispute expect how certain matters would be solved. For example, with rare exception, under FIFA longstanding practice, a player who is not paid salary for a period of three months is entitled to terminate the contract with just cause regardless of the national law which would say opposite.

Article 26.2 of said regulations provide that any other disputes related to the regulation, including disputes regarding training compensation and solidarity contribution, must be solved by the LFF Appeals Committee. Thus, the LFF Appeals Committee acts as the one and only body of the LFF to solve disputes between players or coaches and clubs and between clubs regarding transfer matters and training compensation and solidarity contribution. The decision of the LFF Appeals Committee could be appealed to CAS.

316. In a very recent case of the Court of Appeals[122] the court had to deal with an argument of a football club that agreement between two football clubs to refer any dispute to the LFF was an arbitration clause. The court did not recognize such agreement as arbitration clause. The court emphasized that the statutes of the LFF do not provide that disputes *by two clubs* would be referred to arbitration. However, the statutes of the LFF in general provide that *final decision* of the body of LFF is a subject of arbitration. Thus, if a club submits a dispute to the bodies of the LFF (the LFF Appeals Committee) and then wants to challenge the decision of the LFF body, there is a great risk that the court would refuse to admit the claim due to the potentially existing arbitration clause.

2. Competence of LKF

317. Article 8 of the LKF Transfer Regulations stipulates that disputes related to transfers of players are solved by the competition organizers. If such organizer may not solve the dispute, then such dispute shall be solved by the LKF. The regulations do not provide for any procedure for dispute resolution. It must be stressed that said provision expressively provides that the LKF does not solve disputes related to fulfilment and validity of the contract.

318. In fact, there are very few fields where a dispute may be solved instantly by the LKF. Such matters are related to administration of letter of clearance procedures and assurance that the training compensation for the training of basketball player is paid (in case it is not paid, the licence issued for such a player to play for a new club which fails to pay training compensation would be suspended until the compensation is paid). There are no procedures for appeal as well.

319. Thus, the LKF does not interfere in private disputes and leaves it to means chosen by the parties. It sometimes may cause certain issues. For example, if the club fails to respect its financial obligations, a player can terminate the contract. After termination of the contract, the player would sign a new contract with a new club which would request the LKF to issue a letter of clearance. However, the former club may state that the contract is valid. Due to the fact that the LKF does not solve contractual disputes and leave it to the court or arbitration, the procedure of issuance of letter of clearance may take unreasonably long and the player would lose a significant amount of time of his or her career.

---

122. 20 Dec. 2016 ruling of the Court of Appeals in Civil Case No. e2A-878-407/2016.

Part II. Sports and Employment

320. This part of the monograph will mainly concern what may be referred to as 'professional sports employment', i.e., employment and related relationship between athletes, i.e., the players and the clubs. Relationship between athletes of individual sports and competition organizers or other organizations will not be at the centre of attention. However, certain aspects involving individual athletes will be covered as well.

321. Related aspects of relationship between players and clubs include transfer of players, individual representation of players, social security and taxes related to players. For the sake of clarity, it also should be noted that a 'player' in terms of Part II will mean an athlete who operates under SAA or a 'contract'.[123] Mostly players are basketball, football and other team sports participants.[124]

123. SAA is a definition provided by the Law on Sport. However, such agreements are simply often referred as 'contracts'.

124. Although, some individual sports athletes, such as bicycle riders conclude contracts with cycling teams and represent them in races, such *Giro D'Italia* or *Tour de France*. On the contrary, cycling is no longer considered as an individual sport due to the importance of work carried out by all members of the team.

Chapter 1. General Issues

322. In order to elaborate on general issues of sports and employment in Lithuania, it is necessary to take into consideration the fact that Lithuania regained independence only in 1990. Therefore, Lithuanian legal regulation in this specific field is relatively young. For more than forty-five years Lithuania was occupied by Soviet Russia. Communist regime and its regal regulation influenced every aspect of social and economic life, including sport as well. Even top-level athletes technically were considered as regular employees. Most of the sports clubs, or rather teams, were formed within the organization of various factories and other industrial units.

323. Most importantly, football and basketball players and other athletes could not escape the 'Iron curtain' and to play abroad. This meant that even world-class athletes could not make a decent living. Only in the late 1980s prominent athletes could leave the country and become really well-paid professionals. Lithuanian basketball player Šarūnas Marčiulionis was one of the first athletes who were allowed to leave as he joined NBA franchise Golden State Warriors.

324. After Lithuania regained its independence in 1990, a new model of sports governing as well as including issues related to the employment of athletes began to develop. The market economy started functioning and football and, mostly, basketball clubs began to form and grow. Soon clubs became capable to pay comparably high salaries and professional sports employment market began to emerge. Market and related aspects grew faster than the legal regulation of such aspects. Therefore, many fields were not governed. This also is reflected in sports as well. There was no regulation on the status of athletes; therefore, stakeholders had to solve arising issues without legal guidance. Needless to say, certain mistakes were made.[125]

325. Finally, in 1995 a very first edition of the Law on Sport was adopted. For a very first time, it introduced the concept of professional athletes and professional SAAs. From then clubs and leagues grew stronger, conditions for the development of players, especially young athletes, improved, players were paid more.

326. However, despite the improvement of legal framework and general economic situation, certain issues related to the employment of athletes remained:

- As it will be analysed further, the status of players under SAAs is not yet totally clear. The lack of answer on whether a player under a contract with the club is considered to be a worker or a provider of service creates legal uncertainty.

---

125. In 1994 the LKL decided to arrange LKL Draft, a local copy of NBA Draft despite essential differences between NBA model and Lithuanian situation. Information available online (accessed on 26 Jun. 2021) (http://sportas.lrytas.lt/krepsinis/antrasis-lkl-sezonas-nepavykusi-naujoku-birza-l-kunigelio-debiutas-olimpo-viliones-j-kazlauskui.htm).

- Legal uncertainty of the legal status of a player is related to the issue of the lack of the collective representation of athletes. Despite several initiatives, unions of players (be it basketball or football players) were never really capable of transmitting the sound voice of players.
- Protection of a player in the event of injury or death of an athlete is poor and mainly depends on the agreement of an athlete and a sports organization or existence of a private insurance policy.
- Social security system is less providing to the players.

327. However, the lack of public governance is supplemented by rules and regulations of sports federations, which bring more balance between rights and obligations of clubs and players.

Chapter 2. Public Governance of Legal Status of Players

328. Law on Sport defines[126] athlete as a person who competes with other persons in high performance sports competition and (or) trains in high performance sports practices, high performance sport training camps aimed to prepare for high performance sports competitions. Unlike the previous version of the Law on Sport, the current one does not provide any definition for an amateur athlete who is not dedicated to high performance sport. No distinction is made between professional athletes and amateur athletes as well by the current edition of the Law on Sport as well.

329. Elimination of concepts of professional and amateur athletes and connection of status of athlete with high performance sports competition in the current edition of the Law on Sport show that one of the purposes of the change of the Law on Sport in 2018 is deregulation of matters which are more often governed by sports federations, including status of players.

330. The Law on Sport provides no distinction made in terms of the status of athletes depending on the sport, i.e., individual or team. In accordance with Article 10(1) of the Law on Sport, an athlete can be remunerated for sporting activities in accordance with labour agreement or SAA. It is usual that professional team sports players act under SAAs concluded with the club. However, individual athletes may receive significant amounts of money (e.g., prize money) and still they do not possess written SAA with a single sports organization or do possess more than one agreement at a time. Individual sports athletes may conclude agreements with the competition organizers or other sports organizations, however such agreements differ from SAAs essentially: first of all, a player under SAA usually is not allowed to have the same agreement with another club, meanwhile an individual athlete may be on several agreements at the same time; second, a player's SAA with a club is usually fixed for a considerably long period of time (at least to the end of the season), meanwhile individual athletes participate in certain event and they usually are free to subscribe for another event; third players are usually under a certain level of subordination from the club as they have to follow a schedule determined by the club and obey internal regulations, meanwhile individual athletes plan their activities themselves and are usually independent from sports organization. However, the Law on Sport does not distinguish individual athlete and player under contract with the club and invokes the same definition of 'athlete'.

331. In 2008 Lithuanian State Tax Authority issued comments (consultation) on taxation of athletes. Despite the fact that such comments are not considered as a legal act and therefore the court hearing the dispute would not necessarily take it into consideration, besides, such comments refer to the situation of athletes from taxation point of view, some very important remarks to understand the differences between the statuses of various athletes are provided.

126. Article 2(15) of the Law on Sport.

332. An individual athlete from taxation point of view is considered an athlete who himself or herself is *independent* and does not maintain *labour-alike* relationship with a sports organization: such athlete resolves issues related to his or her activity independently. For example, he or she covers all expenses related to participation in competition. Meanwhile, an athlete under SAA with the club is considered to be in labour-alike relationship.[127] The main element which enables to declare accordingly is subordination: functions of an athlete stipulated in the agreement, obligation of an athlete to comply with the internal regulations of a sports organization, salary of an athlete, health insurance condition, etc. Thus, from a taxation point of view, an athlete under SAA is considered as an employee. The legal consequence of such comments is that a sports organization, mostly a club will be responsible for declaring and paying taxes for the athlete. Meanwhile an athlete who carries out individual activities is responsible for said tax formalities himself.

333. Therefore, the definition of 'athlete' provided by the Law on Sport is very broad and does not necessarily reveal all important aspects. Besides, the Law on Sport does not provide a wide scope of rights and obligations of athletes, and most of them are related to the involvement of funding by the state of high performance athletes. Therefore, the regulations of the federations become very important.

127. It is very important to notice, that labour-alike relationship between the player and the club from taxation point of view *shall not mean* that relationship between the player and the club are labour or civil. The nature of legal relationship between the player and the club needs to be analysed in light of provisions of labour law and civil law. The Supreme Court also noticed that qualification of legal relationship between the player and the club from public law point of view [including tax law] does not have any impact on the qualification of such relationship from private law point of view, *see* 21 Feb. 2011 ruling of the Supreme Court in Civil Case No. 3K-3-65/2011.

Chapter 3. Private Governance of Legal Status of Players

§1. LFF Regulations

334. The main regulations of the LFF governing the status of an athlete, a football player, are the LFF Transfer Regulations. It should be noted that the LFF Transfer Regulations are very similar to the FIFA RSTP and many provisions are moved to the LFF Transfer Regulations from the FIFA RSTP without much of modification.

335. The LFF Transfer Regulations not only specify the status of players but also governs the transfers between clubs, training compensation, solidarity mechanisms, protection of contractual stability, release of players to the LFF association teams and the players' rights to play for such teams. Currently, edition of 7 October 2021 of the LFF Transfer Regulations is in place.

336. The LFF Transfer Regulations clearly distinguish professional and amateur players. In accordance with Article 4.2 of the LFF Transfer Regulations,[128] 'a player who has a contract [i.e. SAA] with a club and *is paid for the sporting activity* at the club is deemed a professional, i.e., a player holding the status of a professional football player'. Important criteria to determine if a player is professional are provided: a player is professional if his or her remuneration is *higher than the expenses* he/she actually incurs for the same purpose. It is further explained that 'the remuneration shall *be deemed* to exceed a player's actually incurred expenses related to his sporting activity at the club when it is no less than the minimal monthly wage payable in the Republic of Lithuania'. Thus, in order to gain professional status, a player must have a written SAA with the club and to be remunerated with an amount at least equal to minimal monthly wage.[129] However, the general rule for distinguishing a professional from an amateur is that a professional receives remuneration which is *higher than the expenses*. Accordingly, it may be concluded that even an athlete who receives less than minimal salary can be considered professional if his/her remuneration is higher than expenses related to sporting activity.

337. According to the LFF Transfer Regulations, there is no rule prohibiting a minor player to obtain a status of a professional. Restriction regarding international transfers does apply to minors in accordance with the FIFA RSTP. In order to consider a minor player a professional, it is sufficient for a player to be remunerated with a salary at least amounting to half of the minimal salary. As mentioned above, as a general rule minor player cannot be part of an international transfer subject to rare exceptions.

---

128. Provisions of the LFF Transfer Regulations are quoted as stipulated in translation of documents by the LFF provided in the LFF website. Source is available online (accessed on 6 Aug. 2021) (https://lff.lt/files/documents/911/Zaideju%20statuso%20ir%20perejimo%20reglamentas%202021.pdf).
129. On 8 Aug. 2022 the amount is equal to EUR 730.

338. An amateur player is a player who does not have a professional status. A status of a player is registered by the federation and may be traced in the player's passport.[130]

339. Status of a professional player is important in several aspects: first of all, professional players have to maintain and respect contractual relationship with clubs. Certain restrictions such as prohibition to terminate the contract (principle of stability of contract) are applicable to professionals. A professional who terminates the contract without just cause can be subject to serious economic consequences and sporting sanctions as well. Professional players are not allowed to switch clubs without the consent of their current club. Professional players also may be loaned to another club subject to consent of both clubs and players. Status of a professional player is also important to determining of the obligation of a club to pay training compensation or solidarity contribution.

340. Special provisions governing the content of an SAA between the club and the player do apply too. LFF Transfer Regulations include a model SAA between a professional player and the club stipulating minimum requirements which must be maintained. SAAs must be registered within the LFF. The LFF has a right to refuse registration of an SAA. In such case SAA would not necessary lose its legal power; however, a player would not be registered for competition, and thus the club would not be able to field the player concerned. Thus, it is highly advisable to at least comply with the essential conditions of a model contract stipulated in the LFF Transfer Regulations.

§2. LKF Regulations

341. The LKF Regulations Governing Transfers of Players and Education Compensation[131] (LKF Transfer Regulations) are a set of rules governing the status of a basketball player within the frame of the LKF. The LKF Transfer Regulations are closely related to the FIBA Internal Regulations. Generally, the latter governs a major part of the relationship and the LKF Transfer Regulations just supplement certain domestic specifics.

342. First, the major difference between LKF Transfer Regulations and the LFF Transfer Regulations is that there is no distinction between amateur or professional players in the LKF Transfer Regulations. However, the LKF Transfer Regulations

130. A player passport in terms of the FIFA RSTP should not be understood as a player's identification document. The player passport contains information on the career of the player: periods of registration with a club, his status (professional/non-professional), contract entry and expiry dates. In general player passports are opened following the first registration of a player to a club or football education entity (academy or school). Player passport is a very important document, in particular when determining football clubs involved in the education of the player. In order to determine the clubs which have to be paid training compensation or solidarity contribution a player passport shall first be examined.

131. Provisions of LKF Transfer Regulations are translated by the author.

distinguishes 'professional contract' and 'education service contract'. Definition of a professional contract (SAA) matches the one provided by the Law on Sport. Education service contract is a type of agreement which is usually concluded by a minor player with a basketball school or an academy for rendering educational services in the field of basketball training. It should be noted that generally the FIBA Internal Regulations forbid players under 18 to conclude contracts. In an event of a player signing a contract for the first time may result in payment of education compensation by the new club to the old club or the basketball school.

343. The LKF Transfer Regulations do not stipulate any requirements for the content of SAA, although a model education contract is attached to the LKF Transfer Regulations. The rest of the LKF Transfer Regulations govern the transfer of players, procedure of issuance of letter of clearance and education compensation.

Chapter 4. The Nature of Relationship Between Players and Clubs

344. In many countries professional players are considered as employees. The clubs and players in Lithuania can also sign labour agreements which are governed by the Labour Code of the Republic of Lithuania ('Labour Code'). However, on 20 December 1995 the Law on Sport was adopted, and thus the definition of the SAA was introduced.

345. In accordance with the previous edition of the Law on Sport (in force before 2018), the SAA was defined as:

> an agreement between a professional athlete, athlete or coach and a sports organization under which the professional athlete, athlete or coach undertakes to prepare for sports competitions or to train athletes, to participate in competitions by adhering to the set internal regulations of the sports organization, and the sports organization undertakes to pay remuneration for sports or coaching activities and guarantees the conditions of training for and participation in competitions, as well as undertakes to implement other terms and conditions provided for in the agreement.

346. Current edition of the Law on Sport does not define the SAA at all. However, Article 10(2) of the Law on Sport sets forth that the SAA contains an agreement of the parties on their rights and obligations, remuneration, liability for breach of obligations set forth in the SAA, duration of the SAA. The SAA shall have to conclude in writing. Parties are free to conclude on other conditions as well.

347. Neither definition provides a clear answer to the question on the nature of such agreement: is it labour agreement or is it the other kind of agreement (e.g., civil service agreement)?[132]

348. This answer is essential. Depending on the nature of the agreement, different laws and provisions may apply to legal relationship. If SAA is considered a labour agreement certain provisions of the Labour Code could be applied. On the contrary, if SAA is considered as a civil agreement, the provisions of the Civil Code would apply. Difference between labour agreement and civil agreement also manifests in other important aspects, such as:

- Liability of an employee is usually limited while in case of civil liability a principle of full compensation of damages applies (thus a player may be in serious financial situation following breach of obligation).[133]

---

132. It should be noticed that in accordance with Art. 10(1), the athletes may be remunerated for their sporting activities in accordance with labour agreement *or* SAA. It may suggest that the clear distinction is established between labour agreement and SAA; however, the specificities of the SAAs must be analysed in order to establish the nature of such agreement.
133. The classic example of such situation is the famous *Mutu* case. Adrian Mutu, notorious Romanian striker was sacked by Chelsea due to a failed cocaine test. CAS awarded to Chelsea from Mutu a

- Procedures of termination of an agreement differ, as an employee can terminate agreement without any cause just complying with the procedure of termination.
- Dispute resolution methods are different.
- Employees have a larger scope of social guarantees.
- Consequences of termination of SAA are defined by the agreement mostly, while employers are obliged by law to perform certain financial obligations towards their former employees.
- Consequences of compensation for the death or injury of an employee are comprehensively governed by laws meanwhile compensation for death or injury of a player is not governed by law and is subject to an agreement.

349. Decision on whether to consider the legal relationship between the player and the club as labour or other kind of relationship could result in different legal consequences. Therefore, interpretation of the nature of SAA is essential. Interpretation of law in Lithuania is a privilege of courts. Further, the evolution of understanding of nature of SAA by courts of Lithuania is provided.

§1. Early Stages

350. On 24 May 2000 the Supreme Court of Lithuania rendered a decision in Civil Case No. 3K-3602/2000. The case concerned an issue whether labour law may be applicable to a contractual dispute between a basketball player and the club in terms of compensation for wrongful dismissal.

351. The court held that professional sport is a *specific activity* of labour for which the player is remunerated. However, since, according to the court, an SAA is concluded in accordance with the Law on Sport, it is governed by this law and therefore labour laws *are not applicable*.

352. On 1 June 2005 the Supreme Court passed an award in a Civil Case No. 3K-3-254/2005 which created confusion. The court backed the decision of courts of lower instances by which the football player was awarded, *inter alia*, compensation for unused holidays, which is only granted for employees under labour laws in Lithuania. The court did not elaborate on the status of the player, however its decisions to apply labour law provisions on certain part of dispute raised questions on the status of SAA.

§2. Depart from Labour Law Application

353. On 21 February 2011 the Supreme Court passed a ruling in Civil Case No. 3K3-65/2011 in the already mentioned case between Kęstutis Marčiulionis and BC Žalgiris. The court held that professional SAAs, taking into consideration its

compensation of around EUR 17 million. *See* further CAS 31 Jul. 2009 award in Case No. CAS 2008/A/1644 *Adrian Mutu v. Chelsea Football Club Limited.*

essence and substance, should be considered *as service agreement* and should be governed by the chapter of Civil Code 'Provision of Charged Services'. Nevertheless, the court still indicated that SAA contains features attributable to labour law. In accordance with the court, SAA is in general a civil contract (service agreement); however, the presence of labour law may not be excluded in future in case some aspects are not governed by agreement.

354. On 22 December 2011 the Supreme Court rendered another important ruling[134] with respect to the status of SAA. The court dealt with the potential invalidity of SAA and did state very important remarks. First of all, the court verified earlier jurisprudence by stating that sport is a particular employment activity for a player for which he or she is remunerated; however, labour law provisions *are not* applicable if SAA compatible with requirements set by the Law on Sport is present. The inclusion of elements which are usually attributed to labour relationship, such as limitation of contract termination, guarantees for employees, right to holidays is a matter subject to free will of parties involved in sports relationship. The court also did acknowledge that professional sports employment relationship is related not to the performance of certain functions (like in labour relationship) but rather to aim for certain sporting result. Sports employment relationship is attributed to such elements like maintenance of sports regime and discipline, health care and insurance, etc. Said elements, in accordance with the court, determine attribution of SAAs to civil agreements. SAA may be considered as establishing labour relationship when the parties agree that such contract is considered as labour agreement. Finally, the court noted that qualification of agreement is subject to the content of the agreement. If a contract pursuant to its terms cannot be attributed to labour agreement then the relationship deriving from such contract will not be acknowledged as labour agreement and should be considered as specific agreement governed by the Law on Sport.

355. Thus, to summarize the jurisprudence and, therefore, the general approach of the courts to SAAs, it can be concluded that in general SAAs are considered as specific agreements governed by the Law on Sport and thus generally provisions of labour law are not applied. SAA is considered as civil contract and thus provisions of the Civil Code are applicable. However, interpretation of the contract depends mainly on the content of the agreement. Said approach is also maintained in relatively recent jurisprudence of the Supreme Court.[135]

356. Therefore, the nature of SAA is not yet clear in Lithuania. It is obviously considered to be more as civil contract and not labour agreement; however, there is space for interpretation. More time and practice is needed to determine these issues.

134. 22 Dec. 2011 ruling of the Supreme Court in Civil Case No. 3K-3-548/2011.
135. 4 Jul. 2019 ruling of the Supreme Court in Civil Case No. e3K-3-227-684/2019.

Chapter 5. Contractual Relationship Between Players and Clubs

357. A career of a professional athlete is relatively short and usually lasts ten to fifteen years. Career of professional athletes carves the human body, and in many cases consequences are felt after an athlete retires. Such relatively short age of a professional life does not leave too much space for employment-related errors. A player may get contracted with a potentially insolvent club, or a player may be abused by unprofessional staff and managers of the club, in some cases a player may lack decent medical care or health insurance. A loss of any period of time in an athlete's career with an improper club may bring significant damage or jeopardize the career of such athlete. Thus, a contract and content of the contract is indeed significant for an athlete.

358. The same applies to the clubs too. Clubs spend huge amounts of money for the salaries of their players in order to pursue sporting success. Football clubs around the world spend significant amounts of money for transfers of their players as well.[136] It is in clubs' interest that a player would fulfil expectations and comply with the standards of the club. Therefore, contractual relationships become an important aspect of the activity of a club.

359. The quality of the relationship between a player and a club mostly lies within the content of the SAA. As mentioned above, SAA in Lithuania is in general not considered as an employment agreement. Considering the civil nature of the SAA, certain principles set out in the Civil Code apply including the principle of freedom of contract. Thus, the responsibility of quality SAA lies upon the parties as they are free to agree on the most important aspects of their contractual relationship.

§1. SAA: Provisions of Law on Sport

360. Article 10(2) of the Law on Sport provides that the SAA contains an agreement of the parties on their rights and obligations, remuneration, liability for breach of obligations set forth in the SAA, duration of the SAA. The SAA shall have to conclude in writing. Parties are free to conclude on other conditions as well. No other provisions are set forth by the Law on Sport in terms of governance of the SAAs.

361. As mentioned, a written form of agreement is required as well. SAAs of minors aged 14 to 18 must be co-signed by his or her parents or guardians. An SAA

136. It must be stressed that the transfer market of football players in Lithuania barely exists. The vast majority of incoming transfers are related to out-of-contract players, or so-called free agents. Clubs pay training compensation only if it is due. However, players from Lithuanian clubs are sometimes sold against transfer compensation to foreign football clubs.

on behalf of a minor who is under 14 must be signed by his or her parents or guardians. Before analysing main rights and obligations of the players and clubs requirements from the LFF and the LKF on SAAs are discussed.

§2. SAA: Regulations of Federations

I. LFF Regulations

362. As noted above, the LFF Transfer Regulations are very similar to the FIFA RSTP. This is also applicable to the provisions governing the regulation of SAAs or contracts. Most of the contract principles laid down in the FIFA RSTP are included in the LFF Transfer Regulations as well.

363. In accordance with the LFF Transfer Regulations, a contract is a written agreement for sporting activity concluded between a club and a player. The LFF Transfer Regulations provides that the shortest term of the contract is the period starting on the day the contract comes into force and expiring at the end of the current season. The longest term of the contract is five years. Minor players cannot conclude professional contracts for a term longer than three years. In the event that a contract is concluded for a term which exceeds the limits, it shall be deemed that the term of such contract is the longest possible term as specified above.

364. Validity of a contract cannot be subject to a successful medical examination and/or the grant of a work permit. Medical examination is the responsibility of a club. Usually, clubs do not sign a contract with a player before medical examination. Only after successful examination a club puts a signature on the contract. It should be noted that in practice the clubs tend to insert clauses allowing clubs not to pay salary or terminate a contract subject to the injury of a player.

365. The LFF Transfer Regulations foresee the same principles as the FIFA RSTP with respect to the contractual relationship between the player and the club. Such provisions establishing a contract stability principle are:

- A contract between a professional and a club may only be terminated upon expiry of the term of the contract or by mutual agreement.
- A party may terminate the contract with just cause without any consequences arising out of such termination. What is considered as a just cause depends on the content of the contract, applicable law and other circumstances. For example, in accordance with long-lasting FIFA DRC jurisprudence,[137] a failure to pay salary for more than three months is usually considered a just cause for a player to terminate the contract.
- A professional who has appeared in fewer than 10% of the official matches in which his club has been involved in the course of a season may terminate his contract prematurely on the grounds of sporting just cause.

137. For example, DRC 15 Mar. 2013 Decision No. 03132433 of the FIFA DRC.

- A contract cannot be unilaterally terminated during the course of a season, except when there is a just cause to terminate the contract, or when the contract is terminated by mutual agreement between the professional and the club.
- A contract can be terminated if the club fails to respect its financial obligations and fails to pay amount equal at least to sum of two monthly salaries.

366. The contract stability principle does not necessarily prevent premature contract termination or breach of contract. It is possible that the club or the player would terminate a contract during the course of the season and the opposing party most probably could not suspend such termination. However, a party in breach would face certain consequences: it could be awarded to pay compensation by the LFF bodies or the court. Moreover, sporting sanctions could be imposed – if a player breaches a contract, such player may be banned from football for a certain amount of time. If a violator is a club, then a club may be fined or banned from registering new players or other sanctions could be applied.

367. It must be stressed that LFF controls prima facie validity of the contract. LFF has the right to refuse the registration of a contract with player and with coach, its annexes, additional agreements, amendments or supplements in the event that the club fails to follow the requirements set forth in the LFF Transfer Regulations and their annexes as well as other rules and regulations adopted by the LFF (Article 12.3 of the LFF Transfer Regulations). Hence, if a contract does not meet the requirements of the LFF, including minimum requirements set forth in the LFF Transfer Regulations, the LFF could refuse registration of the contract. In such case, a contract would not lose its legal power, but for sure a player could not be fielded by the club without a registration, therefore the parties would have to amend the contract accordingly. As well as this, the LFF has a right to reject registration of player contract in case of potential infringement of integrity of the game (Article 12.5 of the LFF Transfer Regulations).

II. LKF Regulations

368. The LKF Transfer Regulations provides definition of the SAA which is identical to the definition set forth by the previous edition of the Law on Sport.[138] LKF Transfer Regulations do not provide any requirements for player and club contract, although it provides a model agreement for the education of minor players.

369. Therefore, basic principles laid down in the FIBA Internal Regulations, Book 3 apply. FIBA sets very few requirements: a contract shall be in written form and respect the laws of the country and the federation of origin. The only specific

138. An agreement between a professional athlete, athlete or coach and a sports organization under which the professional athlete, athlete or coach undertakes to prepare for sports competitions or to train athletes, to participate in competitions by adhering to the set internal regulations of the sports organization, and the sports organization undertakes to pay remuneration for sports or coaching activities and guarantees the conditions of training for and participation in competitions, as well as undertakes to implement other terms and conditions provided for in the agreement.

regulation is related to the duration of the contract: it shall have a minimum duration of one year and a maximum duration of four years.

370. FIBA Internal Regulations, Book 3 sets forth suggestions on potential content of the contract between a player and a club: parties, basic regulations to be referenced in the contract, rights and obligations of players (to give best services and loyalty to the club, to train and play) and the club (to pay salary, provide vacations and release to national team), duration and conditions for premature termination, image rights issues and promotional activities, agent's commission if applicable, applicable law. It is also suggested that the parties would include the arbitration of the BAT clause as for the resolution of disputes.

§3. Collective Bargaining Agreements

371. In accordance with the Labour Code, collective bargaining agreement is an agreement concluded between trade unions, employers and their organizations. A labour relationship element is required to conclude a collective bargaining agreement. Professional athletes are not considered employees; therefore there is no legal ground for conclusion of a collective bargaining agreement between the players or their representatives and clubs or their representatives.

372. Although the current edition of the Law on Sport does not specifically provide so, the players may form an association in order to enhance their status in relationship between them and clubs or association of the clubs. However, the mere formation of association will not guarantee any benefits and may not provide any effective measures for the collective defence of rights. In order to gain some power such association has to be recognized by a federation or should sign an agreement with the association of clubs which would determine the rights of such association. Therefore, a scope of collective defence of rights would depend a lot on the content of agreement between the association of players, the federation or the association of clubs.

373. There was no notable practice of forming of associations by professional athletes in Lithuania until 2020. Association of basketball players did exist; however, it hardly conducted any notable activity in terms of collective representation of players' interests. In 2016 Union of Lithuanian Football Players was established and introduced.[139] However, as well as in basketball, it does not conduct any notable activity, though it was admitted to members of the LFF during 30 September 2017 meeting of the Conference of the LFF. Thus, collective representation of professional players basically barely existed, and the rights of professional players were

139. Information available in online news portal (accessed on 26 Jun. 2021) (http://www.delfi.lt/sportas/futbolas/lff-remiamas-naujadaras-nuo-futbolininku-globos-iki-komercines-veiklos.d?id=72420290).

not subject to collective defence and representation. Due to lack of active player association, no agreements between players' and clubs' organizations are concluded.

374. A positive step in an attempt to collectively represent athletes (football players) was taken in 2020, when several football players founded a Union of Professional Players, an association responsible for safeguarding rights of football players in Lithuania. The newly established organization instantly attracted the attention of football players and now has over 200 active members. Union of Professional Players is recognized by football players, hence it is hardly doubtable that the Lithuanian Union of Football Players, regardless of support from the LFF, will become irrelevant.

375. Basketball players followed football players in establishing a new Lithuanian Professional Basketball Players Association in 2020.

376. Therefore, players will surely have more possibilities to say their word on essential contractual matters, such as minimum salary, contract requirements.

377. In accordance with the Labour Code, only professional unions or their organizations have a right of strike. However, professional unions are organizations of employees and professional players cannot form a professional union in the sense the Labour Code and the Law on Professional Unions of the Republic of Lithuania, 1991. Therefore, the players have no such instrument as strike.

378. It should be noticed that the rights of players can indirectly be protected at certain level by federations. For example, in accordance with the LFF Club Licensing Regulations, LFF monitors how clubs carry out their financial obligations towards players. A failure of a club to meet financial obligations may be subject to sanction. Besides, the LFF Transfer Regulations provide certain minimum requirements for player contracts.

379. However, such measures are usually not sufficient which makes collective protection of players' right ineffective. Despite of existence of associations of players, at the end of the day the players have to defend their rights on personal level. That is why a contract and its content become essential both for the club and for the player.

§4. Main Rights and Obligations of Athletes and Clubs

380. It is important to notice that content and importance of various rights and obligations of the parties mostly depend on the will of the parties. The parties may agree on a very wide range of aspects including on what is to be considered as essential terms of agreement.

381. The way certain provision of an agreement is interpreted depends a lot on the body hearing the dispute. Lithuanian rules of contract interpretation are laid down in the Civil Code. The general requirement is that the contract must be interpreted in accordance with good faith. It is important to seek the real intentions of the parties without being limited by the literal meaning of the words. In the event where the real intentions of the parties cannot be established, the contract must be interpreted in accordance with the meaning that could be attributed in the same circumstances by reasonable persons in the corresponding position as the parties (Article 6.193 of the Civil Code). As well as this, contract conditions must be assessed with a systematic approach.

382. Regardless of the content of contract, general principles of contract performance shall apply to the parties. The parties shall perform the contracts in a proper way and in good faith (*see* Article 6.200(1) of the Civil Code). Parties shall be bound to collaborate and to cooperate with the other party performing the contract (Article 6.200(2) of the Civil Code). The parties shall be bound to use the most economical means in the performance of the contract (Article 6.200(3) of the Civil Code). Finally, where according to a contract or its nature, a party in exercising certain actions is bound to make the best effort in the performance of a contract, this party shall be bound to make such effort as a reasonable person would make in the same circumstances (Article 6.200(4) of the Civil Code).

383. It should be noted that said principles are applicable to performance of the SAAs as well. In its recent case law the Supreme Court[140] underlined the importance of duty of cooperation of the parties (basketball players and clubs). In the said case the Supreme Court stated that the facts of the case and the factual circumstances of the case as established by the courts suggest that both parties to the case have not properly complied with their duty to cooperate (insufficient co-operation in the performance of the sports activity contract: the defendant's breach of this obligation manifested itself in a lack of communication with the plaintiff – the defendant did not (timely) respond to the plaintiff's own-initiative notices on contract performance, training camp). According to the Supreme Court, the lack of cooperation resulted in a need to reduce the amount of compensation requested by the player. Hence, nevertheless, the content of a contract, parties to the contract shall have to adhere to the essential contract performance principles, including the principle of cooperation.

384. Further, the typical contractual obligations of clubs and players as well as peculiarities thereof shall be analysed.

140. 4 Jul. 2019 ruling of the Supreme Court in Civil Case No. e3K-3-227-684/2019.

I. Obligations of Clubs

A. *Financial Obligations*

385. Financial obligations are the most important obligations of a club towards the player. There can be several types of such financial obligations: remuneration, performance bonuses and other benefits.

1. Salary

386. Salary is the amount of money which is paid to the player for his training and participation in competition representing a club, i.e., for his sporting services. Usually, it is a fixed amount paid on monthly, weekly or other periodic basis. Salary is undoubtedly the most important part of financial obligations of the club. Non-payment of salaries for a considerable amount of time can be considered as a breach of essential obligation of a club justifying termination of contract unilaterally and prematurely.

387. Importance of salary paid in accordance with schedule stipulated in contract was underlined by the Court of Appeals.[141] The court made an important statement underlining that the career of a professional athlete is very short, full of risk and is closely related to his state of health, injuries. Therefore, the salary due to the athlete and its payment within the set terms, according to the court, is a very important factor to consider when deciding which club to join and sign a contract with.

388. As mentioned before, in football, especially in FIFA DRC practice, the non-payment of salary for three months is usually considered as a ground to terminate the contract. Lithuanian laws, as well as regulations of sports federations, do not provide what kind of period of non-payment is sufficient to terminate the contract. The parties may agree on the consequences of non-payment of salary in their SAA.

389. It must be stressed that non-payment of salary may not be justified by lack of sporting form or failure to meet certain statistical milestones (goals scored, assists completed, etc.) unless it is established that the athlete had breached essential obligations of contract. The Court of Appeals also stated[142] that it is essential to distinguish obligation to seek for a certain result and obligation to maintain certain level of care. The court made a conclusion that the value of a player and his performance in competition does not depend solely on such attributes of a player like his professionalism, his physical shape, experience. It is also influenced by a number of other factors, such as the role assigned for the player, time spent on the court, passes received from teammates, style of team playing and opposition. Due to said reasons, the court concluded that it was impossible to request from the player to

141. 21 Dec. 2009 ruling of the Court of Appeals in Civil Case No. 2A-726/2009.
142. 13 Sep. 2010 ruling of the Court of Appeals in Civil Case No. 2A-589/2010.

achieve certain statistic indicators or that his team would win certain number of matches. The obligation of the professional player is *to put maximum effort* so his team would benefit from his play. Thus, a lack of endeavour or insufficient efforts could be considered a breach of such obligation but not failure to meet statistic indicators.

390. The ruling of the court is important for another element as well. The court held that if the contract states that salaries are 'guaranteed', then all salaries and bonuses must be paid unless the player does breach the contract in its essence. Even if the player is expelled or released from the team or the agreement is terminated due to insufficient performance, in case of death, illness or injury of a player or any other physical or psychical disability or any other reasons other than the essential breach of contract by the player, the club shall have to pay salary and bonuses to the player.

391. Federations may take an active role in ensuring that clubs comply with payment of salary. For example, obligation to pay salary is monitored by the LFF. In accordance with Article 15 of the LFF Transfer Regulations, any payment by a club delayed for more than thirty days without a just cause as defined in the contract shall result in the sanctions (caution, reprimand, fine, prohibition to register new players for the entire registration period or two consecutive registration periods). Repeated breach of this provision is deemed an aggravating circumstance and may result in the club becoming subject to stricter sanctions.

2. Performance Bonuses

392. Bonuses may be paid to a player in accordance with the contract. Bonuses are usually paid subject to the occurrence of a certain, predetermined condition. Usually bonuses are paid for achieving collective goals (if, for example, a team becomes champion, reaches play-offs, gets into the Group Stage of the UEFA Champions' League, etc.) or personal achievements (e.g., scoring ten goals in a season and maintaining fifteen points per game stats in all seasons). Bonuses can be paid for personal and team efforts combined. Parties may agree on various types of inventive achievements which, if occurred, may later be awarded by bonus payments.

393. In practice clubs tend to agree on bonus as an option but not obligation. Clubs include a clause in an agreement stating that a club has a right to reward a player for collective and/or personal achievements. However, the option for bonuses may not be enforced as it solely depends on the will of the club. However, a clear obligation to pay bonuses can be enforced should the club fail to pay amounts due after the events giving rise to such obligation occur. An obligation to pay bonus has to be drafted clearly without any ambiguity.[143]

---

143. For example, in 12 Dec. 2011 decision in Civil Case No. 2A-480/2011 the Court of Appeals rejected player's argument that certain amount paid by the club to him was not salary but a bonus.

394. Legal acts of the Republic of Lithuania or regulations of federations do not provide if non-payment of bonus may constitute a ground for a player to terminate a contract unilaterally; however, parties may agree upon the non-payment of bonus as an event justifying unilateral termination of contract.

3. Other Benefits

395. Other payments or benefits mean other financial obligations of the club which by nature differ from salary and bonus. One of such obligations may be the signing premium or so-called sign-on fee. When a player signs a contract with a club, a player may be immediately paid a fixed amount of money and thus rewarded for signing the contract. Such money could be considered as salaries since it sums with the general remuneration due to the player. However, a legal meaning of such amounts can be different. For example, depending on factual circumstances at stake failure to pay salary may constitute a right of a player to terminate the contract, meanwhile failure to pay the sign-on fee could not be sufficient enough if the general salary is paid. Sign-on fees are applied when a contract is extended by mutual agreement as well.

396. Payments should be also paid for use of a player's image for promotion activities of the clubs. In practice, a condition that general salary covers remuneration for use of image is included. If it is not stipulated by the contact, a player may request additional remuneration for use of his image. Subject to an agreement, a player may also receive other benefits of financial value from the club, like provision of an automobile, covering accommodation expenses, provision of school for children of athlete, etc.

B. Obligation to Provide Facilities and Other Services

397. An obligation of a club to provide an athlete with adequate facilities and conditions to train and to participate in competitions was stipulated by the previous edition of the Law on Sport; however it was not explained in detail. The current edition of the Law on Sport does not stipulate such obligation; however, the parties may agree on the details of such obligation in the contract as well. The jurisprudence of Lithuanian courts on such provision is not established yet too; however, it is reasonable to expect that the clubs can be required to arrange certain facilities for players:

– Training facilities meeting safety and hygienic requirements. In general, a player should be able to prepare for competition and to play in safe environment. A club

The court stated that a contract did not foresee any bonuses and the club did not indicate that certain amounts were paid as bonuses, thus the court held that paid amounts were part of salary.

should be responsible not only to provide training ground but also to ensure it is safe and it can be used in accordance with its purpose. Same applies to the competition ground used by the club.
- Training equipment (balls, baskets, goals, etc.). It is upon the club to ensure that equipment needed for training or completion is in place and is usable.
- Transportation to competitions. It is upon the club to ensure that player is transferred to club competitions safely.
- A club should provide professional medical assistance. Although such obligation is not provided by the Law on Sport, its importance should be underlined. There is no precise regulation on how the club should protect the health of athletes. The Law on Sport and other regulation[144] provides such obligation to athletes, rather than clubs. National team players have to be examined by team doctors. However, the clubs have no such obligation by law. Federations require that the clubs would submit documents proving that the health of all players registered by competitions is duly examined.

C. Insurance and Compensation in Case of Death or Injury

398. The Law on Sport does not specify the issue related to insurance of players against injuries or death. However, the parties may agree upon such matters.

399. It must be also stressed that the players under SAA have to be insured by their clubs with a mandatory health insurance policy. Thus, the clubs have to pay a certain amount (percentage from the salary) every month in the form of health insurance payment for the player. However, it covers the costs of provision of state healthcare services and compensations for rendered services, medical assistance and medicine only. Standard contract clauses provided by the LFF Transfer Regulations also state that the contract shall explain and outline the health and safety policy of the club in terms of the player. LFF requires the clubs to ensure insurance coverage for the player in case of illness or injury, insurance coverage in case of regular medical/ dental care and ensure that the required medical/dental treatment is provided if such arose due to the player carrying out his professional duties for the benefit of the club.

400. The procedure for compensating for the damage done to the health of the player during the training for competitions and during the competitions is a very important condition for a player. Player's activity is related to a very high degree of risk. A player may be seriously injured while performing his contractual obligations to the club. In some cases, such injuries may have long-lasting effects. It must be stressed that the Law on Compensation of Damages Arising from Accidents in the workplace or Professional Illness of the Republic of Lithuania, 1999 stipulates the

144. 31 May 2000 Order No. 301 of the Minister of Health of the Republic of Lithuania on Preventive Health Inspections at Health Care Institutions.

grounds of liability of employer in case of work-related injury or professional illness. However, said law is only applicable to labour relationship and thus does apply to players under SAA. Therefore, such issues should be considered by the contract.

401. In the absence of certain contractual provisions, a non-contract liability of the club may also arise. Article 6.283 and 6.284 of the Civil Code stipulate provisions governing compensation for damage caused to another person's health and liability to compensation for damage caused by fatal injury. Said provisions would most probably be applied in case the player seeks compensation due to suffered injury. However, in order to apply such provisions against a club, *unlawful act of such club* should be established (breach of legal provision or duty of care). Also, a strict liability could be applied, for example, in the event of collapse of a sports hall owned by a club.

D. Release of Player to the National Teams

402. For most of the athletes, representation of a national team in competition is an ultimate experience. Usually, players do not receive any remuneration from national federations for the representation of their country. Players may be awarded afterwards for successful tournament, but generally training and participation in competition for national team is not rewarded. It is understandable that for most of the players, money may not necessarily be a factor preventing a player from putting on his national team jersey.

403. However, the real employers of the players, the clubs, are usually not keen to allow their players to the national team. The main reason is the risk of injury of a player. The clubs pay significant amounts to their players; thus they are completely not interested that their players would play for other teams. Even if the risk of injury is excluded, an international break in the middle of the season may cause serious player fatigue issues. Especially in cases whereby players, mostly footballers from top European leagues, have to fly over the Atlantic Ocean, play a game or two and come back to Europe in the period of several days.

404. Thus, it can be seen that conflict of players, national associations and clubs arises. In most cases, such conflict is solved by the regulations of international sports federations. International sports federations, such as FIFA or FIBA, are very interested that national associations (national teams) would be represented by the best athletes. For FIFA, a World Cup is an essential event granting funds for operation of organization. If national teams lack their main stars, a commercial gain of such event could drop significantly. Thus, such federations make sure national associations are entitled to call up the best players they can[145] regardless of the content of contract between a club and a player.

145. However, it must be stressed that clubs do not give up easily on this issue. European football clubs now receive money from UEFA for released players. In 2012 FIFA launched FIFA Club Protection

405. FIFA RSTP (Annex 1, Article 1(1)) clearly states that clubs are obliged to release their registered players to the representative teams of the country for which the player is eligible to play on the basis of his nationality if they are called up by the association concerned. Any agreement *between a player and a club to the contrary is prohibited*. The same approach is kept by the LFF Transfer Regulations as well. Article 34 of the FIBA Internal Regulations, Book 3 states that any club which signs a contract with a player is obliged to release that player when he is summoned by a national member federation to play for its national team in any age category in a main official competition of FIBA which is included in the FIBA calendar. Failure to release a player for national football and basketball teams may be subject to sanctions.

406. Therefore, release to a national team is ensured by regulations of international federations and it is not necessary to include such clause in the contract.

II. Obligations of Player

407. The main obligation of a player is to prepare for sports competition and to participate in it. Such obligation first of all consists of the duty of a player to attend activities of the club: practices, training camps, friendly and official matches, be present for team trips, etc. As well as this such obligation includes of the duty of a player to put sufficient amount of effort in his daily routines, look after his physical shape and form, to refrain from certain activities which could cause negative impact to the player's form.

408. The Court of Appeals also stated[146] that the obligation of the professional player *is to put maximum effort* so his team would benefit from the play of the player. Thus, a lack of endeavour or insufficient efforts could be considered a breach of such obligation. A circumstance whether a player maintains his effort or not will depend a lot on the factual circumstances as well as the wording of the contract.

409. A player must also comply with internal regulations of the club. The content of internal regulations is not specified by the Law on Sport or regulations of federations. However, usually, internal regulations govern more specific elements of daily duties of a player which are not necessarily mentioned in the contract. Such elements include rules of conduct during training sessions and matches, duty to obey orders of the coach, rules for the wearing of club's official apparel. Most importantly, internal regulations usually include the club's disciplinary regulations and potential sanctions applicable to the player for breach of such regulation, including fines.

Programme (http://resources.fifa.com/mm/document/affederation/administration/01/64/76/90/technicalbulletinmitcirculare.pdf) which is basically an insurance policy covering certain losses of clubs in case their players get injured while on international duty.

146. 13 Sep. 2010 ruling of the Court of Appeals in Civil Case No. 2A-589/2010.

410. It can be considered that internal regulations are a specific extension of the scope of contract. Due to such importance, a player has to be acquainted with regulations before signing a contract. In order to apply such regulations, the presence of players' consent on the content of regulations is necessary. It is also possible that internal regulations may be amended or new edition of it may be adopted unilaterally by the club. New regulations may foresee different duties for the player which may impact the balance of rights and obligations initially agreed by the parties. The law does not specify whether such new edition of rules would be applicable to the player without his or her consent; however, due to the importance of internal regulation, it should be considered that amendment of such regulations could apply to a player only if he or she consented amended consent.

411. The Law on Sport prohibits a player from violating doping regulations as well as to commit any activity related to manipulation of course and result of match. Such activities may not only be rewarded by sporting and financial sanction from sports federations but may also constitute a serious breach of contract by a player which may lead to the unilateral termination of the contract and, as well as this, to serious financial consequences for a player.

III. Essential Rights of Players

412. Provisions on essential human rights and freedoms are laid down by the Convention of Human Rights and the Constitution, as well as the other legal acts of the Republic of Lithuania. Essential rights and freedoms of a player must be respected and may not be denied by a content of contract.

413. Said sources includes such fundamental rights as the right to private life (personal correspondence, telephone conversations, telegraph messages and other communications shall be inviolable), right to freely express convictions(no one must be hindered from seeking, receiving, or imparting information and ideas), right of free thought, conscience and religion (everyone shall have the right to freely choose any religion or belief and, either alone or with others, in private or in public, to profess his religion, to perform religious ceremonies, as well as to practise and teach his belief). The model contract provided by the LFF Transfer Regulations states that the contract shall include the club's obligation to ensure protection of human rights (e.g., right of free expression of the player, freedom of speech, non-discrimination, etc.). Thus, regardless of the content of the contract, a player is free to defend his or her fundamental rights deriving from the Constitution and other laws.

414. Principles of equality and prohibition of any kind of discrimination (sexual, racial, sexual orientation, religion, etc.) are established by the Laws of the Republic of Lithuania. Discrimination due to nationality, race, sex, origin, religion or other belonging to the other group is a crime under Article 169 of the Criminal Code. Incitement against mentioned groups of people is a crime too in accordance with Article 170 of the Criminal Code.

415. Fight against any type of discrimination is also a core of disciplinary regulations of sports federations. In accordance with Article 42 of the LFF Disciplinary Code, an act of discrimination can lead to disqualification of an athlete and deduction of points for the club. Disciplinary and Ethics Code of the LKF also provides sanctions (financial) for players, official persons and clubs due to an act of discrimination. It must be stressed that failure to comply with anti-discrimination requirements may lead to serious breach of contract. In accordance with the model contract provided by the LFF Transfer Regulations, the player is obliged to comply with the provisions of the anti-discrimination policy of the FIFA, UEFA, and/or LFF and/or the club. Moreover, both a player and a club are obliged by signing the contract to refrain from any racist or discriminating actions and to prevent any such racism and discrimination in football.

§5. Termination of Contract as Measure of Defence

416. Termination of contract is a very important institution of contract law. Its importance in terms of SAA is even more notable. Due to the short career of an athlete, an option to terminate the contract can mean an essential difference between a player being stuck in a club whereby he or she does not get match practice or which is in financial difficulty and therefore is late to pay salaries and a very successful opportunity. Therefore, a termination of contract can be a remedy for the defence of rights of the player. Same applies to the clubs who could no longer stand the player's systematic violations of sports discipline or player's admiration for gambling and betting in the way it effected the performance of the team.

Termination of SAA very much relies on the provisions of the contract itself and provisions of the Civil Code. The Law on Sport does not provide any specific provisions with regards to grounds and procedure of the termination of SAA. Thus, provisions of the Civil Code apply. Regulations of sports federations are important as well.

I. Mutual Termination

417. A principle of freedom of contract allows parties to agree not to be in a contract anymore, i.e., to terminate the contract by mutual consent.

418. It is the easiest and less complicated way to end contractual relationship between a player and a club. An agreement over a fact of termination of contract and corresponding rights and obligations deriving from such termination needs to be concluded by the parties. Additionally, the parties agree upon a solution of remaining issues, such as payment of remaining salary to the player, payment of compensation, or returning gear provided to the player by the club. Parties may agree upon the date which will be considered as day effective of termination as well as other aspects.

419. From the point of view of civil law, mutual consent and written form is efficient to finalize the agreement over termination of SAA. However, certain aspects established in the regulations of the sports federations are important as well. For example, football clubs are forbidden to register a player outside the registration period subject to few exceptions in accordance with the LFF Transfer Regulations. Parties should have in mind that due to registration periods, restrictions to register players during the ongoing season, a player may find himself in difficulty to get registered for a new club once his recent contract has been terminated on mutual consent.

II. Predetermined Contract Termination

420. Pursuant to Article 6.217(5) of the Civil Code a contract may be dissolved unilaterally in the cases provided by law. The parties are free to determine in their contract circumstances which, if they occur, trigger a right for a party to terminate the contract. In the case of a contract between a club and a player, it is very common that a right of a player to unilaterally terminate the contract is related to failure of a club to pay salary or other amounts in certain amount of time. From the club's point of view provisions which allow clubs to terminate the contract unilaterally due to the involvement of a player in match-fixing activities or violation of the anti-doping rule are common too. It is very important for parties to an SAA to carefully draft an agreement and determinate the termination clauses as they have to be transparent and unambiguous.

421. Conditions providing so-called unilateral options are very common in SAAs. Unilateral option is a clause which provides one party a right to unilaterally terminate or extend the contract, without providing the other party an adequate right. Unilateral options are used by clubs very often. For example, a player and a club conclude a four-year contract. However, a clause stating that a club has a right to terminate the contract without any reason whatsoever after the end of every season is included. In the other case, a club and a player may agree for a one-year deal; however, a club possesses a right to unilaterally extend the contract by its sole decision before the commencement of the last match of the season. Players may also have this right. It is widely discussed that unilateral options, if held by a stronger party of the contract, are of *disputable validity*. The FIFA DRC is very strict on the application of unilateral options if they are possessed by clubs solely. In accordance with the FIFA DRC jurisprudence, if the unilateral extension option is unilateral to the benefit of the stronger party in the employment relationship, i.e., the club, there is no apparent gain for the player and therefore the unilateral extension option cannot be valid.[147] In terms of the Lithuanian law, unilateral option could be a disputable clause at certain level if it is not in line with mandatory provisions or public order or it disrupts a balance of contractual obligations.

147. FIFA DRC 18 Mar. 2010 Decision No. 310607 and FIFA DRC 31 Jul. 2013 Decision No. 07132435.

422. Considering conditions to terminate the contract it is also necessary to draft a procedure for the termination of contract. In accordance with Article 6.218(1) of the Civil Code, party shall be bound to give the other party notice of dissolution in advance within the time limit established by the contract. If the contract does not indicate such time limit, the notice of dissolution must be given within thirty days.

III. Unilateral Termination Due to Just Cause

423. Grounds and procedure for unilateral termination of contract are established in Article 6.217 and 6.218 of the Civil Code.

424. In accordance with Article 6.217(1) of the Civil Code, a party may terminate the contract where the failure of the other party to perform it or the defective performance thereof is considered to be *an essential violation of the contract* (material breach). Article 6.217(2) of the Civil Code provides criteria which have to be taken into account in order to determine whether a violation of a contract is essential (material):

- Whether the aggrieved party is substantially deprived of what he was entitled to expect under the contract, except in cases when the other party did not foresee or could not have reasonably foreseen such result.
- Whether, taking into consideration the nature of the contract, strict compliance with the conditions of the obligation is of essential importance.
- Whether the non-performance is made intentionally or with great imprudence.
- Whether the non-performance gives the aggrieved party the basis to suppose that he cannot believe in the future performance of a contract.
- Whether the non-performed party, who was preparing for performance or was effectuating the performance of the contracts, would suffer significant damages if the contract were dissolved.

425. It should also be noted that parties may agree on what kind of violation of contract could be considered as essential (material). It is reasonable to assume that such violation as failure to pay salary for a significant amount of time to the player could be considered as essential (material) violation constituting ground to terminate the contract unilaterally. Same applies to violations of a player related to the use of doping or involvement in match-fixing. However, it is upon the court to interpret the contract after assessment of all related circumstances.

426. In the event of essential (material) violation of agreement, a party can terminate the contract without addressing to the court. As mentioned before, the party shall be bound to give the other party notice of dissolution in advance within the time limit established by the contract, and if the contract does not indicate such time limit, the notice of dissolution must be given within thirty days.

427. In case of lack of essential (material) violation of the contract or a condition stipulated in the contract allowing a party to terminate the contract, an injured party should apply to the court and request the court to terminate the contract. However, the latter option is the least attractive and in order to duly exercise it a significant amount of time may be needed for the court to decide upon the issue in all instances. Time is a very important factor in sports relationships; thus it is advisable to include conditions for premature termination in the SAA.

Chapter 6. Transfers of Players and Compensation Mechanisms

428. A transfer of players is usually understood as the move of a player from one sports organization (releasing club) to another sports organization (new club). The Law on Sport provides no material regulation on the transfer of player thus the regulations of international federations apply.

429. International federations do govern transfers of players, however such regulations are usually applicable to international transfers, i.e., a transfer with an international element. For example, Article 1(2) of the FIFA RSTP states that the transfer of players between clubs belonging to the *same association* is governed by specific regulations issued by the association concerned. The FIBA Internal Regulations, Book 3 (Article 58) establishes a similar approach. Therefore, local transfers are governed by national federations. Transfer regulations of the two most important Lithuanian sports federations, i.e., the LKF and the LFF will be analysed with due attention to international regulation as well.

§1. Transfers in Football

430. Transfers in football are one of the most entertaining and publicly discussed elements of professional football. Legal aspects of players' transfer are no less entertaining and important.

431. The FIFA RSTP is the most important regulation on transfers in international football, and it lays down the essential internationally binding principles on the status and transfers of players. However, the FIFA RSTP does not define what a transfer is.[148] The basic understanding of a transfer is a move of a player from one football club to another club. If a player moves clubs from different jurisdictions then a transfer is international and therefore the FIFA RSTP will apply. If a transfer of players takes place between clubs affiliated to the same association, then a transfer is considered as domestic thus national transfer regulations shall apply.

432. In accordance with Article 1(2) of the RSTP, the transfer of players between clubs belonging to the same association is governed by specific regulations issued by the association concerned which must be approved by the FIFA. The FIFA RSTP states that the national associations cannot divert from certain provisions of the FIFA RSTP, and such provisions must be implemented by national associations. Therefore, national regulations, including the LFF Transfer Regulations, are closely related to the FIFA RSTP and both documents contain several identical provisions. The current edition of the LFF Transfer Regulations closely follows the FIFA RSTP guidelines as the above-mentioned principles are met. Before going into more

148. A transfer is defined as 'an agreement between a player and clubs to change the player's registration from one club to another (loan and definitive transfer)' in study of The Economic and Legal Aspects of Transfers of Players, available online (accessed 26 Jun. 2021) (http://ec.europa.eu/assets/eac/sport/library/documents/cons-study-transfers-final-rpt.pdf).

details regarding LFF Transfer Regulations and national transfers, a more detailed analysis will be conducted on types of international transfers and transfer contract. Major part of transfers involving Lithuanian elements when a transfer fee is paid as part of a transfer agreement is related to players being transferred from Lithuanian clubs to foreign clubs, i.e., following an international transfer.

I. Types of Transfers

433. There is no uniform model to classify international player transfers in association football. However, practical aspects, such as existence or non-existence of player contract, or payment and non-payment of transfer fee, can be considered as criteria for such classification. Therefore, it is possible to distinguish the following transfers:

- Transfer of *out-of-contract player*. The key aspect of such transfer is that the player has no contract with his former club at the moment of transfer. There can be various reasons for such out-of-contract status. First of all, it can undergo natural expiry of term of contract. A contract may be terminated unilaterally by a former club due to various reasons as well. A contract can be also terminated by a player due to several reasons: breach of contract by a club justifying unilateral termination, sporting reasons[149] or exercise of right of contract termination. The latter option may foresee a right of player to terminate contract without any specific reasons. Unilateral termination option may also be related to the payment of a specific amount for a club to legitimately terminate a contract. After termination a player moves as a 'free agent', i.e., out of contract.
- Transfer against payment of a transfer fee. The key aspect of such transfer is that the player is under a contract during the transfer and therefore a new club 'buys out' such a player. It is a type of player transfer when releasing club and the new club agree on the transfer of player, and usually a transfer fee is paid by a new club to the releasing club. A player has to consent the transfer. As a result of such transfer, a player's old contract is terminated and a contract with a new club is concluded. In international practice, it is common that contract between a player and a club includes so-called minimum release clause which stipulates the obligation of the releasing club to arrange the transfer of a player and in fact transfer such a player to a new club subject to offer of a new club to pay an amount for the player set forth in a contract.
- Loan of player. A loan of player is a transfer of a player to a new club on a temporary basis, i.e., for a period not exceeding the length of a player's contract with the releasing club. Usually players are loaned for a period of one season. After the end of the loan period a player returns to his former club. A loan of players

149. Article 15 of the FIFA RSTP states that an established professional who has, in the course of the season, appeared in fewer than 10% of the official matches in which his club has been involved may terminate his contract prematurely on the ground of sporting just cause. However, this clause is a very unpopular ground for termination.

is very popular in case of young players. Clubs tend to off-loan their young players to smaller clubs to ensure their young players gain match practice and return with more experience. A loan can be free of charge or against payment. Clubs and a player also agree upon conditions of payment of salary to a player while on loan (usually a new club covers whole or part of player salary). It is also common that a loan agreement includes a so-called buy-out clause which allows a new club at certain point to acquire the rights to a player on a permanent basis if a new club pays the agreed amount.

- Loan of player. A loan of player is a transfer of a player to a new club on a temporary basis, i.e., for a period not exceeding the length of a player's contract with the releasing club. Usually players are loaned for a period of one season. After the end of the loan period, a player returns to his former club. A loan of players is very popular in case of young players. Clubs tend to off-loan their young players to smaller clubs to ensure their young players gain match practice and return with more experience. A loan can be free of charge or against payment. Clubs and a player also agree upon conditions of payment of salary to a player while on loan (usually a new club covers whole or part of player salary). It is also common that a loan agreement includes a so-called buy-out clause which allows a new club at certain point to acquire the rights to a player on a permanent basis if a new club pays the agreed amount.

434. The list of types of transfers is non-exhaustive. Football market is very flexible and very inventive methods of transferring a player may appear.

II. Transfer Contract

435. Player transfer contract is an agreement between two clubs and a player constituting the transfer of a player to a new club. The subject matter of contract is the obligation of a releasing club to cancel the existing contract with a player and the obligation of a new club to pay the agreed amount to releasing for transfer of player. Consent of a player for transfer is absolutely essential. Without the consent of a player an existing contract cannot be terminated and accordingly a new contract with a new club cannot be concluded and thus a transfer cannot be executed.

436. When a player transfer is announced on media channels a misleading term 'club X bought player Y' is used. However, a player, as a human being cannot be the subject of sale and purchase. A new club acquires sporting services of a player and *a right of registration* of a player for a club to perform in domestic and international competitions. In accordance with Article 5(2), the FIFA RSTP a player can only be registered at one club at a time; thus a right to register[150] a player is essential and constitutes an essential element of transfer. A concept of 'economic rights to a player' is sometimes defined as a separate element of transfer contract. Economic right is a right to receive a transfer fee for the subsequent transfer of a player: a new club may sell rights to the player to a third club after a certain period and

150. Sometimes such right is referred as 'federative rights'.

thus collect transfer fee which may also be higher than the amount the new club had paid to the releasing club. Due to the involvement of player agencies, companies and funds in international transfers, a tendency to distinguish 'economic rights' in a transfer began to appear as certain amounts of future transfer fees were assigned to agents of players or so-called football investment funds. Such practices are called by FIFA as 'third-party ownership'[151] and are now banned.[152] Thus, the right to register a player and so-called economic rights cannot be distinguished.[153]

437. Following elements of transfer contract should be distinguished:

- An obligation of the releasing club to cancel a contract with a player. As mentioned, a player must consent such termination. Usually, termination of contract is made subject to signing of a new contract between a player and a new club and actual execution of transfer.
- An obligation of a new club to conclude a contract with a player. It also requires the consent of a player. Before the conclusion of a contract, a medical examination is usually carried out by a new club. In accordance with the FIFA RSTP, validity of contract cannot be made subject to successful medical examination; thus clubs tend to conduct medical examination before signing a contract.
- Consent of player. A player must consent a transfer, termination of an old contract and signing a new contract.
- Transfer fee. Clubs agree on a transfer fee to be paid by a new club to the releasing club. It can be a lump sum payable immediately or amounts to be paid as instalments in a longer period. Alternative economic benefits can supplement or replace the transfer fee. A so-called sell-on fee is included very often. By such clause, a new club obliges to pay a former club additional amount in case a player is further subsequently transferred to a third club. In such cases, amounts payable to a former club are usually determined by certain percentage as from amount received from a third club by a new club. Clubs may also include players to exchange (swap of players) as well as other benefits, such as arrangement of a friendly match or share of know-how. In accordance with provisions of the FIFA RSTP training compensation or solidarity contribution may be paid as a result of transfer. If clubs do not agree that training compensation or solidarity contribution is included in a transfer fee then a former club can require additional payment of said amounts subject to existence of conditions for the payment of training compensation and/or solidarity contribution.

438. There is no model player transfer contract; thus different clubs use different drafts of contracts. Therefore, the content of player transfer contracts may vary significantly depending on clubs, associations and lawyers who advise parties to a transfer contract.

151. Third-party ownership, also known as third-party investment in players, commonly refers to an agreement whereby a third party provides a club (or player) with money in return for a percentage of a specific player's future transfer fee (i.e., the sum paid by a club to another club for signing a player still under contract, as compensation for early termination of that contract).
152. Articles 20–21 of the FIFA RSTP.
153. Certain amounts of future transfer fees can be paid to former clubs.

III. International Transfer Procedures

439. International transfers in football are governed explicitly and exceptionally by the FIFA RSTP. It contains very strict procedures and provides roles and obligations to clubs, players and associations.

440. The main document confirming that transfer is concluded is the International Transfer Certificate (ITC). Depending on the type of transfer, multiple parties may be included in issuance of the ITC, including both clubs and both associations which the clubs are affiliated to. The ITC is administrated via an online platform called the FIFA Transfer Match System (FIFA TMS) which was introduced by FIFA in 2008. Parties have to enter certain data into their online accounts in order to request the ITC and issue it. It is important that data inserted by the releasing and the new clubs match so the transfer can proceed. The parties have also to upload certain documents, including the transfer contract. The FIFA TMS replaced old-fashioned issuance of the ITC by fax system, and now a player transfer can be confirmed within minutes and not weeks as before. However, even the new system does not prevent the last day transfers from collapsing due to delay of initiation of transfer instruction in the TMS by mere seconds.[154]

441. It is also important to underline the FIFA's rules of registration periods or so-called transfer windows. Every association has to confirm with the FIFA two periods in a year (one lasting four weeks and another twelve weeks) when new players can be registered. Usually, the longer period takes place after between two seasons and the shorter one usually takes place in the middle of the ongoing season. A player cannot be registered outside the registration period subject to rare exceptions.

IV. Football Transfers in Jurisdiction of the LFF

442. Regulation of transfers in accordance with the LFF Transfer Regulations is very similar, or in many cases, is identical to the FIFA RSTP. Articles 13 and 14 of the LFF Transfer Regulations are specifically designated to govern domestic transfers of permanent and temporary basis.

443. The basic requirement is that clubs willing to transfer the rights to the registration of a professional player must obtain the so-called letter of clearance from previous club of the player confirming the inexistence of contractual legal relationship between the player and his/her former club (Article 13.1 of the LFF Transfer Regulations). Should the contract be terminated before term unilaterally or by mutual termination, the letter of clearance is not required.

154. Stories of last minute transfer collapses are available online (accessed on 26 Jun. 2021) (https://www.soccerex.com/insight/articles/2016/resolving-failed-last-minute-football-transfer-deals-lessons-from-the-de-gea-case).

444. A transfer on temporary basis (loan) can take place upon conclusion of the loan agreement between the clubs, including the presence of a consent of the player involved. Additionally, the LFF governs minimum period of loan (time between two registration periods) (Article 14.4 of the LFF Transfer Regulations). Another important provision is that accepting club has no right to transfer a player concerned without written authorization of club loaning a player (Article 14.5 of the LFF Transfer Regulations).

445. All contracts, annexes, amendments and other agreements must be registered within the LFF in accordance with procedures stated in the LFF Transfer Regulations. The same request applies to the conclusion and registration of contracts concluded between the coaches and the clubs. In accordance with Article 12.3 of the LFF Transfer Regulations, the LFF has the right to refuse acknowledgement of contracts with players and contracts with coaches or their respective annexes, amendments and/or supplements if they are not registered with the LFF. Moreover, unregistered contracts with players and contracts with coaches along with their respective annexes, amendments and/or supplements cannot be used against the LFF.

446. Failure to follow formal and substantial requirements for player and coach contract may lead to refusal of the LFF to register the contract which would make the player ineligible to play.

447. As in the case of international transfers, players may only be registered during one of the two annual registration periods. As an exception to this rule, a professional whose contract has expired prior to the end of a registration period may be registered outside that registration period on the condition that due consideration is given to the sporting integrity of the relevant competition (Article 12.5 of the LFF Transfer Regulations). The approach of the LFF on registration of the free agents outside the registration period is very flexible; thus clubs tend to sign free agents even at very late stages of the season.

V. Training Compensation and Solidarity Contribution

448. Training compensation and solidarity mechanism were definitions introduced by early editions of the FIFA RSTP following negotiations with the European Commission on a new regulation after the *Bosman* ruling. In accordance with the FIFA RSTP commentary,[155] the 'system encourages the training of young players and creates stronger solidarity among clubs by awarding financial compensation to clubs that have invested in training young players'. Provisions of the LFF Transfer Regulations on training compensation and solidarity contribution are very similar to the FIFA RSTP provisions.

155. Source available online (accessed on 26 Jun. 2021) (https://resources.fifa.com/image/upload/fifa-rstp-commentary-2006.pdf?cloudid=eeorr2eogoidxzlbwhr8).

A. Training Compensation

449. Training compensation is considered as 'compensation paid to the club to cover the development of young players'. It is more specifically regulated in Annex 3 of the LFF Transfer Regulations.

450. Training compensation is payable by a new club of a player to club or clubs who trained a player when:

- A player is registered for the first time as a professional until the end of the season of his 23rd birthday. When a player is registered as a professional for the first time, a new club is responsible for paying training compensation to every club with which the player has previously been registered (in accordance with the players' career history as provided in the player's passport) and that has contributed to his training starting from the season of his 12th birthday.
- Or a professional is subsequently transferred between two clubs under the jurisdiction of the LFF until the end of the season of the 23rd birthday of a player. In the case of subsequent transfers of a professional player, training compensation will only be payable to his former club for the time he was effectively trained by that club.

451. Training compensation is not payable when:

- a former club terminates the player's contract without just cause;
- player is transferred to a Category 4 club;
- a professional reacquires an amateur status upon such transfers.[156]

452. As a general rule, the player's training and education takes place between the ages of 12 and 23. Training compensation shall be payable up to the age of 23 for the training incurred up to the age of 21 unless it is proved that a player had already terminated his training period before the age of 21. The amount payable is calculated on a pro rata basis in accordance with the period of training that the player spent with each club.

453. As a general rule, the player's training and education takes place between the ages of 12 and 23. Training compensation shall be payable up to the age of 23 for the training incurred up to the age of 21 unless it is proved that a player had already terminated his training period before the age of 21. The amount payable is calculated on a pro rata basis in accordance with the period of training that the player spent with each club.

454. In order to calculate the training compensation due, clubs are divided by the LFF into categories.[157] Training costs are set for each category and correspond

156. In case a player is re-registered as a professional within thirty months of being reinstated as an amateur, his new club has to pay training compensation.
157. Category 3 and category 4 are assigned to football clubs in Lithuania.

to the amount needed to train one player for one year. Training compensation due is calculated by the costs that would have been incurred by the new club if it had trained the player itself.

455. If no club applies for training compensation, the LFF may apply instead. It is very important to notice that training compensations are not payable to public institutions, schools and legal entities if the only stakeholder of such entity is the state, or a municipality, or their branches or agencies. Non-payment of training compensation may result in disciplinary measures.

456. It is very important to notice that training compensation is paid regardless of the type of transfer – free transfer or transfer against payment. If a player is transferred for a transfer fee, parties should consider that failure to mention that transfer fee includes training compensation would allow a former club to require training compensation from a new club additionally.

B. Solidarity Mechanism

457. Solidarity mechanism is 'a system that governs the payments of solidarity contributions to former clubs which contributed to the education and training of the professional player'.

458. The main difference of solidarity mechanism from training compensation is that solidarity contribution is paid only following a transfer against transfer fee (or loan fee). If a professional player moves to a new club during the course of a contract, 5% of any compensation, not including training Compensation paid to his former club, shall be deducted from the total amount of this compensation and distributed by the new club as a solidarity contribution to all the clubs (or club) involved in his training and education. It is paid every time a player is transferred to a new club regardless of the age of the player at the moment of transfer.

459. Solidarity contribution reflects the number of years (calculated pro rata if less than one year) a player in question was registered with the relevant club (clubs) between the seasons of his 12th and 23rd birthdays.[158]

460. As in the case of training compensation, solidarity contribution is also paid to the LFF if no former clubs responsible for training can be traced. Solidarity contributions are not payable to public institutions, schools and legal entities if the only stakeholder of such entity is the state, or a municipality, or their branches or agencies. Moreover, non-payment of solidarity contribution may result in disciplinary measures. The solidarity contribution is not included in the transfer fee; thus in case the parties do not agree, otherwise, the former club can request solidarity contribution from the new club additionally.

158. Seasons of 12th to 15th birthdays – 5% each (i.e., 0.25% from total compensation each) and seasons of 16th to 23rd birthday – 10% each (i.e., 0.5% from total compensation each).

§2. TRANSFERS IN BASKETBALL

461. International basketball transfers are based on 'letter of clearance' system; i.e., a player can be registered for a new club upon issuance of letter of clearance of the national association of a former club.

462. In accordance with Article 56 of the FIBA Internal Regulations, Book 3 (edition 2021), member federations are invited to draw their own regulations governing the transfer of players in the spirit of the FIBA Regulations. On 8 September 2020, the Conference of the LKF adopted the latest version of Regulations on Transfers of Players and Compensations for Trained Player ('LKF Transfer Regulations'). The LKF Transfer Regulations govern transfer procedures, issuance of letter of clearance, protection of minor players, payments of training compensation.

I. Licences and Letter of Clearance System

A. *General Information*

463. The LKF Transfer Regulations does not provide the definition of a transfer. Instead, the regulations provide legal grounds for registration of a player at the club. Once the player is registered, he or she can be fielded, thus a transfer would be held as complete.

464. The essential document proving the right of a certain player to participate in organized basketball competition is the *player licence*. Only players who obtain a player licence are allowed to participate in various levels of organized basketball competition in Lithuania. It is important to notice that the LKF Transfer Regulations do not provide any provisions on the issuance of the player licence and usually player licences are issued by the organizers of competitions (such as leagues). Different competition organizers set their own rules for issuance of the player licence. However, a similar approach is maintained.

465. Clubs registering players and thus willing that licences would be granted have to prove that they are entitled to apply for the licence and field a player to the basketball court; i.e., the club has to prove its legal relationship with the player or provide a copy of the valid contract. The licence, once issued, is usually valid until the end of the ongoing season.[159] If a certain player changes clubs at the end of the season or during the course of the season, such player will need to obtain a new licence. In such case, i.e., the transfer of a player, a national type of *letter of clearance* shall be needed. The letter of clearance is an essential document to complete a transfer of a player, i.e., to move the player from one basketball club to another.

159. Article 3.3 of the LKF Transfers Regulations provides that the licence shall be valid for one basketball season, however no longer than until 1 August of the upcoming calendar year.

466. In accordance with Article 4 of the LKF Transfers Regulations, the letter of clearance is defined as a document governing transfer of a player from one sports organization to another sports organization. A term 'governing' is not too precise. A letter of clearance in practice does not govern anything specific. As it is seen from the standard template of letter of clearance provided by the LKF Transfers Regulations, a letter of clearance is a document issued by the former sports organization confirming the club's understanding that such a club and a certain player are no longer under contract, that the former club does not object that a former player would join a new club. A letter of clearance is a ground to register a player for the new club and issue a player licence.

467. A letter of clearance shall have to be issued regardless of the fact whether the player is transferred *after the expiry* of his contract (i.e., if a player moves clubs as a free agent) or he is transferred under the contract.

468. A letter of clearance must be issued by the club which the player was registered at before moving to the new club. It is not required to obtain a letter of clearance from every club whom the player was engaged with. The letter of clearance cannot be issued to more than one club requesting the letter of clearance (Article 4.1.2 of the LKF Transfer Regulations). Moreover, the letter of clearance cannot be *conditional* (Article 4.1.3 of the LKF Transfer Regulations).

B. Procedures of Issuance of a Letter of Clearance

469. Procedure for issuance of the letter of clearance is initiated by a new club, i.e., a club willing to engage with a player concerned. A new club has to issue and submit a formal request to the club of 'a last registration' of player requesting such club to issue a letter of clearance (Article 4.1.4 of the LKF Transfer Regulations).

470. Upon the receipt of request to issue a letter of clearance an old club has to respond in seven calendar days (Article 4.1.5 of the LKF Transfer Regulations). A former club may (1) accept a request and issue the letter of clearance, (2) ignore a request and not to respond to it at all, (3) to refuse to issue a letter of clearance.

471. In case a former club issues a letter of clearance, the issuance procedure is closed. Unlike international transfers, the domestic transfers taking place within the jurisdiction of the LKF does not require any intervention or cooperation of the LKF in the issuance procedure as a letter of clearance is submitted to the relevant competition organizer and the player concerned would obtain a licence to play.

472. In case a former club fails to reply to a new club within seven calendar days from the receipt of the request, a new club may apply to the LKF and inform on the failure of a former club to respond (Article 4.1.10 of the LKF Transfer Regulations). A copy of communication between two clubs has to be presented to the LKF.

Unless there are no extraordinary circumstances (the regulation does not provide what should be considered as extraordinary circumstances), the LKF will authorize the issuance of a letter of clearance.

473. In case a former club refuses to issue the letter of clearance for a new club, a former club must immediately inform the LKF and communicate reasons of such refusal (Article 4.1.6 of the LKF Transfer Regulations). The only legitimate reason for refusal to issue a letter of clearance is a valid contract between a player and a former club. The refusing club must submit a copy of a valid contract to the LKF. It is very important to notice that under Article 4.1.7 of the LKF Transfers Regulations, ongoing or potential monetary disputes between a player and a club *are not considered a ground to refuse issuance of a letter of clearance* if contract is terminated. In such case, the letter of clearance must be issued and the ongoing disputes will have to be solved separately.

474. It is also important to notice, that the club having a player on temporary basis (loan) cannot issue a letter of clearance to any third club and further transfer the player without the consent of the loaning club (Article 4.1.11 of the LKF Transfer Regulations).

475. As mentioned, the only legitimate reason to refuse issuance of a letter of clearance is a valid contract between a player and a former club. Refusing club is requested to submit a copy of the valid contract to the LKF. Article 4.1.9 of the LKF Transfer Regulations clearly states that all disputes related to the validity of contracts shall be solved by *the competent body stipulated in the SAA*. In accordance with Article 8 of the LKF Transfer Regulations, all disputes related to the transfer of players are solved by competition organizers and, if such disputes are not solved, by the LKF. However, the same Article 8 of the LKF Transfer Regulations clearly states that LKF does not solve disputes related to performance, validity of SAA as such disputes are solved in accordance with the agreement of a player and a club stipulated in SAA. In case of a dispute regarding the validity of a contract, LKF would not solve such dispute and would not issue a letter of clearance, forcing parties to wait for the outcome of the dispute. Depending on the competent body, a hearing of dispute would at least take several months up to close to two years if parties go to a regular civil court and exercise all instances. In the latter case a player could end up in a considerably long period of obscurity: a player would no longer play for his former club and thus would not be able to receive income and he would still not be able to join a new club. In the case of international transfer, FIBA does not prevent itself from authorizing the letter of clearance. In accordance with Article 88 of the FIBA Internal Regulations, Book 3, FIBA solves issues related to the letter of clearance in seven days. Considering the duration of a sportsman's career, such potential period of delay of issuance of the letter of clearance related to dispute over validity of contract could be very harmful.

II. Compensations for Trained Players

476. Legal framework of compensations for a trained player is stipulated by the LKF Transfer Regulations. A general principle is that compensation is paid upon the first registration of the former trainee of a 'sports (basketball) school (club)' (Article 7.1 of the LKF Transfer Regulations). A compensation is paid only once by a basketball club signing a player. Compensation is paid *only for players* who are or who were members or candidates of the Lithuanian national U-16, U-18, U-20 or student team (i.e., such player was included into official application confirmed by FIBA or FIBA Europe). In order to receive training compensation, basketball school must comply with specific criteria.

477. A school is entitled to receive training compensation only if such school did train a player for a period of at least five years or the last two years (players of 12 years old). If a player was trained by more than one basketball school, a training compensation to schools and corresponding coaches is paid by pro rata basis (Article 7.11 of the LKF Transfer Regulations). Training compensation is not payable in case a player moves to a foreign academic institution directly from a basketball school. Training compensation would be payable in case the player signs a club in four years after leaving basketball school.

478. In accordance with Article 7.8 of the LKF Transfer Regulations, only 30% of the compensation is paid directly to the basketball schools. Fifty per cent of the compensation is dedicated to the coach/coaches who did contribute to the training of a player. The latter amount is paid to the bank account of the LKF account and then distributed accordingly. The remaining 20% is paid directly to the LKF as a compensation for funds dedicated to minor basketball league and youth development programme.

479. A training compensation is paid only once, i.e., when a former trainee of a basketball school is being registered by a basketball club. Basketball schools are requested to submit to LKF lists of their graduates on an annual basis and such lists are made available for public by the LKF. Unless parties agree otherwise, training compensation must be paid *before actual* registration of the player at the club and before issuance of a player licence. Competition organizers are requested to ensure that licences are issued only after payment of training compensation. LKF has a right to suspend a player's licence in case a club does not pay training compensation (Article 7.14 of the LKF Transfer Regulations).

480. Following basketball clubs must pay training compensation:

- basketball clubs participating in men's basketball top Lithuanian division;
- basketball clubs participating in men's basketball second basketball division;
- basketball clubs participating in women's basketball top division.

Chapter 7. Player Agents

§1. Player Agents' Status and General Requirements

481. Current edition of the Law on Sport does not set forth any provisions on the issue of representation of athletes. The athletes and players are free to have their own representatives subject to requirements of the regulations of national and international federations.

482. It is important to understand the nature of the legal relationship between the player and his agent. The Law on Sport as well as other legal acts of the Republic of Lithuania provides no clearance on the nature of the representation agreement and the legal relationship between an agent and an athlete. It must be also stressed that Lithuanian courts do not maintain single positions as well. On the one hand, representation agreements are considered as an agreement of services in accordance with Article 6.716–6.724 of the Civil Code.[160] On the other hand, they are considered as commercial representation as per Article 2.152–2.168 of the Civil Code.[161] Finally, the latest jurisprudence of the Supreme Court suggests that provision of Civil Code governing a simple representation apply to the relationship between an athlete and an agent (Article 2.132–2.151 of the Civil Code).[162]

483. Different approach to a player-agent agreement may result in different legal outcome in certain situations. For example, in accordance with Article 6.721 of the Civil Code, a client can terminate the service agreement prematurely meanwhile a client cannot terminate the fixed-term commercial representation agreement prematurely without a serious cause (Article 2.166(1) of the Civil Code). Moreover, in case of commercial representation, a representative has more rights related to the remuneration for his service. For example, a commercial agent shall be entitled to compensation if upon the termination of the contract, the principal has a considerable profit from the business relations established by the commercial agent.

484. It is difficult to predict how courts are going to interpret player-agent agreement as it would mainly depend on several criteria, such as a wording of contract (if the obligations of agent are depicted more as service, it would have more chance to be considered as service agreement), the scope of the agreement (inclusion of multiple type of services, such as legal and financial consulting may help the court deem that the agreement is of a service nature), the 'main activity criteria'[163] (the court would consider if the agent activity is the main activity of the person which is a feature attributable to commercial representation agreements). Thus, the drafting of the agreement may be essential for any potential dispute and assessment of the court.

160. 3 Nov. 2011 ruling of the Courts of Appeals in Civil Case No. 2A-1072/2011.
161. 29 Dec. 2014 ruling of the Court of Appeals in Civil Case No. 2T-96/2014.
162. 22 Sep. 2017 ruling of the Supreme Court in Civil Case No. e3K-3-344-684/2017.
163. 6 Mar. 2016 ruling of the Supreme Court in Civil Case No. e3K-3-411-695/2016.

485. Further, requirements of certain player-agent agreements as per statutes and regulations of the LKF and the LFF are analysed.

§2. The LKF Regulations on Player Agents

486. FIBA has introduced the agent licensing system back in 2007. In accordance with the provision of the FIBA Internal Regulations, Book 3 both the clubs and the player are only entitled to use the services of a licensed agent to represent them or safeguard their interests in negotiations with each other. The agent must be in possession of a valid licence issued by FIBA. Players and clubs are not permitted to use the services of an agent who is not in possession of a valid licence issued by FIBA. If they do so, both players and clubs are subject to serious sanctions which may be imposed by FIBA.[164] The licence-issuing process is centralized and thus is administered and controlled by FIBA.

487. In accordance with Article 292 of the FIBA Regulations, Book 3 any national member federation may establish its own regulations governing players' agents who deal with transfers of domestic players within their own federation. Such regulations must be approved by FIBA and must respect the principles set out in FIBA Regulations.

488. Despite introduction of the FIBA agent licensing system, the LKF at first did not implement any domestic regulation on the players' agents. Therefore, it led to the situation whereby unlicensed persons acted as agents for the players at a domestic level without any particular supervision. However, on 20 April 2014, the Conference of the LKF confirmed the LKF Regulations on the Use of Agents' Services ('LKF Agent Regulations'). The LKF Agent Regulations set the rights and obligations of players, clubs and agents in relation to the use of agents' services within the territory of the Republic of Lithuania.

489. The preamble of the LKF Agent Regulations includes a statement of the LKF that the LKF is not willing to govern player agents' activity in any different means than it is regulated in the FIBA Internal Regulations. It should be noticed that in general the principles laid down by the FIBA Regulations are reflected by the LKF Agent Regulations. The specific provisions are highlighted further.

---

164. The player might be banned from playing and the club might be banned from registering new players.

I. The Definition of a Player Agent; Rights and Obligations of a Player Agent

490. The LKF Agent Regulations defines an agent as a person who is licensed by the FIBA and obtains a valid FIBA agent licence and who acts as an official representative of a player, a coach or a club while concluding SAAs and while performing such agreements.

491. Article II(7) of the LKF Agent Regulations underlines the compulsory requirement for an agent to maintain valid FIBA agent's licence: natural persons are forbidden to engage in the agent's activity if they do not possess FIBA agent's licence or such licence is expired. Other important restrictions are set by Article (II)6 stating that players, coaches and persons engaged in labour or service agreements with the FIBA, the LKF or any other national federation, or league or acting in another position of said entities are not allowed to be engaged in player's agent activities.

492. The LKF Agent Regulations provide the same rights to the agents as stipulated in Article 304 of then FIBA Internal Regulations, Book 3, which are the following:

– a right to approach the player who has no other agent;
– represent any player or club under a request to do so;
– manage personal affairs of the player.

493. As Articles 305 and 306 of then FIBA Internal Regulations, Book 3 the LKF Agent Regulations provide that a written agreement must be signed by the agent and the player. As well as this, the same term of duration of representation agreement (two years) with an option of renewal is set as in the FIBA Regulations.

494. The main obligations of a player agent (which corresponds closely to the ones stipulated by Article 307 of then FIBA Internal Regulations, Book 3) are the following:

– to comply with the regulations of the FIBA and the LKF;
– to refrain from approaching players under a contract with a club or persuade him/her to terminate the contract;
– to refrain from approaching players under a contract with agents or persuade him/her to terminate such contract;
– the amount of remuneration may not exceed 10% as from the value of the SAA;[165]
– to refrain from contacting minor players during competition without prior authorization of the representative of the academy or parents of the player;
– to represent the client properly and to strive for protection of client's interest;

---

165. In general, a sum of all amounts promised by the club to the player in accordance with the SAA.

– to keep the client informed on certain circumstances related to the status of the player.

495. It must be noticed that the LKF Agent Regulations do not foresee any additional sanctions imposable on the agent for the breach of provisions of the LKF Agent Regulations. In accordance with Articles 321–323 of the FIBA Internal Regulations, Book 3 breach of the FIBA Regulations may lead to a sanction for an agent, player or club.

496. It should be noted that LKF is late to implement latest developments of agent regulations by the FIBA. In accordance to changes of the FIBA Internal Regulations, Book 3 introduced in 2022, the clubs can no longer be required to pay agent fees on behalf of the players the agents represent. Such payment could result in breach of prohibition of conflict of interest as per Article 297 of the FIBA Internal Regulations, Book 3.

II. Rights and Obligations of Players, Coaches and Clubs

497. A player, a coach and a club have the same obligations provided by the LKF Agent Regulations: a player, a coach or a club which is willing to negotiate or conclude a contract by the help of an agent, *must only use the services of a FIBA licensed agent* (Article II(1)–II(4) of the LKF Agent Regulations). In case the player or a coach does not have an agent, the club can carry on negotiations and then conclude contracts without the interference of an agent.

498. Thus, a player, a coach and a club may not have an agent at all. However, if they do need services of an agent, such services must be rendered by the FIBA licensed agent only. In case a player, a coach or a club gets involved in a transaction with an agent who has no FIBA licence (or it is expired), a sanction will be imposed. The LKF Agent Regulations basically confirms that the FIBA is competent to impose sanctions on players and clubs who use the service of an unlicensed agent. However, the LKF may impose additional sanctions for such a breach – (1) to issue a reprimand to the player or a coach, (2) to expel the club from the LKF.

§3. The LFF Regulations on Working with the Intermediaries

499. 1 April 2015 was a very special day in the world of football. The new player's *agent* regulations, i.e., FIFA Regulations on Working with Intermediaries (RWI) came into force. Despite FIFA's statement that RWI was not going to mean deregulation of a player's agent activity, the impact of such change was significant. Implementation of RWI and the elimination of existing FIFA Players' Agent Regulations (PAR) brought a shift of responsibilities from FIFA to member associations. FIFA is no longer responsible for issuing the player-agent licence, monitoring how the stakeholders comply with the PAR and, most importantly, solving the disputes among players and agents as well as issuing sanctions for the breaches of the PAR.

500. In accordance with Article 1(5) of PAR, the associations are required to implement and enforce PAR in accordance with the duties assigned in PAR. In addition, they shall draw up their own regulations which shall incorporate the principles established in PAR and may only deviate from these regulations where the provisions of the latter do not comply with the laws applicable in the territory of the association. In accordance with the PAR, the associations had a duty to implement and enforce PAR.

501. Meanwhile, under RWI, the associations are required to implement and enforce at least minimum standards/requirements in accordance with the duties assigned in these regulations, subject to the mandatory laws. RWI provides the associations with a right to go beyond these minimum standards/requirements. Thus, the associations have a huge discretion to govern different issues of working with intermediary issues in their own way.

502. On 21 April 2015 the Executive Committee of the LFF approved the LFF Regulations on Working with Intermediaries ('LFF Regulation on Intermediaries'). Main features of the LFF Regulation on Intermediaries are analysed further.

I. The Scope of the Regulations, Status of Intermediary

503. Although the scope of the LFF Regulation on Intermediaries is not mentioned in the LFF Regulation on Intermediaries it should be considered that such regulations are applicable for the transactions taking place inside the jurisdiction of the LFF.

504. Article 2.1.5 of the LFF Regulation on Intermediaries[166] defines an intermediary as a 'natural or legal person who represents players and/or clubs in negotiations with a view to concluding an employment contract [SAA] or represents clubs in negotiations with a view to concluding a transfer agreement except for the attorneys who represents players and/or clubs in certain negotiations or by provid ing legal services in accordance to legal service agreement pursuant to the requirements stipulated by the Laws of the Republic of Lithuania'.

505. Thus, not only a natural person but also a legal person can conduct activities of a representative under the LFF Regulation on Intermediaries. The regulations *do not* foresee any requirements for natural or legal persons to conclude insurance or obtain bank guarantee.

506. In accordance with Article 3.7 of the LFF Regulations on Intermediaries, the club or the player willing to engage the services of an intermediary must make sure that an intermediary has an impeccable reputation. The definition of 'impeccable reputation' is not provided by the LFF Regulation on Intermediaries; however, Annexes 1 and 2 providing the declaration of an intermediary suggests that in

166. Translated by the author.

order to declare impeccable reputation one has to confirm that no criminal sentence has ever been imposed upon such person for a financial or a violent crime. As well as this, the LFF Regulation on Intermediaries prohibits engagement of officials (i.e., every board member, committee member, referee and assistant, referee, coach, trainer and any other person responsible for technical, medical and administrative matters in FIFA, a confederation, association, league or club as well as all other persons obliged to comply with the FIFA Statutes (except Players)), as intermediaries by players and clubs.

507. The intermediary *is not subject to any sanction*, and the players and clubs must ensure they are using the services of a proper intermediary in compliance with the regulations.

II. General Rights and Obligations of Players and Clubs

508. Players and clubs are entitled to engage the services of intermediaries when concluding an SAA and/or a transfer agreement. In selection and engaging process of intermediaries, players and clubs have to act with due diligence, i.e., the players and clubs have to use reasonable endeavours to ensure that the intermediaries sign the relevant intermediary declaration and the representation contract concluded between the parties. Whenever an intermediary is involved in a transaction, he or she shall be registered pursuant to the LFF Regulations on Intermediaries. Engagement of officials as intermediaries by players and clubs is prohibited. As well as this, the clubs are obliged to ensure that their official persons are not acting as intermediaries as well.

III. Registration of Intermediaries and Disclosure of Information

509. LFF Regulations on Intermediaries do not require any permanent registration of intermediaries. In accordance with Article 4(1) of the LFF Regulations on Intermediaries, intermediaries shall only be registered upon involvement in transaction (contract or transfer). A ground for registration is the submission of intermediary declaration, representation agreement and contract/transfer agreement by the club or the player engaging the services of an intermediary. LFF may request the player or the club to submit additional documents. Players and clubs are requested to inform the LFF upon the amendment or termination of legal relationship with the intermediary.

510. Article 6 of the LFF Regulations on Intermediaries provides sensitive obligation of players and clubs to disclose information on payments made to the intermediaries during the course of their legal relationship. It is important to notice that such data is a subject of public announcement on the LFF website by discretion of the LFF. The aim of such provision is to maintain transparency.

IV. Representation Agreement, Remuneration and Conflicts of Interests

511. In accordance with Article 5(1) and 5(2) of the LFF Regulations on Intermediaries the main elements of the legal relationship entered into between a player and/or club and an intermediary have to be included in writing prior to the intermediary commencing his or her activities. The representation contract must contain the following minimum details:

- Names of the parties.
- Scope of services.
- Duration of the legal relationship.
- Remuneration due to the intermediary.
- General terms of payment.
- Date of conclusion.
- Termination provision.

512. No restriction on the duration of the contract is provided. Players and clubs are requested to inform the LFF upon the amendment or termination of legal relationship with the intermediary.

513. In accordance with the LFF Regulations on Intermediaries, intermediaries are free to carry out their duties even in a situation of formal conflict of interest (representation of different parties in the same transaction) provided that the intermediary obtains the express written consent of all the other parties involved prior to the start of the relevant negotiations or the club and the player willing to use the services of the same intermediary gives their express consent. This simply means that the intermediary may find himself on both sides of the table of negotiation if the represented parties agree so.

514. The new regulation regarding the remuneration is set forth in Article 7 of the LFF Regulations on Intermediaries. In accordance with the LFF Regulations on Intermediaries, the intermediary shall be entitled to remuneration from the player calculated on the basis of the player's basic gross income for the entire duration of a contract. A lump sum (which can be paid by instalments) may be paid to the intermediary by the represented club. Clubs are not allowed to pay payments in connection with the transfer to the intermediary, including future transfer compensation and assignment of claims. The remuneration must be paid directly to the intermediary with provided exceptions (the player may consent the club to pay the intermediary on behalf of the player).

515. Article 7(7) of the LFF Regulations on Intermediaries provides important restriction: no payments are allowed from players or clubs *in case of a transaction (contract or transfer) of a minor*. As well as this, it is important to notice that one of the most controversial novelties presented by the RWI were the recommendations on the amount of remuneration of maximum 3% of the player's basic gross income or the transfer fee. Different from the RWI, the LFF Regulations on Intermediaries do not set the maximum amount of remuneration.

V. Sanctions and Dispute Resolution

516. In accordance with Article 11.2 of the LFF Regulations on Intermediaries sanctions stipulated in the LFF Disciplinary Code may be imposed for the breach of the provisions of the LFF Regulations on Intermediaries. Furthermore, Article 11.3 of the LFF Regulations on Intermediaries states that such sanctions would be communicated to FIFA and announced by the LFF to public. However, the current edition[167] of the LFF Disciplinary Code *does not establish any sanctions* for breaches of the LFF Regulations on Intermediaries. Therefore, at the moment provisions of the LFF Regulations on Intermediaries are hardly enforceable.

517. The LFF Regulations on Intermediaries do not provide any provisions on the resolution of disputes arising from the LFF Regulations on Intermediaries and/ or between intermediaries and clubs or players. Therefore, such disputes should be solved outside the jurisdiction of the LFF (civil courts or arbitration).

167. 12 Jan. 2016 edition.

Chapter 8. Legal Status of Coaches

518. The Law on Sport provides a definition of a coach as 'an expert in high performance sport who train and prepare athletes for high performance sports competition and/or manages athletes in such competition'.[168] In terms of the Law on Sport, a coach is a person responsible for the preparation and management of high performance athletes only. There are no particular requirements set forth for coaches by the Law on Sport.

519. However, the Law on Sport also provides definitions for specialist in high performance sport, sports or physical activity instructor and specialist in physical activity.[169] These persons are responsible for carrying out certain activities which are available for not only professional or high performance athletes (such as, persons attending gyms, students at schools). In accordance with Article 11 of the Law on Sport, certain strict requirements are set for persons willing to conduct such activities.

520. Article 10(1) of the Law on Sport states that a coach can operate under labour agreement[170] or he can conduct an individual activity. In the latter case he or she must conclude an SAA with a sports organization.

521. Regulations of sports federation may determine specific requirements for coaches. For example, in accordance with the LFF Club Licensing Regulations, a club willing to obtain a licence to participate in UEFA competitions and '*A Lyga*' must hire a coach who possesses UEFA Pro licence. A similar approach (with the requirement for lower level of UEFA licence) applies to youth team coaches. Thus, coaches are not able to act in the field of a top football league unless their qualification meets the requirements. LKF provides that only a coach possessing a certificate issued by the LKF may participate in competitions organized by the LKF.

522. As in the case of FIFA RSTP, the new edition of the LFF Transfer Regulations (Annex 2 to the LFF Transfer Regulations) now contain rules applied to contractual relationship between a club (or the LFF) and a football coach. Said rules govern basic requirements of coach contracts, maintaining and termination thereof.

523. Certain laws and public regulations may set further requirements for coaches who act as physical education teachers in education systems or work in public sector institutions (sports centres, schools and academies).

168. Article 2(25) of the Law on Sport.
169. Article 2(5), 2(8) and 2(11) of the Law on Sport.
170. It is very common practice in state and municipality controlled entities, such as football or basketball schools.

Chapter 9. Dispute Resolution

524. The issue related to dispute resolution in the field of sports was analysed in detail in Part I, Chapter 9. Therefore, additional elaboration on the issue in this chapter is not conducted.

525. The issue related to dispute resolution in the field of sports was analysed in detail in Part I, Chapter 9. Therefore, additional elaboration on the issue in this chapter is not conducted.

526. However, it is important to remember that in general athletes are not considered as employees in Lithuania. In case of a contractual dispute between an athlete and a club, the provisions applicable to dispute resolution in labour legal relationship shall not apply. Therefore, as a general rule, a contractual dispute or any other dispute of a civil nature between an athlete and a club will be solved by national courts in accordance with the CPC. However, subject to the existence of a valid arbitrational clause between the parties, a dispute will be diverted to arbitration.

527. Parties, especially under the jurisdiction of the LFF, may divert a contractual dispute to the bodies of the LFF, namely the LFF Appeals Committee. However, even in case of an option stipulated in a contract suggesting that parties did agree to submit the dispute to the body of sports federation, the parties are not prevented from addressing the issue to the court. However, if the sports body takes a decision which is subject to appeal to the court of arbitration, for example the CAS, the intervention of national court may not be possible due to a potentially existing arbitration clause.

528. Disputes related to disciplinary sanctions imposed by bodies of sports federations against an athlete are solved in accordance with the regulations of such sports federation. Yet again, it may foresee that the final decision of a body of sports federation is only subject to appeal to an arbitration institution, namely the CAS. If no arbitration clause is applicable decisions of bodies of sports federations may be appealed in court.

Chapter 10. Social Security of Athletes

529. Lithuanian social security system is based upon the principle of solidarity. Employees or their employers have to pay monthly social security payments. Payments ensure that persons who become pensioners, get ill or get in other social sensitive situations (such as parenthood, loss of spouse) are paid social security benefits.

530. Athletes are under SAAs, i.e., who are considered to be employers from taxation point of view, are insured by compulsory pension, illness, motherhood, unemployment, accidents at work and professional illness social security. Their employers have a duty to pay social security duties on behalf of players. Therefore, in the case of any insured event, such athletes would be subject to payment of social security benefits.

531. Athletes (permanent residents) who are self-employed are insured by compulsory pension, illness, motherhood social security insurance. Self-employed athletes are responsible for payment of social security payments by themselves.

532. The pension accumulation system is first of all based upon payment of compulsory social security payments. Social security payments paid by workers are instantly redistributed for pensions and social benefits; hence working citizens sustain pensioners and other persons in need of social security payments. Citizens may also accumulate their pensions to private pension funds or life insurance companies.

533. It should also be mentioned that former professional athletes who managed to achieve significant results are subject to monthly rent payments (*see* Part I, Chapter 5). Former Olympic or Paralympic prize winners, World champions can be paid state pensions.

534. State health insurance system is separated from social security system. Health insurance system is based upon universality, i.e., all citizens of the Republic of Lithuania and foreigners permanently residing in Lithuania as well as legally employed or temporarily residing foreigners have to pay health insurance payments. Upon the occurrence of an insured event, they would be entitled to receive healthcare services paid from Compulsory health insurance fund. Health insurance payments are paid by clubs on behalf of players (employed athletes). Self-employed athletes have to pay health insurance payments by themselves.

Part III. Doping and Match-Fixing

Chapter 1. Doping: General Global Issues

535. History of doping is as old as the history of sports itself. Some sources suggest[171] that certain forms of doping can be traced back to the authentic Olympic Games in Ancient Greece. Ancient athletes used to take certain kind of food or other nutritional elements in order to enhance their performance.

536. With the increase in public attention towards various competitions of sports nature, new doping cases became public as well. With the birth of modern Olympic movement and rapid increase in popularity of sport, spectators witnessed major doping cases, starting from personal stories of famous athletes like Ben Johnson, Marion Jones, Lance Armstrong to state-controlled doping programmes, such as that of East Germany or Russia as suggested by James McLaren.[172]

537. One of the negative aspects of doping is the element of cheat, i.e., gaining unjustified advantage over clean fellow athletes. Hence, an ethical issue exists. Prominent British sports lawyer and longstanding CAS arbitrator Michael J. Beloff once wrote:[173]

> The objects of doping control are clear. The essence of a sporting contest is that it should be fairly conducted, with the competitor's success or failure being the result of natural talents: speed, skill, endurance, tactical awareness – honed, it may be, by instruction, training and body maintenance in its widest sense. The much-used metaphor – a level playing field – derives from sport. The use of drugs violates all such notions of equality: the drug taker starts with an unfair advantage. Success becomes the product of the test tube, not the training track.

171. Information is available online (accessed on 22 Aug. 2021) (https://www.nationalgeographic.com/history/article/olympics-scandal-doping-ancient-greece-lochte).
172. Information is available online (accessed on 26 Jun. 2021) (https://www.wada-ama.org/en/resources/doping-control-process/mclaren-independent-investigation-report-part-i).
173. Michael J. Beloff, *Drugs, Laws and Versapaks, Drugs and Doping in Sport: Socio-Legal Perspectives Drugs and Doping in Sport: Socio-Legal Perspectives*, ed. by John O'Leary, ISBN 1859416624, pp. 39–56 (Cavendish, 2011).

538. However, cheating element is not the only reason worth fighting against doping in sports. Use of performance-enhancing subjects may cause deaths of athletes.[174] So-called Goldman dilemma[175] proves that athletes of competitive nature are not self-protective and are keen to risk their lives in order to experience victory on the sports field.

539. It was in the 1960s when first steps against doping were taken at a larger scene. In 1960 the Council of Europe presented a resolution against the use of doping substances in sports. In 1967, during the 66th session in Tehran, Iran, the IOC founded a medical commission. The IOC together with the International Cycling Union became the first sports bodies to create such commissions. The primary goal of the IOC commission was to 'set up medical testing service for the 1968 Olympic Games and to study the questions of anti-doping controls and help that could be provided to athletes in developing countries'.[176]

540. A scandal broke through when the new analytical remedies were introduced back in 1983. Introduction of new doping testing systems caused a massive number of positive doping tests in Pan American Games in Caracas.[177] In 1986 the IOC banned blood doping. However, such events as the 1988 case of Ben Johnson, 1998 Tour de France events led to the convening of the World Conference on Doping in Sport in Lausanne in 1999 by the IOC. The Conference gave birth to WADA.

541. It should be noted that initiatives also began at interstate level. In 1989 Anti-Doping Convention was adopted in the framework of the European Council. In 2005 UNESCO International Convention against the Use of Doping in Sport was adopted as well.

542. However, namely adoption of the WADA Code in 2003 was probably the most significant step to unify sports stakeholders' efforts in the fight against illegal use of performance-enhancing substances and methods. The current edition of the

---

174. The first known death from doping occurred back in 1896 when an English cyclist Arthur Linton had died due to alleged use of performance-enhancing materials. One of the most controversial stories was the death of Danish cyclist Knud Jansen during 1960 Olympic Games in Rome due to alleged abuse of amphetamine. The 1960s claimed more lives, including the one of British cyclist Tom Simpson due to use of amphetamines and runner Dick Howard who possibly overdosed heroin. A drink of amphetamine cocktail was lethal for German boxer Jupp Elze.
175. The Goldman Dilemma, which is named under the name of physician Robert Goldman, asks whether athletes would pursue sporting success (an Olympic gold medal) by using banned performance-enhancing drug knowing that such drug would finally cause their death in a period of five years. It is suggested that at least 52% of respondents stated they would take the drug. In order to gain stability in the results of a question, the Dilemma was allegedly offered to athletes in a period of fifteen years.
176. Source available online (accessed on 26 Jun. 2021) (https://stillmed.olympic.org/AssetsDocs/OSC%20Section/pdf/LRes_Fonds_list_Medical_Commission.pdf).
177. Source available online (accessed on 26 Jun. 2021) (https://www.researchgate.net/profile/Jan_Todd/publication/297723914_'The_Event_That_Shook_the_Whole_World_Up'_Historicizing_the_1983_Pan-American_Games_Doping_Scandal/links/56e8a6aa08aea51e7f3b5936.pdf).

WADA Code, which came into force in 2015, sets strict and sometimes uncompromising rules and sanctions regarding the prohibition of performance-enhancing substances and methods.

§1. PRINCIPLES OF THE WADA CODE

543. The purposes of the WADA Code the World Anti-Doping Program are 'to protect athletes' *fundamental right* to participate in doping-free sport and thus promote health, fairness and equality for Athletes worldwide, and to ensure harmonized, coordinated and effective anti-doping programmes at the international and national level with regard to detection, deterrence and prevention of doping'. Such purposes are considered to be so crucial that the means designed to achieve them are sometimes widely criticized for violations of basic human rights of the athletes. In fact, when an athlete commits an anti-doping rule violation pursuant to the WADA Code, there are potentially serious consequences, even for those athletes who commit such violation for the very first time.

544. For a better understanding of how the fight against the doping system works in the world and accordingly in Lithuania, it is important to pay more detailed attention to an anti-doping violation of 'presence' and strict liability of an athlete for such violations stipulated in the WADA Code (and accordingly in the regulations of many sports federations).

I. The Presence Violation

545. The WADA Code provides an exhaustive list of doping violations:

- Use or attempted use by an athlete of a prohibited substance or a prohibited method (Article 2.2 of the WADA Code).
- Evading, refusing or failing to submit to sample collection (Article 2.3 of the WADA Code).
- Whereabouts failures (Article 2.4 of the WADA Code).
- Tampering or attempted tampering with any part of doping control (Article 2.5 of the WADA Code).
- Possession of a prohibited substance or a prohibited method (Article 2.6 of the WADA Code).
- Trafficking or attempted trafficking of any prohibited substance or a prohibited method (Article 2.7 of the WADA Code).
- Administration or attempted administration to any athlete in competition of any prohibited substance or a prohibited method, or administration or attempted administration to any athlete out-of-competition of any prohibited substance or any prohibited method that is prohibited out-of-competition (Article 2.8 of the WADA Code).
- Complicity (Article 2.9 of the WADA Code).
- Prohibited Association (Article 2.10 of the WADA Code).

– Acts by an Athlete or other person to discourage or retaliate against reporting to authorities.

546. But it is the 'presence' which is the most common and obvious violation of doping prohibition. Article 2.1 of the WADA Code provides the definition of violation in question as 'presence of a prohibited substance or its metabolites or markers in an athlete's sample'. The term 'presence' may seem self-explanatory: the existence of prohibited substance in an athlete's sample is an anti-doping rule violation.

547. Article 2.1.1 of the WADA Code provides that it 'is each athlete's personal duty to ensure that no prohibited substance enters his or her body. Athletes are responsible for any prohibited substance or its metabolites or markers found to be present in their samples'. In order to prove the existence of the 'presence' violation, it is necessary to establish that a sample (which is any biological material collected for the purposes of doping control) of an athlete contains a prohibited substance. The jurisprudence of CAS[178] also holds a position that the establishment of presence fact is enough to determine the anti-doping rule violation. Needless to say that the sample testing procedure has to be carried out strictly in accordance with the standards set forth by the WADA Code and corresponding acts, such as WADA International Standard for Laboratories.

548. However, the most important aspect of the Article of 2.1.1 of the WADA Code is that it is not necessary that intent, fault, negligence or knowing use on the athlete's part be demonstrated in order to establish an anti-doping rule violation. Hence, a mere existence of prohibited substance in an athlete's sample is an anti-doping rule violation regardless of intent, fault, negligence or knowing use by an athlete. It can only be justified to the extent where it is considered that no violation took place in case of therapeutic use exemptions, i.e., a certain permission to use prohibited substance for medical or therapeutic purposes which is granted in accordance with the WADA International Standard for Therapeutic Use Exemptions.

549. The nature of provisions set forth in Article 2.1.1 of the WADA Code establishes so-called strict liability of an athlete rule. Athlete's strict liability rule in anti-doping rule violations is one of the most famous principles of established CAS jurisprudence (or *lex sportiva* as it is sometimes referred). The essence of this principle is that in order to determine the violation of a certain rule, as mentioned, *no fault, negligence or intent* has to be proved. The official commentary of Article 2.1.1 of the WADA Code explains that the strict liability makes the athlete responsible, and an anti-doping rule violation occurs, whenever a prohibited substance is found in an athlete's sample.

550. The presence of prohibited substances automatically triggers certain sanctions on the athlete. In accordance with Article 9 of the WADA Code, if the positive

---

178. For example, CAS award of 8 Nov. 2013 in Case No. CAS 2012/A/2979 *World Anti-Doping Agency (WADA) v. Nirupama Devi Laishram & National Anti-Doping Agency of India (NADA).*

sample came from an in-competition test, then the results of that competition *are automatically invalidated.* Meanwhile, in accordance with Article 10.2 of the WADA Code, further sanction – ineligibility is an imposed event on first-time violators. A standard term for first-time violators is four years of ineligibility, however various factors are taken into consideration before determining the final period of ineligibility.

551. One may say that such approach may contradict basic human rights of athletes. Even CAS[179] in its early jurisprudence[180] stated that 'The so-called strict liability rule ... does not, in the Panel's opinion, sufficiently respect the athlete's right of personality ("*Persönlichkeitsrecht*") as established in Articles 20 and 27 et seq. of the Swiss Civil Code which CAS panels are required to apply (Art. 58 of the Code of Sports Related Arbitration).' However, the strict liability rule is well recognized by federations, CAS and, most importantly, the Swiss Federal Court which has to deal with issues of alleged invalidity of CAS awards.

552. The reason behind survival and self-establishment of such uncompromising and strict principle is the aspiration of honest competition and, last, but not the least, protection of an athlete's health and life as well. It is agreed that by having a no strict liability rule, the sport federations would have no sufficient and appropriate remedies to prove the anti-doping rule violation. While establishing the presence fact is rather easy due to developed and still developing scientific testing measure, the federations would undoubtedly struggle to prove the fault or negligence or intent of an athlete. CAS in its 6 February 2012 award in notorious *Contador*[181] case determined:

> The importance and difficulty of the struggle against doping in sport has however brought about a qualification to these two normal indispensable precepts of justice. That qualification is that once a strict liability doping offence is established by demonstrating no more than the presence of a prohibited substance in an athlete's sample, the burden shifts onto the athlete to establish how the substance came into his body and that he bore no fault or negligence for its presence (see Article 296 UCI ADR and Article 10.5.1 WADC). In essence, the athlete must prove his innocence. This significant incursion into the rights of the accused is however justified by the need to protect sport and the difficulty faced by the regulatory authority to actively prove the method of ingestion and the athlete's degree of fault.

179. In most of the cases, the CAS becomes the final institution which solves matters related to doping violations. International and national sport federations foresee that appeals against final decisions of federations in doping matters go to CAS. Thus, jurisprudence of CAS in doping case is essential to understand doping matters.
180. *See* the award of 9 Jul. 2001 in Case No. CAS2001/A/317 A. Fédération Internationale de Luttes Associées (FILA).
181. *See* 6 Feb. 2012 CAS arbitral award in Case No. CAS 2011/A/2384 *UCI v. Alberto Contador Velasco & RFEC & CAS* 2011/A/2386 *WADA v. Alberto Contador Velasco & RFEC.*

553. Mentioned jurisprudence of CAS proves that the need to protect sports from doping and difficulty of disciplinary bodies to prove doping violation justifies the need of the strict liability rule. Moreover, strict liability principle may well work as a tool of prevention. Athletes and their personnel being aware of strict liability and the consequences it brings may reconsider their intents to enhance performance by using prohibited substance. A strict liability rule in case of 'presence' violation shows how particular the fight against doping is from a legal point of view.

II. The Way the WADA Code Works

554. In order for the WADA Code to become a legally binding document one must undertake to be bound by it. If the WADA Code is not implemented and followed by major stakeholders in the world of sports, it would not be possible to maintain a universal approach implemented by the WADA Code.

555. The WADA Code includes a list of obligations for different stakeholders. First of all, the IOC is obliged to adopt and implement anti-doping policies and rules for the Olympic Games which conform with the WADA Code and to require as a condition of recognition by the IOC that international federations within the Olympic movement are in compliance with the WADA Code (Article 20.1.1–20.1.2 of the WADA Code). Moreover, the IOC is obliged to ensure that athletes, coaches, staff and other stakeholders would be bound by anti-doping rules which are in line with the WADA Code as a condition of such participation. This means that an athlete has no option but to be bound by the WADA Code if he or she is willing to participate in the Olympic Games. National Olympic committees are requested to ensure that all their members comply with the WADA Code (Article 20.4.2 of the WADA Code).

556. The Olympic Games take place only once in four years; therefore, it is important to ensure the application of the WADA Code outside the Olympic movement, i.e., in all tournaments and competitions which take place every day. International federations are required to adopt and implement anti-doping policies and rules which are compatible with the WADA Code (Article 20.3.1 of the WADA Code). Moreover, international federations are obliged to ensure that compatibility of policies and rules of national federations is condition precedent to the membership rights of such federations (Article 20.3.2 of the WADA Code). This way the requirement to comply with the WADA Code is transmitted to the national associations. International federations must ensure that all athletes, coaches and staff participating in competitions organized by such international federations comply with the regulations compatible with the WADA Code. International federations are required to ensure that national federations implement this regulation as well. Mostly international and national federations are responsible for the investigation of doping infringements and accordingly adopting sanctions. Mostly final decisions of federations are subject to appeal to CAS. It must be noticed that WADA has a special right to appeal against the decision of bodies of federations.

557. One of the most important means of implementation of the WADA Code is an obligation of signatories of the WADA Code (including IOC, national Olympic committees, international federations) to implement directly without substantive change in certain groups of provisions of the WADA Code (Article 23.2.2 of the WADA Code): Article 1 (Definition of Doping), Article 2 (Anti-Doping Rule Violations), Article 3 (Proof of Doping), Article 4.2.2 (Specified Substances), Article 4.3.3 (WADA's Determination of the Prohibited List), Article 7.11 (Retirement from Sport), Article 9 (Automatic Disqualification of Individual Results), Article 10 (Sanctions on Individuals), Article 11 (Consequences to Teams), Article 13 (Appeals) with the exception of 13.2.2, 13.6 and 13.7, Article 15.1 (Recognition of Decisions), Article 17 (Statute of Limitations), Article 24 (Interpretation of the Code), Appendix 1 – Definitions. Such provision ensures the uniform approach of different sports federations against doping.

558. For example, the FIFA Anti-Doping Regulations are applicable to competitions organized by the FIFA and members of the FIFA. UEFA adopted their Anti-Doping regulations applicable to competitions organized by UEFA, including UEFA Champions' League as well. LFF has no doping regulations; however, Article 39 of the LFF Disciplinary Code stipulates the liability for doping violations and refers to the FIFA Anti-Doping Regulations: in case a doping violation is committed by the player in competition organized by the LFF, the LFF Disciplinary Committee would investigate this violation, however the FIFA Anti-Doping Regulations would be applied as material law. A similar approach is kept by the LKF which does not have its own doping regulations. However, the Disciplinary and Ethics Code of the LKF refers to the FIBA Anti-Doping Regulations, and thus in case the doping infringement is investigated, the FIBA Anti-Doping Regulations would apply.

559. It is necessary to ensure that all the international federations and Olympic committees implement the WADA Code. The implementation of the WADA Code is not an automatic procedure. Even though the WADA Code is designed to protect the integrity of sports and well-being of athletes, it is not guaranteed that all signatories implement the WADA Code without any hesitation. For example, with the 2009 edition of the WADA Code the 'whereabouts rule' was introduced. The rule states that athletes who are included in a so-called registered pool are required to be available all the time for testing – for such reason athletes are requested to provide information of their whereabouts to doping authorities with utmost precision (to disclose the details on where the player is going to be from 6 AM to 11 PM hour-by-hour for months in advance). FIFA and UEFA hesitated to implement the provision.[182]

560. A measure to ensure that the international federations and national Olympic committees implement the WADA Code is set forth in the Olympic Charter. Article 44 of the Olympic Charter states that only sports which comply with the

182. Source is available online (accessed on 22 Aug. 2021) https://www.uefa.com/insideuefa/protecting-the-game/news/01d7-0f85b3dce788-1e846955c942-1000--fifa-and-uefa-reject-wada-whereabouts-stance/.

Olympic Charter and Code are eligible to be in the Olympic programme. If the international federation of a certain sport does not implement the WADA Code, such sport will not be a part of the Olympic movement.

Chapter 2. Doping and Lithuania

§1. General Introduction

561. Despite certain negative stories of athletes caught with doping[183] in their systems, Lithuania in general is devoted in its fight against doping.

562. On 1 April 1993 Lithuania signed the Anti-Doping Convention of the Council of Europe which took effect on 1 July 1996 (additional protocols were signed in 2012). In 2005 Lithuania signed the International Convention against Doping in Sports. It was ratified by the Parliament of the Republic of Lithuania on 2 May 2006 and it took effect on 1 January 2007.

563. In 2005, Lithuanian Anti-Doping Agency was established. It was founded by the KKSD. One of the most important reasons behind the establishment of Lithuanian Anti-Doping Agency is the direct implementation of certain tasks of the International Convention against Doping in Sports and the Anti-Doping Convention of the Council of Europe. The primary goal of the Lithuanian Anti-Doping Agency was to implement both of the mentioned international conventions. The main tasks of the Lithuanian Anti-Doping Agency are to carry out doping tests during international and national competitions, to train doping control officials, coordinate their activities, organize anti-doping education and informative activities, educate athletes, coaches, physicians, prevent usage of doping among athletes and coordinate relationship with sporting organizations. One of the main functions of the Lithuanian Anti-Doping Agency is to run the testing of athletes in Lithuania. The other important function is informative – the agency is responsible on spreading the news on doping regulations, information regarding testing, provision of the updated prohibited list and, importantly, the list of doping incidents including names of athletes. Activities of the Lithuanian Anti-Doping Agency related to implementation of the WADA Code are directly financed by budget funds of the state in accordance to national anti-doping programme.

564. LTOK and the national sports federations are bound to the WADA Code due to regulations of the IOC and the international sports federations. They ensure that the provisions of the Code are respected and abided.

183. The very first Olympic gold medal winner after the re-establishment of independent Lithuania, Romas Ubartas (discuss event in Barcelona, 1992), was caught positive with the steroid boldenone after his fourth-place finish in World Championships in Stuttgart, Živilė Balčiūnatė, a marathon runner, was tested positive for excessive levels of testosterone and epitestosterone and she was stripped from her European champion title and was banned for two years.

§2. Lithuanian Public Regulations

565. Article 3(3) of the Law on Sport sets a general principle of anti-doping: this principle requires certain stakeholders to take all actions necessary provided in the UNESCO International Convention against the Use of Doping in Sport to fight against the use of doping in sports.

566. At the moment use of doping is not criminalized in Lithuania. However, activity of illegal disposition of materials provided by the Law of the Republic of Lithuania on the Control of Various Doping Materials with the intention of distribution is considered a crime due to 2015 amendments of the Criminal Code (Article 276^1–276^3 of the Criminal Code). The Law of the Republic of Lithuania on the Control of Various Doping Materials was also adopted in 2015. Doping materials concerned are included in the list of International Convention against Doping in Sports. The main purpose of the law is to protect the health and life of athletes and other persons as well and thus limit the availability of certain materials in the market. The intention of the lawmakers[184] was to restrict the supply of such materials to purely pharmaceutical or scientific reasons and to diminish possibilities that such materials could be used.

§3. Provisions of LTOK and Federations Against Doping

567. In accordance with the statutes of LTOK, one of the tasks of LTOK is to fight against the use of WADA prohibited substances. The role of LTOK in this field is a reflection of the functions assigned by the WADA Code to the national Olympic committees. LTOK ensures that all participants of the Olympic Games delegated by Lithuania comply with the WADA Code.

568. National federations either include references to the Anti-doping rules adopted by the Lithuanian Anti-Doping Agency or refer to anti-doping rules of related international federations.[185]

569. Lithuanian Anti-Doping Agency adopted its own Anti-doping Rules. The structure and the content of the Anti-doping rules are very similar to the structure and content of the WADA Code. In fact, the main parts (such as the doping violations, proofs of doping, sanctions) are identical to the WADA Code. The principal goal of the Anti-doping Rules is to ensure the uniform approach of the WADA Code within Lithuania. All recognized sport federations are required to acknowledge the

184. Online source is available (accessed on 26 Jun. 2021) (https://lrv.lt/uploads/main/Posed_medz/2014/140430/13.pdf).
185. For example, Art. 46 of the LFF Disciplinary Code of the Lithuanian Football Federation provides that sanctions for doping violations shall be applied in by the LFF Disciplinary Committee in accordance with the FIFA Anti-Doping Regulations. Art. 17 of the Disciplinary and Ethics Code of the LKF provides that sanctions for doping violations shall be applied by the FIBA. In accordance with the Statues of the Lithuanian Athletics federation, doping violations are dealt with in accordance with anti-doping regulations of the IAAF.

Anti-doping regulations and to insert the rules in their regulations and by-laws or to refer to the rules. Failure to acknowledge such rules may lead to certain consequences, including the stopping of state funding of certain federations. However, the recognition of such regulation in by-laws of federations is not common. As mentioned, most national federations are bound by the rules issued by international federations and the latter are applied in the event of doping violations.

570. However, Anti-doping Rules also stipulate certain provisions on national disciplinary procedures in doping violations establishing certain rights of Lithuanian Anti-Doping Agency as well. Such rules could be applicable for federations which did not set-up their own specific procedural or material regulations on the investigation of doping violation. However, since national testing is assigned to the Anti-Doping Agency, their rules are important in terms of procedures as from the stage of the test result management to the phase of appeal to CAS.

Chapter 3. Fight Against Match-Fixing

§1. General Introduction

571. Official term of 'match-fixing' is 'manipulation of sports competitions'. The latter is defined by the Council of Europe Convention on Manipulation of Sports Competitions ('Match-fixing Convention') as '*intentional* arrangement, act or omission aimed at an improper alteration of the result or the course of a sports competition in order to remove all or part of the unpredictable nature of the aforementioned sports competition with a view to obtaining an undue advantage *for oneself or for others*'. There are various forms and methods of match-fixing and different jurisdictions, sports federations define such activities differently as well.

572. Traditionally, match-fixing is related to betting activities. A player in a football match may bet against his/her own team and therefore act in the field accordingly. Moreover, players are often approached by outsiders who conduct illegal betting activities and are 'bribed' to perform on the pitch in a manner which would secure the intended outcome or course of the match. A referee can be paid or rewarded to affect a match in accordance with his power as well. However, match-fixing is not necessarily related to ongoing betting – several players of one team may be approached by the other team officials with a proposal not to perform well so a second team could advance further to other stage of tournament or to secure a higher place in the league without any element of betting. Not only affecting the final outcome is considered match-fixing. Course of the match may also be affected. Betting companies offer various types of events to bet for, including a number of fouls, scores after certain parts of a game. Thus, a player may not necessarily be interested in losing a game, but he or she may attempt to keep certain score after a part of the game, to intentionally collect fouls in order to trigger betting milestone. However, all these types of activities have a common feature – such activities eliminate unpredictability and integrity of sports competition.

573. One of the most important challenges of the states and sports federations in the fight against manipulation of sport is to detect a potential violator and, most importantly, to collect sufficient evidence to prove the violation and to sanction the violator accordingly. It is important to notice that standards of proof may differ depending on the type of liability.[186] In CAS practice[187] (when dealing with the decisions of sports federations) usually a standard of comfortable satisfaction is applied. Said standard of proof is not as soft as 'balance of probabilities' which is usually applicable in civil cases, but not as strict as 'beyond reasonable doubt' which is applicable in criminal cases. Regardless of applicable standard of proof, in

---

186. Standard of 'beyond reasonable doubt' is applicable to criminal cases and standard of 'balance of probabilities' is applicable to civil cases.

187. For example, 15 Apr. 2010 CAS award in Case No. CAS 2009/A/1920 *FK Pobeda, Aleksandr Zabrcanec, Nikolce Zdraveski v. UEFA*, 5 Dec. 2013 CAS award in Case No. CAS 2013/A/3139 *Fenerbahçe SK v. UEFA* the CAS, 23 Jan. 2014 CAS award in CAS 2013/A/3258 *Besiktas Jimnastik Kulubu v. UEFA*.

general it is very difficult to catch a perpetrator due to the specific nature of the violation: agreements to manipulate a match are not obvious and for a non-expert it is not easy to distinguish intentionally bad performance of a player on the pitch from just a bad luck or lack of health. Therefore, in most of the times special measures of criminal intelligence have to be invoked. It is not rare that match-fixing investigations are unwrapped during investigation on other potential crimes, such as organized crime. Number of cases in CAS related to match-fixing also includes specific evidence, such as telephone conversation transcripts and other material collected by law enforcement bodies.[188] Lack of legal framework enabling the gathering of sufficient evidence as well as general lack of legal attention to such activity may lead to an increase in match-fixing events.

574. First notorious and quite obvious match-fixing scandal in Lithuania did occur in April 2011, in LKL match between the local team Palanga and BC Žalgiris. A local team lost by thirty-seven points. The difference between both teams was evident well before the match, however several players of Palanga allegedly acted suspiciously in the last quarter in order to lose a game by a bigger margin. Soon it was confirmed that some of Palanga's players placed bets against their team to lose the game by more than thirty points.[189] Players were sanctioned by LKL and club. However, no public legal measures were taken. This event gave birth to discussions on the general situation of integrity of sports and seriousness of such activities. A level of involvement of law enforcement bodies in the fight against manipulation in sport was also discussed. Some suggested that players should be brought to criminal charges, however it was not done due to alleged lack of legal basis, i.e., specially drafted body of crime in the Criminal Code.

575. In 2014 the Lithuanian branch of Transparency International, published report 'Unfair Agreements in Sport'.[190] The goal of the report was to determine the level of manipulation in sports in Lithuanian football and basketball. Football and basketball players were surveyed. The results of the investigation were very sound: it was discovered that 42% of surveyed football players and 27% of surveyed basketball players considered that manipulation in sport was spread. Moreover, almost 26% of players considered manipulation in sport as a 'big problem' and 28% of football players and 44% of basketball players admitted that they were aware of colleagues being part of such activities. What is more, about 21% of football players and 15% of basketball players admitted of being aware that manipulation activities were going on in a match they had played. Finally, 42.1% of football players and 38% of basketball players stated they had experienced pressure to commit such activities. Mostly economic reasons were mentioned as a cause of involvement of

188. For example, 18 Jan. 2011 CAS award in Case No. CAS 2010/A/2172 *Mr Oleg Oriekhov v. UEFA*, 5 May 2011 CAS award in Case No. CAS 2010/A/2266 *N. & V. v. UEFA*, 5 Dec. 2013 CAS award d in Case No. CAS 2013/A/3139 *Fenerbahçe SK v. UEFA*, 23 Jan. 2014 CAS award in Case No. CAS 2013/A/3258 *Besiktas Jimnastik Kulubu v. UEFA*.

189. Online source is available (accessed on 26 Jun. 2021) (https://m.basketnews.lt/news-38465-skandalas-lkl-naglio-zaidejai-state-pries-savo-komanda-papildyta-komentarai.html).

190. Online source is available (accessed on 26 Jun. 2021) (http://www.transparency.lt/susitarimai-sporte/).

athletes in this kind of activities – 52% of athletes considered such activities as a source of extra income and 16% indicated that the reason behind such activities was simply bad personal financial situation of athletes while 13% stated that the over-due salaries were to blame.

576. Results of the Transparency International report clearly indicated that the integrity of most popular sports in Lithuania, such as basketball and football, is in serious danger. This resulted in active discussions on the fight against match-fixing in both, i.e., private and public sections. While discussions on possible remedies in public section were concentrated on the issue of what to do with the criminal aspect of manipulation in sports, the federations and leagues implemented their own remedies to fight against manipulation in the sports issue.

§2. Match-Fixing: Public Regulations

577. On 18 September 2014 Lithuania signed the Match-fixing Convention. The Match-fixing Convention aims 'to combat the manipulation of sports competitions in order to protect the integrity of sport and sports ethics in accordance with the principle of the autonomy of sport'. The main objectives of the Match-fixing Convention are to prevent, detect and sanction national or transnational manipulation of national and international sports competitions and to promote national and international cooperation against manipulation of sports competitions between the public authorities concerned, as well as with organizations involved in sports and in sports betting. First important note of the Match-fixing Convention is that it defines manipulation in sports competition. Second, it provides a vast number of remedies to tackle manipulation of sports competitions in international level, including establishment of national platforms (an institution which is responsible[191] to, *inter alia*, serve as an information hub, coordinate the fight against manipulation of sports competitions, cooperate with all organizations and relevant authorities at national and international levels, including national platforms of other signatory states).

578. After signing of the Match-fixing Convention, Lithuanian lawmakers took an additional step further to tackle match-fixing. On 30 June 2016 the Parliament adopted amendments on the Criminal Code, the Law on Sport and, as well as this, the Law of Criminal Intelligence of the Republic of Lithuania, 2012. All three amendments are related to the introduction of criminalization of match-fixing or manipulation in sport. The amendments took effect on 1 January 2017 and from then on, an activity of manipulation in sports may lead to conviction and, accordingly, to imprisonment.

579. As it was mentioned before, the events of *Palanga v. BC Žalgiris* sparked discussions on whether such conduct should be a subject of criminal investigation and criminal charges. At the time the position of prosecutors was that legal regulation was not sufficient to bring criminal charges against a person involved in

191. Article 13(1) of the Convention.

match-fixing as the Criminal Code did not foresee any special composition of a body of crime. Discussions spread whether such activity needed a special provision at all or it could fall in the scope of Article 182 of the Criminal Code (the fraud or swindling) which provides that a person who, by deceit, acquires another's property for one's own benefit or for the benefit of other persons or acquires a property right, avoids a property obligation or annuls it is subject to criminal punishment. Prosecutors did not agree that manipulation in sports can be subject to Article 182 of the Criminal Code. Meanwhile, Lithuanian authors believe[192] manipulation in sport could have fallen under Article 182 of the Criminal Code.

580. The difference of opinions on how to criminalize the manipulation in sport was obvious during the phase of drafting the amendments of the Criminal Code. Various different drafts were prepared and negotiated by the lawmakers.[193] Finally, Article 182^1 was adopted to constitute the crime of manipulation in sports competitions. It consists of three provisions. Article 182^1(1) states that one who *illegally influenced* fair course or result of *professional* sports competitions shall be punished with community service or fine, or restriction of liberty or imprisonment up to four years. Article 182^1(2) sets the exemption from criminal liability for persons who although had committed the criminal act described in Article 182^1(1) but who did report it voluntarily to the law enforcement institution before being recognized as suspect and who actively collaborated in finding out such activity. Article 182^1(3) sets that legal persons may also be held responsible for activities set in Article 182^1(1).

581. At the moment there is no jurisprudence on the application of such amendment of the Criminal Code, and therefore it is difficult to discuss the content of objective and subjective attributes which forms the body of said crime. However, it is clear that there will be several issues. One issue is that amateur sports competitions do not fall in the scope of Article 182^1(1). Yet again, the Criminal Code does not provide for the distinction from professional and non-professional competitions. Moreover, the Law on Sport does not provide such distinction as well.

582. The previous edition of Law on Sport was amended in order to synchronize it with the new edition of the Criminal Code and such amendments took effect on 1 January 2017 as well. The essence of such amendment lies within the introduction of the definition for the 'manipulation in sports competition'. As well as this, restriction for athletes to take part in such activities was introduced. Finally, an important amendment was made governing a cancellation of the right of an athlete to receive rent in case of disqualification and annulment of results of such athlete giving ground to rent payment due to the involvement of such athlete in manipulation of sports competitions. In accordance with Article 2(13) of the current edition of the Law on Sport, the definition of 'manipulation of high performance sports competition' was introduced. Manipulation of high performance sports competition

---

192. Salomėja Zaksaitė, *Sukčiavimo sporto srityje paplitimas ir prevencijos problemos: PhD dissertation* (University of Vilnius, 2012).
193. Ramunė Bistrickaitė, *Lithuania Criminalises Match-Fixing* (EPFL Legal Newsletter, 2016).

is considered as intentional agreement, act or omission aimed to influence the course or result of high performance sports competition with an aim to fully or partially eliminate the unpredictability of such competition and to gain or provide unjust advantage to oneself or others. Prohibition of manipulation of sport is one of the main principles of sport set forth by the Law on Sport.

583. The Law on Criminal Intelligence of the Republic of Lithuania was amended accordingly too. The crime of manipulation in sports competitions (Article 182[1] of the Criminal Code) was included in the list of crimes which can be investigated by means of criminal intelligence investigation. The status of criminal intelligence investigation allows the law enforcement bodies to operatively use special measures to investigate potential crimes (e.g., gathering information from entities providing electronic communication services, use of special technical devices, etc.). This amendment of Law on Criminal Intelligence of the Republic of Lithuania is very important for proper implementation of Article 182[1] of the Criminal Code. Potential application of criminal intelligence investigation to such activities might increase chances of the law enforcers to collect necessary evidence, to determine violators and bring them to justice.

§3. Match-Fixing: Private Regulations

584. As it was underlined in previous chapters, the spread of manipulation in sports competition in Lithuania is really worrying in accordance with statistics and various surveys. Since public bodies, including the prosecution office, were not very keen to investigate various possible match-fixing cases due to alleged lack of specific crime description in the Criminal Code, the federations, namely the LFF and the LKF had to amend their disciplinary regulations.

585. The LFF did take a stronger effort in the fight against manipulation in sports in terms of implementation of certain investigation and procedural measures and more strict sanctions. It is fair to mention that the remedies available to the LFF from its partners (such as UEFA or SPORTRADAR) are significant to establish the potential cases of match-fixing and to punish violators. It is also important to mention that the system of the LFF established in its Disciplinary Code has successfully passed the exam of the CAS Appeals Division.

I. Regulations of the LKF

586. The CDE establishes disciplinary match-fixing fighting remedies. The CDE does not specify or define the concept of manipulation in sports competition or match-fixing, but it establishes related activities.

587. Article 8 of the CDE establishes a general rule of fair play, which could also be applied to the extent of manipulation in sports. Paragraphs 8–11 of Article 8 of the CDE specify what is considered to be unsporting and impropriate conduct:

- Direct or indirect receipt, request, demand, offer, giving or acceptance to give or acceptance to receive any form of reward which could be considered as a measure to influence the course or result of the match or/and any other acts which are aimed to infringe the ethics of sport or course or results of a match.
- Direct or indirect offer, promise or provision of any form of gain to the competitor on behalf of oneself or any other person urging to infringe provisions set in the CDE, regulations of the LKF and/or FIBA, FIBA Europe and/or acceptance to receive any form of gain, promise to provide or accept any form of gain.
- Direct or indirect participation in any kind of betting related to the competitions.
- Direct or indirect provision of information or advice to competitors or third persons, including betting operators.

588. All the above-mentioned activities are subject to identical sanctions, i.e., a fine from EUR 286 to EUR 2,857 or suspension (disqualification) of competitor for a period of time determined by the disciplinary bodies. The possible length of suspension is not stipulated by the CDE.

589. It is very important to notice that potential violations of paragraphs 8–11 of Article 8 of the CDE are investigated and possible disciplinary procedures have to be conducted by the leagues. The LKF, namely, the Committee for Discipline and Ethics of the LKF, acts as an appeal body only following the examination of appeals against decisions taken by disciplinary bodies of the leagues concerned. The leagues are obliged to include the same provisions to their regulations as the CDE. And only in cases when the league regulations are not harmonized with the provisions of the CDE, the CDE directly applies and the disciplinary procedures are instigated and initiated by the LKF.

590. Paragraphs 8–11 of Article 8 of the CDE are transplanted in regulations of most leagues, including the LKL. Only the severity of the terms of sanctions differs. For example, the LKL defines that direct or indirect participation in any kind of betting related to the LKL competitions may result in disqualification for one to two years which suggest that other activities are considered as less harmful.

II. The LFF Regulations

591. The LFF took serious efforts to challenge the increasing amount of potential cases of match-fixing in Lithuanian football matches. It is important to understand that since the position of law enforcement institutions was not very active, it became evident that the federations will have to develop their way to tackle the issue without the interference of law enforcers. As mentioned before, one of the biggest problems in the fight against match-fixing is the difficulty to collect proof. Thus, having no potential help from law enforcement authorities, federations had to apply a different approach.

592. First of all, the LFF secured assistance from prominent partners, namely the UEFA and the SPORTRADAR.[194] With the help of these partners, the LFF obtained a way to secure important data on suspicious matches which could later be considered as evidence. SPORTRADAR generates reports on suspicious matches accompanied with a very comprehensive analysis of betting patterns and anomalies which suggest certain irregularities of a specific match.

593. Second, the LFF adopted provisions in the LFF Disciplinary Code which are aimed to fight manipulation in LFF organized and recognized football competitions. It sets a system recognizing two general types of participation in match-fixing activities.

594. Article 38(1) of the LFF Disciplinary Code established the definition of manipulation in sports. It states that participants have to refrain from any type of behaviour damaging or possibly causing damage to the integrity (fair play) of the competition and/or matches, including but not limited to violation of the principles of sports ethics, and behaviour influencing or possibly impacting the results and/or the course of the competition and/or matches. The violator is subject to *any sanctions* indicated in the LFF Disciplinary Code, including ban of a significant length.

595. Article 38(2) explains the type of behaviour which is prohibited, i.e., defines what is, *inter alia*, considered manipulation in sports by the LFF Disciplinary Regulations:

- Direct or indirect participation in any betting or similar activities related to the competition or the match that the clubs/teams or the LFF selected teams are taking part in.
- Use of any information or its disclosure to third parties, when such information cannot be accessed publicly and is acquired (received) due to the status held in football, if such disclosure is damaging or could possibly damage the integrity (fair play) of the competition or matches.
- Failure to immediately and voluntarily present to the LFF any information known or related to the infringements or prohibitions set forth herein, especially in cases of anyone contacting a participant with the offer to commit the infringements or breach the prohibitions laid out herein.

596. It is important to notice that not only 'active' participation is punishable, but 'passive' (failure to inform on ongoing activities) is also subject to sanctions. In order to sanction a certain person, the LFF must prove that such person has committed a violation of Article 38(1) and 38(2) of the LFF Disciplinary Regulations which requires certain amount of evidence.[195] Therefore, to tackle this issue, the

---

194. Information available online (accessed on 26 Jun. 2021) (http://lff.lt/prieziura/saziningas-zaidimas/).
195. The LFF Disciplinary Code does not establish the standard of proof like for example UEFA's regulations.

LFF established a rule defining so-called presumed match-fixing, i.e., a violation which is slightly different from 'regular' match-fixing offence.

597. Article 38(4) of the LFF Disciplinary Code states that in the case when there is sufficient data to confirm that a match *has been manipulated*, the participant of the match whose behaviour during a match (as shown by the analysis of the match) *allows presuming* that such participant could have committed the infringements specified in Article 38(1) such participant shall be sanctioned with match suspension (disqualification) from twenty matches and/or a ban from taking part in a particular or any football-related activity up to five years. This rule says that in order to sanction a person in accordance with Article 38(4) Disciplinary Code, the LFF has to prove following elements: (1) the match was manipulated, (2) available data allows presuming that the person involved could have committed a breach stipulated in Article 38(1). While the issue related to establishment of fact of a fixed match is not detailed in the LFF Disciplinary Code, the remedy to prove that a person was involved in a wrongdoing is established in Article 62 of the LFF Disciplinary Code.

598. Article 62 of the LFF Disciplinary Code governs the functions of the so-called Match Investigation Expert Team. The team investigates football matches and searches for any clues of suspicious behaviour of a violator. Article 62(3) of the LFF Disciplinary Code states that the Match Investigation Expert Team analyses the match and the behaviour of its participants and then presents conclusions on the behaviour of an investigated participant during the respective match and on assumptions of the said participant possibly committing the infringements laid out in Article 38 of the LFF Disciplinary Code. Article 62(4) is very important – it states that the conclusion of the Match Investigation Expert Team that the behaviour of the participant of the match during the respective match allows making an assumption that such participant could have committed the infringement specified in Article 38(1) constitutes the *basis for applying the sanctions established* in Article 38(4) and Article 38(5).

599. Similar practices are also used by the UEFA too, however, not to impose a sanction but to prevent suspicious (but not yet convicted) cubs to enter UEFA competition.[196] Such practices are used not in disciplinary but in administrative procedures. A CAS decision in *Skenderbeu*[197] case confirmed that such practices are valid. Before *Skenderbeu* decision, CAS examined very similar matter involving a Lithuanian club and decisions of the LFF disciplinary bodies which will be discussed further.

600. However, certain means of the LFF to tackle alleged match-fixing might be less convincing. For example, in accordance with Article 8^1(1) of the LFF Transfer Regulation, the LFF has the right to *refuse* to register a player if the department of the LFF responsible for the registration of players *believes* that such registration

196. *See*, 21 Nov. 2016 CAS award in Case No. CAS 2016/A/4650 *Klubi Sportiv Skenderbeu v. UEFA*.
197. *Ibid.*

and/or participation of the player in club activities *may violate or negatively influence* the reputation and integrity of the respective club, LFF, competition of the LFF, other clubs participating in the competition of the LFF or football itself as sport. Part 2 of said Article provides that appeals against the decision of the department of the LFF responsible for the registration of players to refuse to register the respective player may be lodged to the Executive Committee of the LFF. The decision passed by the Executive Committee of the LFF shall be final.

601. Said provisions are questionable due to the fact there are no criteria provided to assess on what basis the LFF can come up with a conclusion on the potential danger of player to the integrity of the game. It is left to the *belief* of the LFF which may be not supported by any evidence whatsoever. Moreover, there is no indication of what happens if a player is not allowed to be registered for a club. Such measure is equal to the most severe sanction which can be applied by disciplinary bodies, i.e., disqualification. However, in this case, no formal procedure is conducted, the player is not provided any right to submit his or her statement, besides the duration of such measure is not provided as well. Therefore, such provisions could constitute situations where players are forbidden to carry out their activities for an undetermined amount of time without any evidence whatsoever.

III. The FK Kruoja Case at CAS

602. In 2016 the disciplinary system of the LFF against match-fixing was a subject of legal test at the CAS. It was the first and until now the only Lithuanian match-fixing case which was heard by the CAS Appeals Division following the decisions of the LFF Disciplinary Committee and the LFF Appeals Committee. The subject matter of the case concerned two matches of '*A Lyga*' during 2015 season. Both matches were played between the same teams FK Kruoja and FK Šiauliai. The first match took place on 27 May 2015. Home team FK Šiauliai beat FK Kruoja 1:0. The second match took place on 16 August 2015. Host team FK Kruoja suffered another loss against FK Šiauliai, this time by a result of 2:3 despite having 2:0 early lead.

603. Soon after the matches the LFF received information, including the UEFA Betting Fraud Detection System (BFDS) reports on both matches suggesting that the matches were manipulated in order to secure fraudulent betting profits.

604. In accordance with the BFDS reports, betting patterns for the first match (1:0 to FK Šiauliai) were odd. Prematch active betting for FK Kruoja not to win was followed by more intense betting for FK Kruoja to actually lose the match allegedly without any reasonable justification of sports nature. The odds of FK Šiauliai were decreasing from 2.40 to 1.62. A large number of bookmakers removed the offer from betting. What is more, the betting offers of match suspiciously generated ten times more income than usual. The anomalies in betting market led to the conclusion of the BFDS that the matches were manipulated in order to secure fraudulent betting profit by FK Kruoja.

605. In the second match, home team FK Kruoja, a clear favourite, took comfortable early lead by the result of 2:0, both goals scored in a gap of two minutes (on fourteenth and fifteenth minute respectively). Despite having control of the match FK Kruoja managed to let two quick goals in (thirty-third and thirty-fifth minute respectively), the latter one being scored from the penalty spot. As from the sixty-first minute, FK Šiauliai started to create a number of goal opportunities which finally resulted in the third and final goal. The final score was 2:3.

606. As in the case of the first match, the latter meeting of both the teams attracted the attention of the BFDS again. Suspicious action allegedly began to take place well before the match. The prematch betting clearly favoured FK Kruoja not to win and then to lose the match. Chances of FK Šiauliai winning before the match declined from 5.10 down to 2.00. Such rapid change of betting offers was allegedly hardly justified by sporting reasons – on the day of the match FK Šiauliai was at the bottom of the table having a horrible away game form (eight losses out of the last ten games) and very poor overall form (two wins out of twenty-two matches). Besides FK Šiauliai had won only one match against FK Kruoja in the last nine matches. Despite this the betting marked clearly favoured an underdog FK Šiauliai.

607. The unusual course of the match corresponded with unusual events in the betting market as well. At the beginning of the second half (at the time the score was at 2:2) punters began placing bets against FK Kruoja causing the increase in odds for FK Kruoja. In the meantime, the chances of FK Šiauliai were increasing from 1.75 to 1.82. And it all happened in a single minute of a game (during the sixty-second minute). However, until that particular moment of the match, few events suggested that FK Šiauliai might actually break through. Nearly 20% of bookmakers withdrew the match from offer before it actually started meanwhile six out of ten bookmakers withdrew the match offer from their live betting during the course of the match. BFDS also noted the poor defence of FK Kruoja failing to maintain the comfortable lead in a negligent fashion. Thus, BFDS concluded that it had no doubt that the match had been manipulated to secure fraudulent betting profit by FK Kruoja.

608. The BFDS reports were considered sufficient enough for the LFF Disciplinary Committee not only to start disciplinary procedures but to conclude that the matches were in fact manipulated. Now it was the turn of the Match Investigation Expert Team to investigate actual events on the pitch and to determine if any suspicious conduct of players during both matches did happen. The Match Investigation Expert Team concluded that in both matches behaviour of certain players of FK Kruoja team was suspicious. Totally nine players of FK Kruoja were indicated in both matches.

609. Possessing mentioned data, the LFF Disciplinary Committee imposed sanctions on nine FK Kruoja players and the club itself under the strict liability rule. All players appealed the decision of the LFF Disciplinary Committee to the LFF Appeals Committee which dismissed the appeal. The LFF Appeals Committee declared that both of the conditions to apply Article 44(5) of the LFF Disciplinary

Code (Article 44(4) of the current edition of the LFF Disciplinary Code),[198] i.e., the presence of manipulated match fact and a suspicious behaviour of certain players, were present.

610. All nine players of Kruoja and the club filed appeals to the CAS Appeals Division. The appellants argued that the LFF had insufficient evidence to conclude the breach of the LFF Disciplinary Code. They also challenged the position of the LFF that it was sufficient enough to suspect the illegal conduct of the players in order to establish the breach of the regulations. Moreover, the appellants challenged the conclusion of the LFF that the matches were in fact fixed. Finally, the appellants questioned the selection of sanctions as well as alleged procedural flaws allegedly committed by the LFF bodies.

611. The panel of the CAS dismissed the appeal and confirmed the decisions of the LFF bodies.[199] First of all, the panel took the effort to identify the meaning of Article 44 of both the editions of the LFF Disciplinary Code. The panel concluded that Article 44 of the LFF Disciplinary Code contains *two different violations*: first of all, Article 44(1) of the LFF Disciplinary Code established an actual commission of match-fixing, for example direct or indirect participation in any gamble or similar activities related to the competition or the match that the clubs are taking part in. Such infringement is defined by the CAS as a very serious disciplinary violation which could result in any sanction.

612. Meanwhile, Article 44(5) (Article 44(4) of the current edition of the LFF Disciplinary Code), in accordance with CAS, consists of so-called *presumed commission of a match-fixing*. In order to convict the player with such violation, a match-fixing must be established and the behaviour of the player in question during the match is identified, which allows the presumption that such player could be responsible for the match-fixing. In such case, the sanction of a limited period of disqualification is provided. In the first event, the direct involvement of a player is required to prove factual infringement. In the second event, it is required to find a suspicious conduct of the player. It must be stressed that the CAS pointed out that such conclusion does not mean that any lower standard of proof should be applied in the event of the latter infringement: the panel must be *comfortably satisfied* (i.e., a standard of comfortable satisfaction must be applied) to conclude that the infringement was in fact committed.

613. The panel rejected arguments of the appellants regarding the alleged lack of evidence to find players guilty. The panel underlined that it is in line with the LFF Disciplinary Code to hold a player responsible for presumed match-fixing when the finding of an actual match manipulation is not possible. The panel concluded that

198. It should be taken into consideration that both matches did take place during power of different editions of the LFF Disciplinary Code. When the first match took place the old version of the LFF Disciplinary Code (adopted on 25 Feb. 2015) was in legal power with a relevant rule being stipulated in Art. 44(3). The second match took place after the new edition of the LFF Disciplinary Code was adopted (30 Jul. 2015) a rule in question was stipulated in Art. 44(5).
199. 13 Jul. 2016 CAS award in Case No. CAS 2015/A/4351.

the BFDS reports and supporting explanations of experts *confirmed* that both matches were fixed. Moreover, the panel concluded that the report of the match investigation expert group was sufficient enough to conclude suspicious behaviour of each of the players involved since the appellants had failed to present any evidence to support their counter position. The panel also rejected arguments related to alleged procedural flaws and improper application of sanction.

614. Thus, the very first Lithuanian match-fixing case deriving from the decisions of bodies of the national sports federations successfully passed the exam of CAS. What is noteworthy is that the FK Kruoja case was not one of the traditional match-fixing cases we see being heard by CAS which usually includes hard evidence, like transcripts of telephone conversations, data collected by criminal intelligence or statements of witnesses. LFF developed the concept of fight against match-fixing by distinguishing the actual match-fixing from presumed match-fixing. It obviously has a major weakness – persons committing such infringements are not sanctioned as the one participating in match-fixing activities should be: the actual match-fixing is usually met with severe sanctions including a lifetime ban from football activities, whereas the LFF Disciplinary Code provides limited and a slightly lesser period of disqualification. Thus, a violator is not actually radiated from football and there is a chance of his or her repeated offence. However, the advantages are obvious too: it is easier to prove the wrongdoing of presumed manipulation: the body has to prove the match-fixing fact with the help of the BFDS and prove the suspicious behaviour of the player with the help of the Match Investigation Expert Team. Besides, the recidivism increases the volume of potential second sanction and could also cause contractual problems for the player;[200] thus the preventive nature of sanctions still remains.

615. This case allows concluding that the sports federations can establish their own means to fight against match-fixing without interference from the law enforcement bodies. Needless to say, it is important to have good organizational means and human resources to ensure proper supervision of the integrity of particular sport.

200. Clubs and players tend to agree in their contracts that a match-fixing commitment is a serious breach of contract which constitutes the ground for the club to terminate the contract unilaterally and then request.

Part IV. Commercial Matters

Chapter 1. General Introduction

616. It is suggested that one of the main causes of development of sports law as an area of law was the general commercialization of sport: a larger concentration of money in the field of sports required more intense intervention of law and legal regulation.

617. In accordance with the Study on the Contribution of Sport to Economic Growth and Employment in the EU conducted by the European Commission,[201] in 2005, sport-related gross value added (direct effects) amounted to EUR 112.18 billion according to the narrow definition and EUR 173.86 billion with respect to the broad definition. For the statistical definition of sport, it was EUR 28.16 billion. The direct effects of sport, combined with its multiplier (indirect and induced) effects, added up to 2.98% (EUR 294.36 billion) of overall gross value added in the EU. For the EU as a whole, the contribution of sport-related employment to total employment is 2.12%. In absolute terms, this is equal to 4.46 million employees. This demonstrates the impact of sports business to the whole EU.

618. However, in Lithuania, the contribution of sport to economic growth and employment is below the EU average.[202] Such situation is also reflected in the level of commercialization of sport. It should be noted that in general, Lithuanian market is relatively small and therefore it does not generate such income in sports as in bigger EU countries. Moreover, different from countries such as France, Germany, Italy, Spain or UK, the level of domestic football and in particular football clubs and leagues, is considerably low. Average attendance of football matches in top Lithuanian football league, '*A Lyga*', is just 464 spectators per game.[203] Such approach to domestic football (unless the national team is playing) is also reflected in the size of the TV audience. Although basketball in Lithuania is far more important, both from sports and organizational point of view, the general level of professional club football in Lithuania determines the lack of known attributes related to commercialization of sports, such as huge player contracts, collective sale of TV and media rights,

201. Study on the Contribution of Sport to Economic Growth and Employment in the EU, 2012. Source is available online (accessed on 26 Jun. 2021) (http://ec.europa.eu/assets/eac/sport/library/studies/study-contribution-spors-economic-growth-final-rpt.pdf).
202. *Ibid.*
203. Source available online (accessed on 26 Jun. 2021) (http://www.european-football-statistics.co.uk/attn.htm).

sponsorship of players and clubs, player transfer market. Nevertheless, specific issues related to commercial matters which can also be attributed to sports do exist and they have to be analysed in more detail.

Chapter 2. Public Regulations

§1. TV Broadcasting

619. General grounds and requirements to carry out broadcasting activities are governed by the Law on Information to the Public of the Republic of Lithuania, 1996. The Law does not specify any specifics in terms of broadcasting of sports events.[204] Broadcasting is closely related to advertising, which will be analysed further.

620. It is important to notice that in accordance with Article 33(9) of the Law on Information[205] to the Public of the Republic of Lithuania, Radio and Television Commission of Lithuania may, at the broadcaster's request, grant it the status of a must-carry programme which is rebroadcast and/or disseminated via the Internet and provide that the said programme must be rebroadcast and/or disseminated via the Internet free of charge by programme rebroadcasters and other persons providing users of the Republic of Lithuania with the services of dissemination of television programmes and/or individual programmes via the Internet. Only special culture, education, science, knowledge, *sports* or religion television programmes shall be recognized as must-carry television programmes which are rebroadcast and/or disseminated via the Internet.

621. One of the events when a compulsory broadcast of sport competition was considered is related to EuroLeague competition. EuroLeague competition is very popular in Lithuania due to regular performance of BC Žalgiris.[206] However, the EuroLeague competition could watched via satellite channels against payments. Alleged necessity to provide the general Lithuania audience with a possibility to watch the EuroLeague competition, the Government proposed an amendment for the Law on Information to the Public of the Republic of Lithuania in order to declare EuroLeague competitions as an event of social importance enabling free broadcasting. However, the model was not implemented.[207] Nevertheless, the national broadcaster, the Lithuanian Radio and Television acquired rights to broadcast Žalgiris' EuroLeague games as from 2020/2021 basketball season.

622. TV broadcasting and media rights are closely related to the protection of intellectual property. As it is noted by the World Intellectual Property Organization, advances in communications technologies have revolutionized broadcast sports coverage and enabled billions of people around the world to take part in the spectacle

204. Except certain requirements for advertising in sports which are analysed further.
205. Official translation provided in website of the Seimas (accessed on 26 Jun. 2021) (https://e-seimas.lrs.lt/portal/legalAct/lt/TAD/2865241206f511e687e0fbad81d55a7c?jfwid=1clcwosx33).
206. BC 'Lietuvos Rytas' and BC 'Neptūnas' also did take part in certain editions of the EuroLeague, however BC 'Žalgiris' is the only Lithuanian club which is regular participant of the tournament.
207. Source is available online (accessed on 26 Jun. 2021) (http://www.delfi.lt/krepsinis/naujienos/nemokamos-eurolygos-transliacijos-ilgai-lauke-dar-palauksime.d?id=61319829).

and excitement of major sporting events.[208] In general, a sports competition, such as football or basketball match should not be considered as intellectual creation (unless certain artistic element is included, such as specific moves in dance competition or synchronized swimming). However, in accordance with decision of the EU Court of Justice in *Murphy* case,[209] 'it is permissible for a Member State to protect sporting events, where appropriate by virtue of protection of intellectual property, by putting in place specific national legislation, or by recognizing, in compliance with European Union law, protection conferred upon those events by agreements concluded between the persons having the right to make the audiovisual content of the events available to the public and the persons who wish to broadcast that content to the public of their choice'. However, in accordance with Lithuanian regulation, such protection is not provided. A TV broadcast is considered as an object of related rights in accordance with the Law on Copyright and Related Rights of the Republic of Lithuania. Therefore, certain protection provided by the Law on Copyright and Related Rights of the Republic of Lithuania applies.

§2. Advertising

623. Advertising is one of the key aspects of commerce in sport. Without a possibility to advertise a trademark, a product or a service, a sponsor would not be interested to support an athlete, a club, an arena or a sports event. Possibility to place an advertisement notable during grand sports events can generate a significant amount of income. Therefore, a regulation of advertising in the field of sports is important.

624. There is no special legal act specifically governing advertising related to sports. In Lithuania, a special legal act governing basic principles of advertising activities exist – the Law on Advertising of the Republic of Lithuania, 2000 ('Law on Advertising'). It must be also stressed that special cases of advertising in television are also governed by the Law on Information to the Public of the Republic of Lithuania.

625. The Law on Advertising defines advertising[210] as 'information disseminated in any form and by any means and relating to a person's commercial and economic, financial or professional activities, where it promotes the purchase of goods or use of services, including the purchase of immovable property and the takeover of property rights and obligation'.

---

208. Source is available online (accessed on 26 Jun. 2021) (http://www.wipo.int/ip-sport/en/broadcasting.html).
209. *Football Association Premier League Ltd and Others v. QC Leisure and Others* (case C-403/08) and *Karen Murphy v. Media Protection Services Ltd* (case C-429/08).
210. Official translation provided in website of the Seimas (accessed on 26 Jun. 2021) (https://e-seimas.lrs.lt/portal/legalAct/lt/TAD/dd69e1e2a58711e59010bea026bdb259?jfwid=q86m1vre1).

626. The key requirements for advertising are that advertising must be proper and accurate and clearly recognizable. Article 4 of the Law on Advertising provides general requirements for advertising. The following types of advertising are prohibited:

- which violates principles of public morality;
- which degrades human honour and dignity;
- which incites national, racial, religious, gender-related or social hatred and discrimination as well as defames or misinforms;
- which promotes coercion and aggression and gives rise to panic;
- which promotes behaviour which poses a threat to health, security and the environment;
- which abuses superstitions, people's trust and their lack of experience or knowledge;
- which makes a reference to the name and the surname of a natural person without his consent, presents his opinion, information about his private or public life and property and makes use of the natural person's image;
- which uses special subliminal means and technologies in advertising dissemination;
- which uses advertising material which has been prepared in violation of copyright to works of literature, art and science and/or related rights;
- which scorns religious symbols of the religious communities registered in Lithuania.

627. As well as this, a misleading advertising is prohibited as well. Article 5 of the Law on Advertising provides criteria to assess whether advertising should be considered as misleading. Surreptitious advertising is prohibited as well. However, a comparative advertising is allowed.

628. In accordance with Article 9 of the Law on Advertising, advertising disseminated in any form and by any means of advertising transmittal shall be prohibited in cases when one seeks to advertise:

- the activity which is prohibited by law or is unlawful;
- the goods or services, the production and/or sale/supply whereof are prohibited by law;
- the goods which have been withdrawn from civil circulation.

629. It is very important to underline subjects that *cannot* be advertised:

- In accordance with Article 17 of the Law on Control of Tobacco, Products of Tobacco and Related Products,[211] 1995, advertising of tobacco is prohibited subject to very rare exceptions.[212] Electronic cigarettes are not to be advertised as well.
- In accordance with Article 29 of the Law on Control of Alcohol,[213] 1995, advertising of alcohol is forbidden. It should also be noted that alcoholic drinks stronger than 7.5 cannot be sold *during sports* events.
- In accordance with Article 14(5) of the Law on Advertising, advertising of energy drinks or reference to drinks as sponsors is restricted to minors.
- In accordance with Article 10(9) of the Law on Gaming of the Republic of Lithuania,[214] 2001, the advertising of gaming is prohibited in the territory of the Republic of Lithuania, except where it contains only the name of a gaming company, types of gaming. Any type of information on gaming is restricted in websites dedicated to minors. It should be noted that betting falls in the scope of the definition of gaming. Thus, betting companies should be allowed to place their logos on the shirt of football or basketball teams as long as such advertising complies with the further regulation.

630. The failure to meet the above-mentioned requirements may result in sanctions applicable to the violator.

§3. Sponsorship and Merchandising

631. 'Sponsorship' is a term better known in public life than developed by the Laws of the Republic of Lithuania. The Laws of the Republic of Lithuania do not specify any particular form of sponsorship in the field of sports as well. Therefore, Lithuanian regulation does not provide any specific concept of sponsorship in sports.

632. Specific models of sponsorship in sport (which receives certain level of advertising against payment) including sponsorship of legal persons such as football or basketball club or other sponsoring of the athlete are implemented through various agreements which are analysed further.

I. Agreement of Financial Support

633. Barely all Lithuanian football and basketball clubs (as well as other clubs) operate under a legal form of association or a public institution. None of the clubs

211. Official translation provided in website of the Seimas (accessed on 26 Jun. 2021) (https://e-seimas.lrs.lt/portal/legalAct/lt/TAD/TAIS.30929?jfwid=-fxdp7906).
212. For example, certain information on tobacco products is allowed in retail sale places.
213. Official translation provided in website of the Seimas (accessed on 26 Jun. 2021) (https://e-seimas.lrs.lt/portal/legalAct/lt/TAD/47009fe079f111e4a8a7b07c53dc637c?jfwid=rivwzvpvg).
214. Official translation provided in website of the Seimas (accessed on 26 Jun. 2021) (http://www.elibrary.lt/resursai/DB/LPD/Istatymai/Istatymai/pd_39a.pdf).

are joint-stock companies. Although, it is very common that a public institution is owned by a joint-stock company or a joint-stock company holds certain part of stake of public institution. Same applies to associations – limited liability companies may be direct members of associations and thus control it. One of the reasons for this notable popularity of such legal forms of clubs is the fact that public entities and associations may receive funds from state entities and, most commonly, municipalities.

634. Another very important reason behind the popularity of associations and public institutions is that in accordance with the Law on Charity and Sponsorship of the Republic of Lithuania ('Law on Charity'),[215] only public entities and associations as well as other forms of very specific legal forms of non-profit legal persons, may receive financial support from providers of such support, or 'sponsors'. In order to do so, associations and public entities have to gain a status of 'receiver of financial support'.

635. A 'sponsorship' deal between a sponsor and a club of legal form of association or a public entity is done by concluding a *financial support agreement.* The Law on Charity and Sponsorship provides conditions for financial support agreement. As well as this, financial support agreement is subject to formal requirements of provisions of the Civil Code applicable to donation agreements.

636. In accordance with Article 2(2) of the Law on Charity and Sponsorship, a financial support is considered to be voluntary and *free* provision of objects of financial support to receivers of supports, with an exception of certain obligations of the receivers of support.

637. The main obligation of a sponsor is to provide certain object of support. In accordance with the Law on Charity and Sponsorship, such object is not only money but also any other asset including goods and services. In practice, the most common form of support is money; however sports clubs receive other types of support, including refreshment drinks, medication, services (travel organization, MRI tests, etc.).

638. The main obligation of the receiver of support is to ensure that the received support is used strictly for the fulfilment of the purposes of activities laid down in the Law on Charity and Sponsorship and in founding documents of such receiver. The sponsor may specify how the support should be used, and in such case, the receiver would have to use such support precisely in the foreseen way. For example, a sponsor may include a clause requesting a football club to divert all received financial support to the development of a youth team. The use of funds provided by

215. The term 'sponsorship' is provided by official translation by the Seimas. Online source is available (accessed on 26 Jun. 2021) (https://e-seimas.lrs.lt/portal/legalAct/lt/TAD/TAIS.281044?jfwid=rivwzvpvg).However, a term 'sponsorship' should be understood as 'financial support' as it corresponds more accurately to Lithuanian term of '*parama*'.

a sponsor is a subject of monitoring and control. The receiver of support has to submit reports to the sponsor depicting the use of received financial support. Should the receiver of support fail to use it within the set purpose a sponsor will be able to request the return of provided support.

639. The sponsors would probably not be interested in the provision of financial support under financial support agreements if there is no element of advertisement. Article 8(1) of the Law on Charity and Sponsorship provides a list of permitted obligations of the receiver of financial support towards a sponsor. One of such obligations is the obligation of a receiver of support to '*publicize information about the sponsor*'. Provisions of legal acts governing advertisement are applied *mutatis mutandis* to the events of such publication of the information about the sponsor; thus it is important to follow general requirements of the Law on Advertising.

640. Therefore, a financial support agreement which includes the obligation of the receiver of support to publicize (or more simply, to advertise) the provider of the funds can be considered of what is understood as sponsorship agreement.

641. Besides requirements set forth above, financial support agreement is also subject to provisions governing donation agreement. First of all, it should be noted that formal requirements are applicable – financial support agreement of a value exceeding EUR 1,500 must be concluded in a written form. Moreover, if a real estate is a subject of a financial support agreement or the amount of agreement exceeds EUR 14,500 then the sponsorship agreement shall have to be confirmed by the notary public. Usually, top clubs are supported with amounts exceeding far more than EUR 14,500; thus such agreement is a subject of confirmation of notary public.

642. In accordance with Article 6.467(1), a person, in gifting the property, may establish a condition for the property to be used exclusively for a definite purpose without prejudice to the rights and lawful interests of another person. In accordance with Article 6.467(2) in the event when the receiver fails to perform a condition established in the contract of gift, the donor may demand within judicial proceedings the compliance with that condition or annulment of the contract of gift and return of the property. Thus, in case a club sponsored by a club does not use the donated funds in accordance with the set forth purposes, donation (financial support) agreement may be terminated and donated amounts could be collected back from the club. What is more, failure to use financial support in accordance with assigned purposes may lead to cancellation of tax privileges and sanctions by state authorities.

643. Another particular issue related to the consideration of financial support agreement as donation agreement is that donation agreement is a 'real' agreement. Its conclusion moment corresponds to the moment of transfer of asset. Therefore, financial support agreement is considered as concluded only upon the transfer of money (or other object of donation, e.g., goods or services). On many occasions, clubs and their sponsors conclude financial support agreements which provide payment schedule, i.e., donation of funds in several instalments. From contractual law point of view, even if the agreement provides the obligation of a sponsor to donate certain amount of money on the determined dates, the club would not be in a position to request such donation if a sponsor decides not to pay a part of the amount of money[216] without specific reason. Therefore, it can be concluded that financial support agreements foreseeing payment schedules are hardly enforceable. The club would be only able to request damages for a breached promise. Therefore, such regulation increases the potential financial fragility of clubs.

However, it should be noted that the issue of enforceability of the financial support agreement is now a matter of the court case presented by Lithuanian top tennis player Ričardas Berankis who argues that the decision of this sponsor to suspend payments under financial support agreement is illegal.[217] The Lithuanian Court of Appeals rendered final ruling in favour of the athlete and provided important considerations as to sports sponsorship contracts.[218] The defendant (company which undertook to provide sponsorship) argued that legal relationship of donation was established between the parties. Meanwhile the athlete maintained that the parties were bound by 'commercial sport sponsorship' legal relationship which was not directly governed by Lithuanian law. The Court of Appeals analysed various international sources (including Code of sponsorship of the International Chambers of Commerce, papers of scholars) and came to the conclusion that sports sponsorship contract is a transaction between a sponsor and a sponsored party (athlete, sports team, organization, etc.) under which the sponsor provides financial or other support to the sponsored party for its sporting activities and specific transferable rights. The support provided by the sponsor can be broadly understood and interpreted not only as a sponsor fee, but also as other benefits to the sponsored party that have value (e.g., products, services). According to the court, the features of the sports sponsorship agreement have been clearly distinguished from the donation (support) legal relationship. Accordingly, the court upheld position of the athlete as to qualification of the agreement and ordered payment of amounts stipulated in the sponsorship agreement. This case should be considered as a cornerstone in legal understanding of sport sponsorship in Lithuania. The ruling changed the old perception of relation between athlete and sponsor whereby the sponsor could relatively easily seize payments of stipulated amounts due to further lack of will to 'donate' certain amounts. The ruling brings commercial aspect and from now on sponsorship agreement may be viewed as a mutual consensual contract whereby reluctancy of the sponsor to actually provide amounts as per the agreement will no longer be tolerated. However, the content of the contract remains paramount.

216. 28 Dec. 2011 Ruling of the Supreme Court in Civil Case No. 3K-3-549/2011.
217. Online source is available (accessed on 26 Jun. 2021) (https://www.delfi.lt/sportas/tenisas/berankis-padave-i-teisma-pazadu-neivykdziusius-remejus.d?id=80771561).
218. 29 Oct. 2020 ruling of Lithuanian Court of Appeals in Civil Case No. e2A-689-881/2020/.

II. Use of Image of an Athlete

644. One of the alternative sources of an athlete's income is promotional activity. World-famous football players like Lionel Messi or Cristiano Ronaldo in fact make more money from the advertising of sponsor products and services than from their play of football.[219] Athletes are very good advertising materials as they are admired and followed by many people. Athletes in Lithuania are targeted by various companies as potential advertising partners as well.

645. Different from financial support agreements between clubs and sponsors, the Laws of Lithuania do not foresee any specific type of contract in the case of player – sponsor relationship. Instead, such contract depending on the content and rights and obligations of the parties may include elements of various contracts governed by the Civil Code: for example, a service agreement. Thus, in order to understand the nature of such possible contract, it is necessary to distinguish what is required to be performed by the athlete and the sponsor in specific relationship.

646. Probably the most important element of such contract would be a provision of right to use the image of a player of the club. It is very unlikely that without possibility to promote an image of a player next to the product or the service of the sponsor such sponsor would be interested in paying a player an agreed amount. In order to gain such right, a sponsor and a player must agree upon the use of the image. The issue of a use of an image of an athlete is governed by general provisions of the Civil Code and, as well as this, by specific provisions of the Law on Advertising.

647. In accordance with the Law on Advertising (Article 4(1)(7)), any type of advertising is forbidden if a name and a surname of a natural person, his opinion, information on his private and social life, wealth, his image are used *without the consent* of such natural person. A single count of a violation of said provision may result in serious financial sanctions. Illegal use of an athlete's image could also result in civil action and potential reward of damages. Thus, it is necessary to obtain consent from a natural person, including an athlete.

648. A right to a name and an image is considered to be part of fundamental right of a natural person to privacy. Such rights are protected by Article 2.21 and 2.22 of the Civil Code. Article 2.22 of the Civil Code states that a picture, portrait or any other image of a natural person can be reproduced, sold, exhibited, printed subject to a consent of such person. A natural person may be photographed if his or her consent is present as well (with an exception to the cases whereby taking photography is related to the social activity of a person, his office or following a request of law enforcement institution or a photography is taken in a public space). In any case, a commercial use of photography or other means of image of a natural person

---

219. Online source is available (accessed on 26 Jun. 2021) (https://www.forbes.com/sites/christinasettimi/2017/05/26/the-worlds-highest-paid-soccer-players-2017-cristiano-ronaldo-lionel-messi-lead-the-list/#15fb256210e7).

requires consent from a person. A natural person whose right to an image is violated has a right to apply the court request to seize illegal action and to compensate monetary and non-monetary damages.

649. Issues of the use of an image for commercial purposes were analysed by courts as well. First of all, a general agreement of an athlete to associate his image with a specific company and its service or product should be mentioned. In accordance with the jurisprudence of the Supreme Court,[220] a right to waive a part of his privacy is provided to the holder of such right, i.e., the natural person. Thus, before agreeing he or she must decide if it is correct for such person to participate in commercial activity and if it is in general acceptable for such person to advertise certain person, good or service. Moreover, a person is required to consider other circumstances which are individually important to such person and to choose conditions for participation in such activity. Also, it should be mentioned that stricter standards of care are applicable to persons who may have certain experience in such commercial activity (e.g., models). A popular professional athlete subject to his past experience may be considered as a person holding specific experience; thus he may be expected to act with a higher degree of care than a regular person.

650. Thus, when an athlete and an organization is about to agree on the use of an image of such athlete, it is very important to draft certain aspects with due care. Even though in accordance with the jurisprudence of the Supreme Court, consent may be given orally or by concerted action,[221] it is advisable to draft it in written form. Consent of the use of an image includes several important elements:

- The parties should agree upon the scope and methods the image can be used. Currently there are many different ways an image can be used and exposed: photography, video material, GIF, cartoon, audio of a voice of a person, a reproduction of photography, a painting, etc. With the constant improvement in technology, it may be difficult for parties to draft an excessive list of means an image can be used. Thus, the parties should take it into consideration.
- It is important to define the exact brand, trademark, product or service which would be advertised by using an image of the player. From an athlete's point of view, it is important to understand precisely what services and products are going to be advertised. The vacuum of regulation or broad definition of products and services to be advertised may lead to the situation when the athlete's image is used to promote items the athlete is not willing to advertise at all.
- Terms and conditions for payment of remuneration have to be agreed as well.
- It is very important to agree upon the term of use of an image. In accordance with the jurisprudence of the Supreme Court,[222] it is possible for parties to agree that the image would be used without any restrictions in terms of time. It also should be noted that the absence of the clause governing the term of use of an image may be interpreted in the way that such right is provided without any restrictions in

220. 13 Feb. 2012 ruling of the Supreme Court in Civil Case No. 3K-3-22/2012.
221. *Ibid.*
222. *Ibid.*

terms of time. In case a person decides to use his image for a commercial purpose, he or she must consider the term of such use since termless use of an image for commercial purposes may affect the right of privacy. However, in accordance with the Supreme Court,[223] even in cases whereby a natural person agrees that his or her image would be used for commercial purposes without a clause on the term it is not reasonable to conclude that such consent of a natural person is irrevocable in every case. When a right to privacy of a natural person collides with a right of entity to satisfy its economic interest by using an image of a natural person, a right to privacy prevails. Thus, it is important for both parties to clearly agree upon the precise duration for the use of an image

III. Merchandising: Licence Agreement

651. A term of merchandising is not defined by the Laws of the Republic of Lithuania. However, understanding of merchandising is related to the use of the trademark of another entity for commercial purposes. In order to gain such right, a licence agreement has to be made. A simple example in sports would be the permission of a sports club (football or basketball or other) to use its trademark and name on certain products (apparels, toys, food, etc.) made by another company.

652. In accordance with Article 14(2) of the Law on Trademarks of the Republic of Lithuania, 2001 ('Law on Trademarks'), the proprietor of a registered mark shall have an exclusive right to prevent all third persons *not having his consent* from using in the course of trade any sign:

– which is identical with the registered mark in relation to goods and/or services which are identical with those for which the mark is registered;
– where, because of its identity with, or similarity to, the registered trademark for identical or similar goods and/or services, there exists a likelihood of confusion on the part of the public, which includes the likelihood of association with the registered trademark;
– which is identical with, or similar to, the trademark in relation to goods or services which are not similar to those for which the trademark is registered, where the latter has a reputation in the Republic of Lithuania and where use of that sign without due cause takes unfair advantage of, or is detrimental to, the distinctive character or the repute of the trademark.

653. In accordance with Article 38(3) of the Law on Trademarks, the proprietor of the mark may prohibit the:

– affixing of the sign to goods or the packaging thereof;
– offering the goods or putting them on the market or stocking, renting, lending or in any other form disposing of them for these purposes under that sign, or offering or supplying services thereunder;

---

223. *Ibid.*

– importing or exporting goods under that sign;
– using the sign-on business papers and in advertising;
– manufacturing the sign or keeping specimens thereof with the intention of performing any of the actions specified above.

654. In accordance with Article 27(1) of the Law on Trademarks, the proprietor of a mark may issue to a third party a voluntary *exclusive or non-exclusive* licence for marking some or all goods and/or services for which it is registered and for the entire or part of the Republic of Lithuania. In accordance with Article 27(2) of the Law on Trademarks of the Republic of Lithuania, licensing contract data shall be recorded in the Register of Trade Marks of the Republic of Lithuania on request of the parties to the contract.

655. A sublicensing agreement may also be concluded in accordance with the requirements of Article 27(9) of the Law on Trademarks of the Republic of Lithuania.

656. An issue related to trademarks and alleged unfair competition recently has sparked a conflict between two football clubs from the Lithuanian top-tier league. One of the clubs is the famous FK Žalgiris. Another club was named originally named Spyris but the club was indirectly acquired by the notorious basketball club BC Žalgiris which decided to provide the same name for the acquired football club. Both clubs attempted to prevent each other from using trademark 'Žalgiris' in football activity; however both claims were rejected.[224]

§4. Gaming, Gambling and Betting

657. There are two different legal acts governing betting, gaming and lotteries. First, of all, the Law on Gaming of the Republic of Lithuania, 2001 ('Law on Gaming') regulates conditions for organizing gaming. The second act, the Law on Lotteries of the Republic of Lithuania, 2003 ('Law on Lotteries') governs specifically conditions and terms of lottery organizing in Lithuania.

I. Gaming and Betting

658. The Law on Gaming establishes conditions and procedures for the operation of gaming in the Republic of Lithuania. It is important to understand what does fall into the scope of the term 'gaming'.

659. Gaming is defined by law as the playing of a game or mutual betting in accordance with the established regulations where the participants seek to win

224. Source available online (accessed on 26 Jun. 2021) (https://www.15min.lt/sportas/naujiena/futbolas/teismo-verdiktas-klubu-gince-zalgiriu-gali-buti-daug-24-918500).

money by voluntarily risking a stake and where wins or loses depend on chance, an occurrence of any event or the outcome of a sporting event.[225]

660. In accordance with the Law on Gaming, the following types of games are allowed.

Machine gaming:

(a) Games by gaming machines of category A are played when tokens are inserted into the gaming machine and the winnings are paid out in tokens by the machine. The result of the game and the amount of winnings are determined by the gaming machine.
(b) Games by gaming machines of category B are played when coins and (or) tokens are inserted into a gaming machine and the winnings are paid out in money or tokens. The result of the game and the amount of winnings are determined by the gaming machine.

Bingo is a game which is played with cards bearing numbers and a scoreboard; the amount of winnings depends on the total amount of stakes and the combination of numbers selected at random. The total bingo winnings fund shall comprise at least 50% of the total amount of stakes.

Table games:

(a) Roulette is a game which is played by guessing in which slot a ball dropped on a spinning wheel will stop; the amount of winnings depends on the total amount of stakes and the winning ratio fixed in advance.
(b) Card or dice game is played when the winner and the amount of winnings is determined on the basis of symbols of the cards dealt or the score of dice.

661. Totalizator is a game which is played by guessing the result of *a sporting event* where the amount of winnings depends on the ratio between the bet size fixed in advance by totalizator operators and the winnings fund. The total totalizator winnings fund shall comprise at least 50% of the total amount of the bets made.

662. Betting means mutual betting on the outcome of an event based on guessing where the amount of winnings depends on the amount of the bet made and the betting ratio fixed in advance by the betting intermediary.

663. Remote gaming – is a game where bets of punters are accepted and prizes are paid by use of means of remote communication. Internet games are considered to be remote gaming.

225. Article 2 of the Law on Gaming.

664. Sport betting has no specific regulation and it falls within the scope of definition of gaming by the Law on Gaming.

665. In order to organize one of the above-mentioned games, an organizer must obtain a licence for each type of game. It is possible for one organizer to obtain licence to organize more than one or even all of the mentioned games. Licence is issued by the Gaming Control Authority in accordance with the licensing rules adopted by the Government.

666. A public limited company incorporated under the Laws of the Republic of Lithuania or a subsidiary of foreign company may be an organizer of games. As mentioned, a licence must be obtained. As well as this, an organizer must issue a gaming regulation which is subject to the confirmation of the Gaming Control Authority. The Law on Gaming provides requirements for minimal authorized capital of organizers of the games, and it varies from EUR 144,000 (horse racing totalizator) through EUR 289,000 (betting company) to EUR 1,158,000 (casino).

667. Companies operating games in gaming machine halls, bingo, table games, totalizator and betting shall not have the right to engage in other economic and commercial activities, except for the rent of premises at which the company operates gaming for economic and commercial activities (Article 14 of the Law on Gaming).

668. The Law on Gaming provides strict restrictions on the organization of gaming. First of all, Article 10(2) provides prohibition to organize games in terms of place (e.g., schools, universities and healthcare institutions), restrictions on advertising, restrictions on the persons who are able to participate in gaming (in terms of age or status)[226] and other requirements.

669. Important requirements are set forth in Article 10^1–10^3 of the Law on Gaming. Article 10^1 of the Law on Gaming provides requirement to place information on the potential harm of gaming in the gaming activity areas. Article 10^2 of the Law on Gaming stipulates very important restriction: persons who can directly (such persons participate directly) or indirectly (family members of such persons participate) influence the result or event of a sports competition are forbidden to take part in betting for such sports competitions. As well as this, family members of such athletes are also forbidden to take part in betting. The betting companies must not accept bets from such persons and all bets made against such provision shall have to be annulled. As well as this, betting on events which contradict public order is also forbidden.

670. Articles 15–17 of the Law on Gaming provide requirements for premises and equipment of gaming. Article 18 of Law on Gaming sets up requirements for

226. For example, a person who submitted a request not to allow him to enter a casino or a gaming house may not be allowed.

the gaming regulations. As mentioned, gaming regulations is a key document and must be confirmed by the Gaming Control Authority. Gaming regulations establish order and rules of certain game.

671. Important part of the Law on Gaming is regulation of remote gaming. Remote gaming services are services which include placing of an amount of money in betting via remote means of communication in accordance with the remote gaming agreement. A company which is willing to organize an online remote game has to obtain a licence to organize a certain game (e.g., table game or totalizator) and a specific licence to organize such game remotely.

672. In accordance with Article 8^1 of the Law on Gaming, a company can only be permitted to organize a remote game if such company has already opened not less than one casino, or not less than five horse totalizator spots, or not less than ten gaming machine halls, or not less than twenty betting points or gaming spots. If an organizer intends to organize all of the allowed games online, a minimum authorized capital of EUR 1,158,000 shall have to be formed.

673. Article 20^1–20^3 of the Law on Gaming provide specific requirements for organization of remote games. Such requirements include the obligation to control the data of an online punter in order to comply with age restrictions. Requirements and essential conditions of the remote gaming agreements are provided as well. An ordinary agreement (written agreement) may be concluded as well as the electronic one with a punter, natural person and gaming company. Only subject to a valid agreement a punter can participate in remote gaming. Article 20^4 of the Law on Gaming establishes requirements for technical aspects of remote gaming. The main requirement of the equipment is the ability to collect and store required data. As well as this, certain measures to protect punter's rights (such as setting up a maximum amount which can be bet) are established as well.

674. Article 20^7 of the Law on Gaming establishes measures for the Gaming Control Authority to tackle illegal remote gaming. If an event of illegal remote gaming in Lithuania is established the Gaming Control Authority has a right to request credit institutions to withhold payments and financial operations related to illegal gaming, issue orders to information hosting service provider and/or network service provider to remove information which is stored in order to conduct illegal remote gaming or to remove possibility to reach such information. However, such actions are only possible subject to permission issued by Vilnius District Administrative Court.

675. The Gaming Control Authority supervises how the organizers comply with the Law on Gaming. In accordance with Article 28 of the Law on Gaming, the Gaming Control Authority has important duties and a number of specific remedies to implement such duties (including collecting information, control activities, issue certain order, etc.).

676. It is observed that during recent years, an activity which can be defined as 'poker staking' became apparent in Lithuania. A poker staking contract, in practice, is an agreement between a poker player and stake provider whereby the poker player undertakes to play in professional poker tournaments (usually, remote poker tournaments available on famous remote gambling websites) and the stake provider allocates the money needed to access such tournaments. According to such contracts, typically, in case of a winning of a monetary prize in a tournament, such moneys are shared between the poker player and the stake provider. Typically, in the event of lack of success in a tournament, the moneys provided to the poker player are considered to be lost and the poker player is not required to refund it to the stake provider.

677. However, poker staking practice in Lithuania included a contractual obligation of the poker player to return moneys he or she had received from the stake provider in case the poker player is not successful in the tournaments. Lithuanian courts (including the Supreme Court) have already dealt with several cases related to poker staking contracts, and on number of occasions declared such contracts null and void. Mainly, such contracts were declared null and void due to the fact that said contracts are aimed at objectives which are not compatible with the goals of state policy in the field of gambling. According to the Supreme Court,[227] such agreements encourage persons to take part in gambling which is against the aim of the state to preserve the financial status, health and life of a person. In accordance with the Supreme Court, such contracts are against public policy and thus must be declared null and void as per Article 1.81 of the Civil Code. Besides, in the other case, the Supreme Court[228] considered the poker staking contract null and void, *inter alia,* due to the reason that the contracts contained obligation of a poker player to play in online poker tournaments organized by service providers which are considered illegal in Lithuania. Hence, poker staking is an activity which is, if *per se,* not illegal but very complicated to carry out in Lithuania.

II. Lottery

678. Lottery business is an activity important to sports in Lithuania. Income received from lottery is a source of funding of sports. In accordance with the Law on Sport, 10% of the collected lottery tax is reserved for the financing of sport. Moreover, the activities of the LTOK are financed by the private limited liability company UAB 'Olifėja' partially owned by the LTOK (the main and only activity of the said company is organizing lotteries). Finally, 8% of income has to be provided for financial support in accordance with the Law on Financial Support and Charity. Thus, sport clubs may benefit from such rule as well.

679. Lottery is defined by law as a game of tickets purchased for monetary and/or material winnings and/or gratuitous services incidental to ticket data.

227. 9 Mar. 2022 ruling of the Supreme Court in Civil Case No e3K-3-46-469/2022.
228. 4 Nov. 2021 ruling of the Supreme Court in Civil Case No e3K-3-252-969/2021.

680. The Law on Lotteries[229] provide the following types of lotteries according to their nature:

- circulation lottery: lottery in which a number and/or other signs are selected on the lottery ticket or a lottery ticket with pre-printed numbers and/or other signs is selected and the winning and its size is determined by the lottery ticket price and coincides with the player's chosen or pre-printed the number of drops and/or other signs;
- instant lottery: a lottery, the information about the winnings and their amount is indicated on the lottery tickets before they are sold, and the player finds out about the winnings as soon as he buys the lottery ticket and checks it in accordance with the lottery rules;
- sports lottery: the lottery, the winning and its size of which is determined by the number of correctly selected numbers and/or other tokens in the lottery ticket, depending on the end of the sports competition and indicating their result.

681. The lotteries are also divided in accordance with the manner of distributing lottery tickets, data processing and paying out prizes (remote communication lotteries, offline lotteries, telephone lotteries, online lotteries).

682. As well as this, 'small lottery' and 'grand lottery' are distinguished depending on the nominal amount of edition of lottery tickets. If the amount is not higher than EUR 30,000, the lottery shall be considered small. In order to obtain licence to run such lottery, an organizer (a legal person incorporated in Lithuania or a subsidiary of a foreign legal person acting in Lithuania) must apply the municipality. In order to run a grand lottery, a licence must be granted from the Gaming Control Authority.

683. Organizers of the lottery may not engage in activities other than the organization of lottery. Strict reputation requirements are applied to the members of governing bodies of an organizer company. Moreover, a requirement of minimum authorized capital is set by the law: minimum amount of authorized capital of an organizer of a small lottery is EUR 14,000; meanwhile, minimum amount of authorized capital of grand lottery is EUR 144,000.

684. Activities of organizers are supervised and controlled by municipalities (small lottery) and Gaming Control Authority (grand lottery). They may request for any type of information from organizers, to examine if the organizers comply with the law, assess financial activities of the organizer, invoke sanctions (such as withdrawal of licence), etc.

---

229. Official translation provided in website of the Seimas (accessed on 26 Jun. 2021) (https://e-seimas.lrs.lt/portal/legalActPrint/lt?jfwid=rivwzvpvg&documentId=TAIS.254080&category=TAD).

§5. Club Ownership and Competition

685. Interaction between the sports law in competition law is best seen by the help of development of the EU law. Economic activities related to sports fall within the scope of the EU law. In terms of EU competition law, in accordance with the EU Commission,[230] the following fields should be underlined:

- Joint sale of sport media rights.
- Ticket sales arrangements.
- Regulatory/organizational issues. Following highly discussed Meca-Medina decision,[231] the sporting rules, such as doping regulations, are subject to EU competition law.

686. Lithuanian antitrust regulation is embodied in the Law on Competition of the Republic of Lithuania. Law on Competition of the Republic of Lithuania governs the following fields:

- prohibition of abuse of dominance;
- prohibition of agreements restricting competition;
- control of concentrations;
- unfair competition.

687. In Lithuanian practice sports matters so far have avoided the application of legal provisions related to the above-mentioned fields of regulations of the Law on Competition of the Republic of Lithuania. However, disputes between clubs arise out of Article 15(1) of the Law on Competition of the Republic of Lithuania,[232] undertakings shall be prohibited from performing any actions contrary to fair business practices and good usages if such actions may be detrimental to the competitive potential of another undertaking, including unauthorized use of a reference mark identical or similar to the name, registered trademark or unregistered well known trademark or any other reference mark having a distinguishing feature of another undertaking, if this causes or is likely to cause confusion with that undertaking or its activity. As mentioned in §3,C of Part IV, a dispute related to the allegedly illegal use of the trademark of Žalgiris arose between the two clubs. However, it is one of the rare examples when public regulation of competition manifests in matters related to sport.

Sports clubs in Lithuania are highly dependent on financing from state or municipality authorities. However, until now, state and municipality funding of sports clubs has escaped the control of competition authorities. However, latest plans of Vilnius municipality to grant support for Vilnius-based professional sports clubs, FK Žalgiris and BC 'Lietuvos Rytas', EUR 500,000 each was met by a statement

230. Online source is available (accessed on 26 Jun. 2021) (http://ec.europa.eu/competition/sectors/sports/overview_en.html).
231. Case T-313/02 *David Meca-Medina and Igor Majcen v. Commission* [2004] ECR II-3291 and Case C-519/04 *David Meca-Medina and Igor Majcen v. Commission* [2006] ECR I-6991.
232. Official translation provided in website of the Seimas (accessed on 26 Jun. 2021) (https://e-seimas.lrs.lt/portal/legalAct/lt/TAD/49e68d00103711e5b0d3e1beb7dd5516?jfwid=q8i88mh0m).

of the Competition Council of the Republic of Lithuania stating that such potential support would be illegal subject to the absence of consultation with the European Commission. Thus, it is very likely that public funding of sports club will face more intense control and scrutiny from institutions ensuring fair competition.

Chapter 3. Private Regulations

§1. TV Broadcasting and Media Rights

688. A private entity which sets up an event which can be later broadcasted has a right to issue permission for its broadcast as well as exercise related media rights such as sell advertising space for sponsors. Same applies to the sports organization, clubs or federations. Since the clubs are members of federations or other organizations of clubs, such as leagues, the issue of exploit of broadcasting and media rights is often a matter of regulations of federations or leagues.

689. UEFA organizes important continental club competitions, such as the UEFA Champions' League or the UEFA Europa League, as well as national team competition. The UEFA Champions' League 2021/2022 Regulations define media rights as 'the right to create, distribute and transmit on a linear and/or on-demand basis for reception on a live and/or delayed basis anywhere in the world by any and all means and in any and all media, whether now known or devised in the future (including all forms of television, radio, mobile, wireless and internet distribution), digital, audiovisual, visual and/or audio coverage of the competition and all associated and/or related rights, including fixed media, download and interactive rights'.

690. In accordance with Article 65.02 of the UEFA Champions' League Regulations all media rights in and to the competition, excluding any qualifying phase matches, are exploited by the UEFA. UEFA has the exclusive right to exploit all other commercial rights and to appoint partners for the competition. Any such partners appointed by the UEFA (and any other third party designated by the UEFA) may have the exclusive right to exploit certain commercial rights (including in respect of their products and/or services) in and to the competition and matches. However, the clubs are allowed to advertise on players' kits. In accordance with Article 66.01 of the UEFA Champions' League Regulations, member associations and their affiliated organizations and/or clubs are authorized to exploit the commercial rights of the *home qualifying phase matches* which take place under their respective auspices. Thus, the UEFA owns all media and broadcasting of the tournament except the qualifying round games.

691. UEFA distributes the income from exploitation of broadcast and media rights through its sophisticated distribution scheme. The amounts clubs receive from the UEFA Champions' League main tournament media rights are significant. For example, Real Madrid and Manchester City each received over EUR 80 million.[233] None of the Lithuanian football clubs has ever got to the Group Stage of the UEFA Champions' League thus they do not participate in the distribution scheme. However, Lithuanian clubs participating in UEFA competitions receive participation bonuses and may also add in some income from the exploitation of media rights in the qualifying phase as it is allowed by the UEFA regulations. Success of the latter

233. Source is available online (accessed on 26 Jun. 2021) (http://www.uefa.com//MultimediaFiles/Download/competitions/General/02/41/82/55/2418255_DOWNLOAD.pdf).

hugely depends on the opponent club. If an opponent is from a football prone country with important TV attendance considerably large amount of income may be made.

692. Generally, broadcast and media rights and distribution of income for the clubs is one the most important and often discussed issues. For example, English Premier League champions 2016/2017 Chelsea collected more than GBP 150 million in a single season, i.e., almost twice the amount of a Champions' League winner. However, football in Lithuania is lacking such importance. Due to lack of general attendance, Lithuanian clubs are very rarely rewarded for a right to broadcast their competitions.

693. In accordance with the LFF Statutes, LFF is a rightful owner of all organized competitions and other events without any restrictions of the content or venue. LFF owns all financial rights, audiovisual and radio recording, reproduction and broadcasting rights, multimedia rights, marketing and promotional rights, trademark rights and other rights to be granted by the Law on Copyright and Related Rights of the Republic of Lithuania, the Law on Trademarks and other legislation,[234] The Executive Committee of the LFF decides on the use of said rights and only the Executive Committee decides whether these rights can be used unilaterally or jointly with a third party, or only by a third party. Thus, the LFF is sole holder of the all broadcast and media rights of the tournaments organized by the LFF or by other persons authorized by the LFF, including '*A Lyga*' tournament. LFF can authorize certain persons to exploit broadcasting and media rights. For example, the LFF can authorize the Lithuanian Football Club Association to exploit the rights related to '*A Lyga*' in accordance with an agreement.

694. In accordance with the LFF Competition Regulations, each club must reserve certain space for LFF advertising. The broadcasting and media rights may be assigned to other organizations, such as Lithuanian Football Club Association. No more matters are governed by the LFF Regulations.

695. It should be noticed that advertising is not comprehensively governed by the regulations of the national sports federations. For example, the LFF Competition Regulations state that the LFF has a right to use at least ten advertising boards placed on the perimeter of the pitch. The LFF does not govern this issue any further. It should be noted that in accordance with the agreement of the LFF and the Lithuanian Football Club Association advertising policies may be governed further. For example, the UEFA Champions' League Regulations and related rules[235] govern such area to much more precise detail. However, in accordance with regulations of basketball bodies, advertising matters are assigned to the leagues. The LKL Competition Regulations provide much more extensive regulation on advertising and

234. Article 74 of the LFF Statutes.
235. Such as the UEFA Kit Regulations, edition 2012.

commercial matters than the one in football. The LKL Competition Rules[236] govern various aspects of the commercial matters in the top basketball club competition in Lithuania:

- First of all, the rules govern, *inter alia*, the advertising on basketball kits. In general, the advertising area is not limited as far as the numbers and the player's name can be seen (Article 17).
- Article 23 of the rules provides a ground for so-called commercial time-outs. In case a match is broadcasted by an official broadcaster of the league, a certain number of time-outs are dedicated for commercial purposes (in general for a match to be stopped in order to provide a time frame to broadcast commercials). Such time-outs are not taken by one of the teams but are announced by the match secretary when the ball is not in play.
- Rules introduce certain requirements for technical equipment, such as LED advertising boards, relates advertising to the equipment (e.g., advertising on backboard is forbidden).
- Article 45.3 of the rules provides a right of the LKL to use names and trademarks of all clubs for self-advertising activities. As well as this, the LKL has a right to use images of all players of the clubs for promotion and commercial activities. However, the clubs are also granted a right to use the name and the brand of the LKL.
- Members of the teams have to participate in commercial activities of the league such as playing in video commercials (Article 42.4), participating in commercial events.
- In case a match is broadcasted by an official broadcaster of the league, each club receives certain amount of time (forty seconds each) to be filled by commercials of clubs' sponsors during pauses of the broadcasts (e.g., a time-out, etc.).
- Article 45 of the rules provides a very extensive list of requirements for advertising. It provides requirements for advertising on the playing court, basketball equipment, provides the status of what is called 'official league basketball', use of commercial space on the LED boards for LKL sponsors, use of clubs' and LKL trademarks for merchandising, etc.

696. Failure of basketball clubs and other participants to comply with the said regulations may result in financial sanctions applied by the LKL. Domestic basketball competitions gather much more TV audience than football; therefore the commercial aspect of competition becomes more relevant, and thus it is governed with more precision.

§2. Club Ownership Rules and Fair Competition

697. Regulations of sports federations aim to ensure fair competition among the clubs. The example would be the famous UEFA rule forbidding multi-owned clubs

236. The rules governing season 2020/2021 are quoted.

to participate in single competitions. Such rule is stipulated in Article 5.01 of the UEFA Champions' League 2020/2021 Regulations:

> To ensure the integrity of the UEFA club competitions, the following criteria apply:
>
> a) no club participating in a UEFA club competition may, either directly or indirectly:
>   i) hold or deal in the securities or shares of any other club participating in a UEFA club competition;
>   ii) be a member of any other club participating in a UEFA club competition;
>   iii) be involved in any capacity whatsoever in the management, administration and/or sporting performance of any other club participating in a UEFA club competition, or;
>   iv) have any power whatsoever in the management, administration and/or sporting performance of any other club participating in a UEFA club competition;
>
> b) no one may simultaneously be involved, either directly or indirectly, in any capacity whatsoever in the management, administration and/or sporting performance of more than one club participating in a UEFA club competition;
>
> c) no individual or legal entity may have control or influence over more than one club participating in a UEFA club competition, such control or influence being defined in this context as:
>   i) holding a majority of the shareholders' voting rights;
>   ii) having the right to appoint or remove a majority of the members of the administrative, management or supervisory body of the club;
>   iii) being a shareholder and alone controlling a majority of the shareholders' voting rights pursuant to an agreement entered into with other shareholders of the club; or;
>   iv) being able to exercise by any means a decisive influence in the decision making of the club.

698. Said rule was subject to investigation of CAS[237] which stated that: 'if clubs with the same owner can take part in the same competitions, whether national or international, doubts may arise as to whether the outcome is really undecided in advance. The challenged UEFA Rule is therefore an essential feature for the organization of a professional football competition and is not more extensive than necessary to serve the fundamental goal of preventing conflicts of interest which would be publicly perceived as affecting the authenticity, and then the uncertainty, of results in UEFA competitions'.

237. 20 Aug. 1999 CAS award in Case No. CAS 98/200 AEK Athens and SK Slavia Prague/Union of European Football Associations (UEFA).

699. The LFF Regulations, as well as the UEFA regulations, provide restrictions of a situation whereby a single person (legal or natural) owns or controls more than one football club participating in the same competition. Article 34 of the LFF Competition Regulations, edition 2021 provides that none of the clubs participating in certain competitions cannot directly and indirectly own shares of other clubs participating in the same competitions, as well to take part in governing and administration of such club or to have any related rights. No one can take part in governance, administration and sports activity in more than one club. No legal or natural person is allowed to control or influence more than one club participating in certain competition, including the decision-making right. Article 15 of the LFF Competition Regulations, edition 2021 provides that only one team of a club may participate in the same competition.[238]

700. The LKL Competition Regulations provide a very similar approach. In accordance with Article 3.2 of the LKL Competitions Regulations, clubs (legal persons) participating in LKL competitions cannot be holders of shares or stakes of any other LKL clubs and cannot take part in the management of such club by any means. Natural persons who control LKL clubs, shareholders or stakeholders of clubs, members of governing bodies of the clubs, employees of clubs in the same period cannot be controllers, shareholders or stakeholders of clubs, members of governing bodies of the clubs, employees of any other LKL clubs. The restriction of an employee of one club to work in other clubs should be especially noticed.

---

238. The clubs may field their reserve teams in lower leagues though.

Part V. COVID-19 and Sport

Chapter 1. General Remarks

701. At the time of writing (June 2021), COVID-19 was playing a paramount role in the daily life of the whole world. The outbreak of COVID-19 caused enormous social and economic effects, not to mention its direct impact on the health and life of people. Needless to say, the sport was affected significantly.

702. COVID-19 pandemic hit Lithuania at the beginning of March 2020. Sports organizations of Lithuania had reacted to increasing confusion even before official state measures were taken.

703. Following reports of positive COVID-19 cases in Lithuania, on 12 March 2020, the LFF issued a statement informing that all football competitions, including top-tier 'A Lyga' competition, were suspended due to the COVID-19 outbreak a few weeks before the start of the games (Lithuanian football season follows spring–autumn system and usually starts on February or March).

704. On the same day, i.e., on 12 March 2020, the LKL (top-tier men's basketball league) took an even more drastic step and decided to terminate the 2019/2020 basketball season due to COVID-19 outbreak. The teams were awarded final places in the league according to the regular-season league table at the time. No games, including play-off games, took place following the decision of 12 March 2020. EuroLeague also cancelled its season. Generally speaking, basketball season was terminated before the most entertaining and important phase thereof, the play-offs. It is evident that such chain of events had its toll on financial situation of leagues, clubs and players.

705. On 14 March 2020, the Government adopted Decision No. 207 'On the announcement of quarantine in the territory of the Republic of Lithuania'. During the period of quarantine, Decision No. 207 served as the main legal instrument to control the scope of quarantine and restrictions thereof.

706. In accordance with Article 3.2.2 and 3.2.3 of the very first edition of Decision No. 207, all public indoor and outdoor events, including sports events (training, practices, matches, competition, etc.), were strictly prohibited as of 14 March 2020. Pursuant to Article 3.4 of Decision No. 207, provisions of non-emergency health services were also prohibited. Following the adoption of mentioned provisions, both professional and amateur sporting activities were suspended.

707. Depending on the intensity of pandemics, Decision No. 207 was subject to regular amendments. During, so-called, the first wave of the COVID-19 which lasted from March 2020 to June 2020, twenty-five editions of Decision No. 207 were adopted. Provisions on activities of sports and restrictions thereof were constantly amended as well.

708. As the first COVID-19 wave dropped, initial strict measures were gradually relieved and sporting activities slowly came back to life. Professional athletes and teams were allowed to conduct training. Amateurs were also allowed to conduct exercises subject to certain conditions.

709. As of 31 May 2020 'A Lyga' was allowed to continue. A limited number of spectators were permitted to attend the matches in the stadiums. Qualification rounds to UEFA competitions involving Lithuanian clubs also did take place in the summer of 2020 without any major health or safety concerns.

710. The 2020/2021 basketball season started without any major disruptions and a limited number of spectators were allowed to attend games indoors.

711. However, a very strong second wave of COVID-19 hit the country again in autumn 2020 which resulted in the reintroduction of quarantine and another major lockdown.

712. On 4 November 2020, the Government adopted Decision No. 1226 'On the announcement of quarantine in the territory of the Republic of Lithuania'. Pursuant to Decision No. 1226, high-skill sports exercises, individual (per visitor) physical activity sessions provided by a physical activity or sports specialist, instructor or physical activity or sports specialist service provider were allowed.

713. Despite the reintroduction of the quarantine state, professional sport competitions and matches took place without spectators subject to strict conditions. As in the case of Decision No. 207, Decision No. 1226 was and still is subject to regular amendments and updates depending on the level of the pandemic situation.

714. Vaccination management in Lithuania throughout 2021 was relatively successful which allowed relieving restrictions as to sports as well.

715. Currently, pursuant to Government Decision No. 1226, an unlimited number of people can attend events organized in open air (subject to certain restrictions), including sporting events. Up to two thousand spectators are allowed to attend indoor events, including a sporting event. A special treatment was applied to

FIBA Olympic Qualifying Tournament which took place in Kaunas, Lithuania, in July 2021. Spectators were able to fill up to 75% of the arena capacity. The tournament took place in the Žalgiris Arena, thus more than eleven-thousand fans attended final matches

716. It is difficult to predict the further development of COVID-19 and how it will affect sport. However, the impact of COVID-19 on various aspects of sport was paramount. Further, it shall be elaborated on the impact of COVID-19 to sport in Lithuania and state remedies aimed to help sport.

Chapter 2. State Remedies During COVID-19

717. There are no official statistics on economic impact of COVID-19 as to sport in Lithuania and analysis thereof. However, considering suspension of competition (football), postponement of Olympic Games or total termination of the season (basketball), it is very unlikely that stakeholders, in particular clubs and athletes, were immune to economic impact of COVID-19.

718. Due to termination of basketball seasons, the clubs were deprived of important amount of match day and sponsor-related income. This forced clubs to shrink their budgets for upcoming seasons. Even though football season was resumed following less than two months as of the first quarantine wave, stakeholders of football faced serious financial problems as well.

719. Sports was not the top priority of the Government in terms of COVID-19 management. First, the Government was engaged in developing and implementing measures to control the spread of COVID-19. It is fair to state that there were no significant remedies from the state specifically addressed to support sport.

720. The Government and municipalities introduced a number of business support measures (such as specific loans, rent fee compensations, tax reliefs) which could also be invoked by sports organizations and clubs. However, no specific significant remedies were addressed to sport.

721. One of few special remedies for sport and athletes was amendment of the Law on Sport which enabled extension of state scholarship for participation in sports events postponed due to COVID-19, including Olympic Games.

722. It is not known now what kind of remedies will be made available for sport in the future as it is clear that the impact of COVID-19 shall persist in the foreseeable future.

Chapter 3. COVID-19 and *Pacta Sunt Servanda*

723. Sudden and unprecedented developments caused by COVID-19 raise a question of whether failure in performance of contract and breach of *pacta sunt servanda* can be justified by COVID-19 and impact thereof.

724. Some global sports federations and dispute resolution bodies, including BAT and FIFA, adopted special set of documents which deal with the issue of COVID-19 and, *inter alia*, its importance on performance of contracts.

725. On 20 April 2020, the BAT issued COVID-19 Guidelines confirmed by the BAT President, Vice-President and Arbitrators. Bearing in mind that most basketball players, coaches and clubs in Lithuania are very keen to agree on BAT as dispute resolution option, the BAT COVID-19 Guidelines are quite an important source of law for Lithuanian basketball community.

726. In accordance with the preamble of the BAT COVID-19 Guidelines, it was recognized that professional basketball had been significantly affected by the crisis, especially in that most competitions have been suspended or even terminated early.

727. Pursuant to Article V.1 of the BAT COVID-19 Guidelines, the principle of *pacta sunt servanda* shall be generally upheld in a manner consistent with the standing jurisprudence of the BAT in times of the COVID-19 crisis. Consequently, a contract is not automatically terminated because of the pandemic. Neither does the COVID-19 crisis gives either party just cause to unilaterally terminate the contract.

728. Pursuant to Article II.2 of the BAT COVID-19 Guidelines, amicable settlements are the preferred means of resolving disputes arising out of the COVID-19 crisis. Parties are under a duty to renegotiate in good faith the terms of their contract in order to resolve on an amicable basis contractual issues arising from the pandemic. Pursuant to Article II.3 of the BAT COVID-19 Guidelines, any breach of this duty may be taken into account by the arbitrator when deciding the merits of the case and when deciding on arbitration costs, legal fees and other expenses.

729. The above-mentioned provisions of the BAT COVID-19 Guidelines show clear position of the BAT: COVID-19 cannot serve as an excuse not to perform a contract. Such position was later confirmed by the BAT case law. The BAT emphasized that the BAT Guidelines make perfectly clear that COVID-19 cannot be the basis for a unilateral termination of a professional basketballer's (same should be applicable to coaches) contract, which is in accordance with general considerations of justice and fairness (*see* paragraph 56, 28 August 2020 BAT award in BAT 1545/20).

730. On 6 April 2020 Bureau of the FIFA Council made several decisions regarding regulatory and legal issues as a result of COVID-19. It was determined that the COVID-19 outbreak was a matter not provided for and a force majeure situation for FIFA and football generally. The Bureau did not determine that the

COVID-19 outbreak was a force majeure situation in any specific country or territory, or that any specific employment or transfer agreement was impacted by the concept of force majeure. However, the Bureau declared that clubs or employees cannot rely on the Bureau's decision to assert a force majeure situation (or its equivalent).

731. Hence, the approach of major decision-making in football and basketball as to COVID-19 impact is similar: the impact of COVID-19 is definitely recognized; however, COVID-19 per se does not release the parties from contractual obligations. Similar approach is kept in Lithuanian contract law.

732. *Pacta sunt servanda* is a vital principle of contract law in Lithuania. In accordance with Article 6.189(1) of the Civil Code, a contract, which is concluded in accordance with the provisions of laws and is valid, shall have the force of law between its parties. The contract shall bind the parties not only as to what it expressly provides but also to all the consequences deriving from its nature or determined by laws.

733. Article 6.200 of the Civil Code provides key principles of performance of the contract. The parties shall perform the contracts in a proper way and in good faith. Parties shall be bound to collaborate and to cooperate with the other party performing the contract. The parties shall be bound to use the most economical means in the performance of the contract. Finally, where according to a contract or its nature, a party in exercising certain actions is bound to make the best effort in the performance of a contract, the party shall be bound to make such effort as a reasonable person would make in the same circumstances.

734. Pursuant to Article 6.212(1) of the Civil Code, a party shall be released from liability for failure to perform a contract if it proves that the contract was not performed due to circumstances beyond its control and reasonably foreseeable at the time of the conclusion of the contract and that it could not prevent those circumstances or their consequences (force majeure).

735. The Supreme Court in its case law[239] formed a rule that in case of force majeure, the release of the party from liability for non-performance of the contract means that the non-performance of contractual obligations is justified and cannot cause the defaulting party normal consequences of non-performance of the contract. The right of the creditor (the injured party to the contract) to the protection of the rights violated by the breach of the contract is accordingly restricted.

736. The case law recognizes that circumstances of force majeure are qualified by the following features: (1) the circumstances did not exist at the time of the conclusion of the contract and their occurrence could not be reasonably foreseen; (2) due to the circumstances, the contract cannot be performed objectively; (3) the party who has not performed the contract could not control those circumstances or could

239. For example. 24 Feb. 2021 ruling in Civil Case No. e3K-3-38-248/2021.

not prevent them; (4) the party has not assumed the risk of the occurrence of those circumstances or their consequences. In the absence of all those criteria, the facts cannot be regarded as force majeure. Each individual case must be evaluated on a case-by-case basis.

737. Hence, the concept of force majeure requires existence of special set of circumstances. It allows one to conclude that fact of COVID-19 alone does not per se constitute a force majeure event and, thus, does not release the party from performance of the contract. Yet, it is possible that COVID-19 can contribute or cause force majeure situation together with other circumstances.

738. On 24 March 2022, the Supreme Court passed a ruling[240] concerning COVID-19 as force majeure for the very first time. The court had to deal with an issue whether COVID-19 and subsequent acts of the Government to limit specific economic activities can be considered force majeure or *rebus sic stantibus*.

739. In the context of the COVID-19 pandemic, the panel underlined that force majeure is not only defined as cases of objective impossibility but also as other forms of impossibility caused by external factors which are recognized in modern contract law, such as the economic (practical) impossibility of performing the contract or the frustration of the purpose of the contract. The panel established that a pandemic or the measures taken to control it cannot, in themselves, be regarded as a force majeure or a material impediment to the performance of the contract. This means that the impact of a pandemic or the measures taken to control it must be assessed individually in relation to each contractual relationship. While some contractual relations may be substantially constrained or rendered unenforceable by the pandemic or its management measures, other contractual relations may be less or not substantially affected at all. The Court founded that the temporary defeat of the purpose of the contract may be classified as both a temporary force majeure and a material impediment to the performance of the contract. In the specific situation of the case (the right of the shop owner to invoke force majeure against the landlord of the premises due to prohibition of activity by the Government following pandemic), the Court did state that, in the absence of the possibility of carrying on business in the rented premises, the injured party is entitled to rely on the defence of force majeure if the totality of the conditions for its existence is established.

740. At the moment, the case law related to COVID-19, including disputes over sport contracts, is just at the initial stage. However, first developments suggest that COVID-19 alone will not be sufficient for a party to justify its failure to perform a contract. For now, it is fair to say that *pacta sunt servanda* prevails over COVID-19.

240. 24 Mar. 2022 ruling of the Supreme Court in Civil Case No e3K-3-66-313/2022.

Conclusions

741. Sports law in Lithuania is not yet recognized as a specific established field of law. One of the reasons for the slightly slower development of sports law in Lithuania is a general lack of elements which are considered to have contributed to the development of sports law in other jurisdictions: general commercialization of sports, domestic market of player transfers, collective sale of broadcasting and media rights of domestic sports competitions, significant amount of sports-related disputes between athletes and clubs. However, further progress of national and EU markets and economic development are likely to increase the legal regulation of sports-related matters. Lawmakers and courts tend to recognize specific elements related to sports. It is very likely that the sports law will take further steps to widen recognition in Lithuania in the near future.

742. Two basic sources of legal regulation related to sports can be distinguished. The first source is state governance of sports matters. The second source is governance of national sports federations. State governance determines the level of involvement of the state in the field of sports. The Constitution obliges the state to support sports. Therefore, public financing of sport is one of the hottest topics in Lithuania. The state further provides a legal framework for the operation of sports federations and clubs, and professional athletes. As well as this, the state interferes in essential matters related to sports, such as integrity of sports competitions. National sports federations enjoy wide discretion and general autonomy from the interference of state. Federations govern matters involving their direct and indirect members and athletes. Fields as the structure and competence of bodies of federations, the status and transfers of players, disciplinary matters are governed by national federations.

743. Legal framework in Lithuania provides several dispute resolution options for parties to a sports-related dispute. Simple disputes between clubs and athletes are usually solved in civil courts. Lithuanian legal system respects arbitration agreements and arbitral awards. Courts maintain an arbitration-friendly approach to foreign arbitral awards and arbitral awards are not recognized under exceptional circumstances only. Sports federations, in particular the LFF, offer their internal systems for dispute resolution. Sports federations contain disciplinary bodies which hear disciplinary matters. Torts related to sports matters may result in various types of liability, including criminal liability, civil liability and disciplinary (sporting) liability.

744. One of the most important issues related to sports is the status of the athlete. It is not ultimately clear what is the legal nature of the relationship between an athlete and a club under the SAA. However, recently the courts tend to consider SAAs as agreements of a civil nature. Players are not represented collectively in sufficient matter, the unions of players barely conduct any activities and, moreover, they are hardly recognized by federations. Therefore, an SAA, or a contract, is a very important element for the balance of rights and obligations of an athlete and a sports club. Important aspects of the relationship between clubs and players or between clubs are governed by the regulations of national sports federations. Such aspects include certain elements of the status of players, compensations for the training of players, solidarity mechanism and transfers of players.

745. Lithuania is devoted to the fight against the use of doping in sports. Lithuania is a member of important international anti-doping conventions, and important notable remedies have been implemented to fight against the use of doping in Lithuania. Match-fixing was criminalized in Lithuania in 2017. The framework to use criminal intelligence to fight match-fixing was launched as well. Moreover, federations, namely the LFF, are also active in the fight against integrity issues in competitions. The model to tackle manipulation in sports implemented by the LFF was successfully examined by CAS.

746. Commercialization of sports in Lithuania is not at the same level as in the biggest EU countries; therefore, interference of commercial law in sports matters is not equally intense. However, certain matters, such as broadcasting, advertising, organization of betting and gaming, using trademarks, sponsorship, and using an image of an athlete, are governed sufficiently. Additional governance is provided by federations, including club ownership rules and distribution of media rights.

747. Sport in Lithuania, as well as other industries, was significantly affected by the COVID-19 outbreak. The state could not provide specific remedies of support for sport, except for general remedies available to all businesses. Hence, clubs face financial difficulties which will cause issues related to contract performance. At the moment there are no grounds to conclude that COVID-19 could stand as a sole reason to establish force majeure and to justify non-performance of contract. Thus, the contracts shall have to be performed regardless of COVID-19. Accordingly, mutual understanding and good faith of all stakeholders are going to be paramount.

Selected Bibliography

Books

Armanas Abramavičius et al., *Baudžiamoji teisė: bendroji dalis: vadovėlis* (Eugrimas, 2003).

Linas Baublys et al., *Teisės teorijos įvadas* (Mes, 2012).

Toma Birmontienė et al., *Lietuvos konstitucinė teisė* (Mykolo Romerio universitetas, 2012).

Genovaitė Dambrauskienė et al., *Lietuvos Respublikos Konstitucijos komentaras* (K. Jovaišos PĮ, 2000).

Frans de Weger, *The Jurisprudence of the FIFA Dispute Resolution Chamber*, 2nd edition, ASSER International Sports Law Series (Asser Press, 2016).

Simon Gardiner, *United Kingdom*, in International Encyclopaedia of Laws: Sports Law, Frank Hendrickx (ed.) (Kluwer Law International, 2014).

Edward Greyson, *Sport and the Law,* 2nd edition (Butterworths, 1994).

Vytautas Piesliakas, *Lietuvos baudžiamoji teisė: pirmoji knyga* (Justitia, 2006).

Vytautas Piesliakas, *Lietuvos baudžiamoji teisė: antroji knyga* (Justitia, 2008).

Robert C.R. Siekmann, *Introduction to International and European Sports Law*, ASSER International Sports Law Series (Asser Press, 2012).

Robert C.R. Siekmann & Janwillem Soek (eds), *Lex Sportiva: What Is Sports Law?*, ASSER International Sports Law Series (Asser Press, 2012).

Egidijus Šileikis, *Alternatyvi konstitucinė teisė* (Teisinės informacijos centras, 2003).

Periodicals

Michael J. Beloff, *Drugs, Laws and Versapaks, Drugs and Doping in Sport: Socio-Legal Perspectives Drugs and Doping in Sport: Socio-Legal Perspectives*, John O'Leary (ed.), ISBN 1859416624 (Cavendish, 2011).

Ramunė Bistrickaitė, *Lithuania Criminalises Match-Fixing* (EPFL Legal Newsletter, 2016).

Aurelijus Gutauskas & Linas Žalnieriūnas, *Fizinio smurto sporte baudžiamasis teisinis įvertinimas*, ISSN 1392–6195, 2014 21 (3), Jurisprudencija (2014).

Algis Norkūnas, *Kaltė kaip civilinės atsakomybės sąlyga*, 28(20); 112–118, Jurisprudencija (2002).

Vytautas Sinkevičius, *Konstitucinių įstatymų samprata: teoriniai aspektai*, ISSN 1392-6195, 2008 2(104), Jurisprudencija (2008).

Selected Bibliography

Salomėja Zaksaitė, *Nusikalstamas elgesys sporto srityje*, ISSN 1392–1274, 2010 74, Teisė (2012).
Salomėja Zaksaitė, *Sukčiavimo sporto srityje paplitimas ir prevencijos problemos*: PhD dissertation (University of Vilnius, 2012).

Index

The numbers here refer to paragraph numbers.

www.ingramcontent.com/pod-product-compliance
Ingram Content Group UK Ltd.
Pitfield, Milton Keynes, MK11 3LW, UK
UKHW020141290926
15471UKWH00004B/633

9 789403 515960